ADVERTISING AND HOTEL MANAGEMENT

ADVERTISING AND HOTEL MANAGEMENT

M. C. METTI

ANMOL PUBLICATIONS PVT. LTD.
NEW DELHI - 110 002 (INDIA)

ANMOL PUBLICATIONS PVT. LTD.

H.O.: 4374/4B, Ansari Road, Darya Ganj,
New Delhi-110 002 (India)
Ph.: 23278000, 23261597

B.O.: No. 1015, Ist Main Road, BSK IIIrd Stage
IIIrd Phase, IIIrd Block
Bangalore - 560 085 (India)
Visit us at: www.anmolpublications.com

Advertising and Hotel Management

ISBN 978-81-261-3251-5

PRINTED IN INDIA

Printed at Mehra Offset Press, Delhi.

Contents

Preface

Advertising and promotions is bringing a service to the attention of potential and current customers of hospitality industry. Advertising and promotions are best carried out by implementing advertising and promotions plan. The goals of the plan should depend very much on the overall goals and strategies of the hotel, and the results of the marketing analysis, including the positioning statement.

The plan usually includes what target markets you want to reach, what features and benefits you want to convey to them, how you will convey it to them (this is often called your advertising campaign), who is responsible to carry the various activities in the plan and how much money is budgeted for this effort. Successful advertising depends very much on knowing the preferred methods and styles of communications of the target markets that you want to reach with your ads. A media plan and calendar can be very useful, which specifies what advertising methods are used and when.

For each service, carefully consider: What target markets are you trying to reach with your ads? What would you like them to think and perceive about your products (this should be in terms of benefits to them, not you)? How can you get them to think and perceive that? What communications media do they see or prefer the most? Consider TV, radio, newsletters, classifieds, displays/signs, posters, word of mouth, press releases, direct mail, special events, brochures, neighborhood newsletters, etc.

What media is most practical for you to use in terms of access and affordability (the amount spent on advertising is often based on the revenue expected from the product or service, that is, the sales forecast)? You can often find out a lot about your customers preferences just by conducting some basic market research methods.

Traditionally, the term "management" refers to the activities (and often the group of people) involved in the four general functions: planning, organizing, leading and coordinating of resources. Note that the four functions recur throughout the organization and are highly integrated. Emerging trends in management include assertions that leading is different than managing, and that the nature of how the four functions are carried out must change to accommodate a "new paradigm" in management. This book will help the reader accomplish broad understanding of hotel management and advertisement, and the areas of knowledge and skills required to carry out the major functions of hotel management advertisement.

Author

Chapter 1

Advertising

INTRODUCTION

Advertising is not modern in origin. It undoubtedly began at the earliest time when competition caused each man to make efforts to gain prominence – a process of human nature which has gone on ever since. Competition naturally arose at the earliest time of civilization when communities were brought together and each individual followed the urge to better himself. In present context, without advertising a business cannot run successfully. Before going in depth of what advertising industry is, lets have a brief view of what a hotel normally provide and how it functions.

A comfortable room, good food, and a helpful staff can make being away from home an enjoyable experience for both vacationing families and business travellers. While most lodging managers work in traditional hotels and motels, some work in other lodging establishments, such as camps, inns, boardinghouses, dude ranches, and recreational resorts. In full-service hotels, lodging managers help their guests have a pleasant stay by providing many of the comforts of home, including cable television, fitness equipment, and voice mail, as well as specialized services such as health spas. For business travelers, lodging managers often schedule available meeting rooms and electronic equipment, including slide projectors and fax machines.

Lodging managers are respons'' for keeping their establishments efficient and profitable. In a small establishment with a limited staff, the manager may oversee all aspects of operations. However, large hotels may employ hundreds of workers, and the general manager usually is aided by a number of assistant managers assigned to the various departments of the operation. In hotels of every size, managerial duties vary significantly by job title.

General managers have overall responsibility for the operation of the hotel. Within guidelines established by the owners of the hotel or executives of the hotel chain, the general manager sets room rates, allocates funds to departments, approves expenditures, and ensures expected standards for guest service, decor, housekeeping, food quality, and banquet operations. Managers who work for chains also may organize and staff a newly built hotel, refurbish an older hotel, or reorganize a hotel or motel that is not operating successfully. In order to fill entry-level service and clerical jobs in hotels, some managers attend career fairs.

Resident or hotel managers are responsible for the day-to-day operations of the property. In larger properties, more than one of these managers may assist the general manager, frequently dividing responsibilities between the food and beverage operations and the rooms or lodging services. At least one manager, either the general manager or a hotel manager, is on call 24 hours a day to resolve problems or emergencies. Assistant managers help run the day-to-day operations of the hotel. In large hotels, they may be responsible for activities such as personnel, accounting, office administration, marketing and sales, purchasing, security, maintenance, and pool, spa, or recreational facilities. In smaller hotels, these duties may be combined into one position. Assistant managers may adjust charges on a hotel guest's bill when a manager is unavailable.

An Executive Committee made up of a hotel's senior managers advises the general manager, assists in setting hotel policy, coordinates services that cross departmental boundaries, and collaborates on efforts to ensure consistent and efficient guest services throughout the hotel. The Committee may be comprised of the department heads for housekeeping, front office, food and beverage, security, sales and public relations, meetings and conventions, engineering and building maintenance, and human resources. Executive committee members bring a different perspective of guest service to the total management objective reflecting the unique expertise and training of their positions.

Executive housekeepers ensure that guest rooms, meeting and banquet rooms, and public areas are clean, orderly, and well maintained. They also train, schedule, and supervise the work of housekeepers, inspect rooms, and order cleaning supplies. Front office managers coordinate reservations and room assignments, as well as train and direct the hotel's front desk staff. They ensure that guests are treated courteously, complaints and problems are resolved, and requests for special services are carried out. Front office managers may adjust charges posted on a customer's bill.

Convention services managers coordinate the activities of various departments in larger hotels to accommodate meetings, conventions, and special events. They meet with representatives of groups or organizations to plan the number of rooms to reserve, the desired configuration of the meeting space, and banquet services. During the meeting or event, they resolve unexpected problems and monitor activities to ensure that hotel operations conform to the expectations of the group.

Food and beverage managers oversee all food service operations maintained by the hotel. They coordinate menus with the Executive Chef for the hotel's restaurants, lounges, and room service operations. They supervise the ordering of food and supplies, direct service and maintenance contracts within the kitchens and dining areas, and manage food service budgets. Catering managers arrange for food service in a hotel's meeting and convention rooms. They coordinate menus and costs for banquets, parties, and events with meeting and convention planners or individual clients. They coordinate staffing needs and arrange schedules with kitchen personnel to ensure appropriate food service.

Sales or marketing directors and public relations directors oversee the advertising and promotion of hotel operations and functions, including lodging and dining specials and special events, such as holiday or seasonal specials. They direct the efforts of their staff to purchase advertising and market their property to organizations or groups seeking a venue for conferences, conventions, business meetings, trade shows, and special events. They also coordinate media relations and answer questions from the press.

Human resources directors manage the personnel functions of a hotel, ensuring that all accounting, payroll, and employee relations matters are handled in compliance with hotel policy and applicable laws. They also oversee hiring practices and standards and ensure that training and promotion programs reflect appropriate employee development guidelines. Finance (or revenue) directors monitor room sales and reservations. In addition to overseeing accounting and cash-flow matters at the hotel, they also project occupancy levels, decide which rooms to discount and when to offer rate specials.

Computers are used extensively by lodging managers and their assistants to keep track of guests' bills, reservations, room assignments, meetings, and special events. In addition, computers are used to order food, beverages, and supplies, as well as to prepare reports for hotel owners and top-level managers. Managers work with computer specialists to ensure that the hotel's computer system functions properly. Should the hotel's computer system fail, managers must continue to meet the needs of hotel guests and staff.

THE BEGINNINGS OF ADVERTISING

Advertising, then, is nearly as old as civilization. There are records more than three thousand years old of announcements advertising for runaway slaves, written on papyri and exhumed from the ruins of Thebes. The Greek and Roman advertisements of gladiatorial exhibitions are reminiscent of the modern "billing" of circuses. There is linguistic proof of the existence of the town crier in early

Hebrew civilization, and of hawkers of retail wares in Roman times. The excavations of Pompeii have revealed various "bills" – tablets attached to pillars – on the walls of that ancient city, and there are records in literature of signs over shops and stalls in Rome advertising crafts and merchandise.

As early as the late seventeenth century, advertising was already a source of profits for the first newspapers. From the first daily published in England in Queen Anne's time until the nineteenth century, newspaper advertising was limited to announcements identifying craftsmen, merchandise and services for sale. Even in the early nineteenth century, the newspaper was a local venture usually religious or political in nature. Few had large circulations. If a company wished to advertise, it dealt 6 directly with the paper. There was no particular skill involved in newspaper advertising in the early stages. A simple announcement served both the advertiser and the public.

After the phase of Great Expansion – industrial, geographical and modern mass production methods – production facilities were greatly in excess of natural demand. This brought about the necessity of the persuasive sales appeal – the need to create new markets and new customers. The businessman began to feel the need to *persuade* prospective customers. The businessman *and* the periodicals felt the need to cover wider geographic areas in a more persuasive manner. The problems and profits inherent in this situation were the foundations of the modern advertising agency.

The Rise of the Agency

The first advertising agent was a middleman or jobber in advertising space. He contracted space from publishers, which in turn he retailed to advertisers at a profit.

In 1820 there were about 360 newspapers published in the United States. In 1830 there were over one thousand. In 1841 there is the first definite record of the advertising agent, who, according to Rowell, was Volney B. Palmer. Palmer set himself up in Philadelphia as an agent for country newspapers, obtaining orders for advertising, forwarding the copy to the paper and collecting payment.

Palmer was closely followed by others and before long there were a number of agents in the business. Only a few years passed before the jobbers changed their methods of operation. They soon began to act as space brokers. They made contracts for space on their own accounts and resold the space to advertisers. The early days of the agency business occupy a unique position in business history in that the affairs were conducted in confused state. The early agents were at once agents for the advertiser and for the publication, and space brokers on their own behalf, while some dealt also in printers' materials; and, finally, a few published their own periodicals, selling advertising in these periodicals to the same newspaper for which they acted as agent and whose space they brokered. It was indeed a catch-as-catch-can business, with payments sometimes being made in "supplies" and with great "flexibility" of rates, etc.

Yet since about Palmer's time, for over a hundred years, the agency has been the nerve-center of the advertising business. But it is only today that the advertising agent has achieved the stature of a professional man. The last lap in the progress of the agency began about 1930. It was a fork in the road for the agency: Either fold-up or gear-up. Business couldn't depend on old-fashioned methods to help push it out of the red. The agency had to devise new ways to serve. That agency which was able to gear-up to the new demands of the early '30'$ was the agency which was successful. It is that agency which represents what is typical in the new attitude of the agency business which has made a simple sales job into a complex professional service.

THE EVOLUTION OF ADVERTISING

In the nineteenth century a substantial part of advertising consisted of what would now be termed announcements and of items we now find in the classified advertising section of newspapers. In addition to these, however, the advertising agencies sold a quantity of space to the "patent medicine" business. During the period around 1870, modern medicine was in its infancy. As a result there was a considerable field for the sale of all sorts of remedies. These accounts, which almost any agency would frown on today, were perhaps the backbone of the early agency business.

Those were the days of rugged individualism, not of professional ethics. It was the pioneering period. There was no social legislation and, looking backward, it appears that there was little conscience or application of a moral standard in most business. Thus it was natural that the advertising agency seldom investigated the merits of the product it advertised. Actually, it can scarcely be said that the agency was responsible for the advertising that it sold and placed. In most cases, the advertiser and not the agency prepared the copy for the advertisement. All the agent did was to sell the space, forward the advertising copy and instructions to the publisher, and collect for the advertisement.

In addition to the classified and patent medicine advertising, the early agency placed what we today might consider legitimate advertising, including local notices and the advertising of farm implements and a few other products. Mail-order houses and manufacturers of farm products, books and machinery were some of the first industries to use advertising as a sales tool. The 1870 advertisement is a far cry from the elaborately designed advertisement for the same store today; while the 1911 advertisement for the Buick Motor Company shows that the trend was beginning to change into what is used in present-day styles of advertising.

The nature of the advertising agency business, as it was first constituted, was bound to cause trouble. Nearly all agencies were committed for large amounts of space in the publications which they represented. Consequently, it was profitable for them to urge their clients to use those particular papers. This, of course, was not economically sound. In addition, if the advertiser wanted to use space in periodicals that the agency did not have direct representation for, it was necessary for the agent to try some makeshift negotiations for the space. Agencies were in constant competition with each other in an effort to secure the space that an advertiser wanted. At the best, the agencies' basis of operations was not conducive to creating confidence between the advertiser and the agent since it was never clear to whom the agency was responsible.

This confused state of affairs finally stimulated a clarification of the business, and toward the close of the nineteenth century the agencies began to give up the position of space jobber by instituting what was called the open contract.

The Open Contract

Under the open contract plan, the agency became the representative of the advertiser. The open contract provided that the advertiser have free access to all of the information available to the agency. The agency promised to buy the space needed by the advertiser at the lowest possible rates, and in return charge a commission for its services. The agency began to promise the advertiser unbiased recommendations concerning circulation, population, general reputation of the paper, etc.

The open contract clearly was the beginning of the system existing today for remunerating advertising agencies through a commission paid by the publication.

In 1891, George Batten opened an agency in New York City. From the very beginning, he adhered to the new principle of buying space for the advertiser at the lowest possible cost. To this cost he added fifteen percent for his services. In contrast to the questionable speculative profit that agencies had received when they jobbed space, this new basis provided a reasonable profit margin. It placed the agency in a more secure position and enabled it to develop services for the advertiser. As agencies throughout the country began to adhere more and more to the open contract system, two important developments occurred:

1. They had made their decision to work for the advertisers' interests exclusively.

2. In addition to buying space for the advertiser at the lowest possible cost, they began to provide additional services and to be known as service organizations.

It is during this period that we first hear of "copywriters." Simultaneously with this development in the advertising agency business, publishers began to stabilize their rates so that those agencies which still acted as space brokers had difficulty in buying space below the market. By about 1890, many newspapers had arranged to pay advertising agencies a commission of fifteen percent on the space placed. National magazines at that time were paying agencies a commission of ten percent. During the period from 1890 to about 1930 when agencies were making the transition from space brokers to service organizations, there were many agencies and advertisers who still were wedded to the old idea of buying space below the market. This brought about the vicious practice of price cutting, which the agencies accomplished by rebating a part of their commissions to the advertisers. In 1910, out of twenty-five reasonably large advertising agencies doing business with the Curtis Publishing Company, ten were suspected of rebating commissions. In 1920, six of these ten price-cutting agencies were still in business, but by 1930 only one of them remained.

During the period from 1890 to 1930, publishers began to see that the advertising agency was a valuable tool for legitimately creating advertising business. There was a real incentive for them to protect the agency from price cutting and unsound competition, for the publisher wanted the advertiser to get his money's worth. Since the publishers were not in a position to conceive the advertising campaign, select the media, prepare the copy and visualize the art work, the advertising agency was the perfect answer to their problem.

In 1893, the American Newspaper Publishers' Association adopted a resolution which provided that agencies' commissions be paid only to advertising agencies and that no similar price reduction be allowed to advertisers. The Curtis Publishing Company in 1901 put into effect a new contract arrangement with advertising agencies. This new contract provided for a commission of ten percent to approve advertising agencies. To be approved the agencies agreed to charge advertisers the full card rate, less only the cash discount for prompt payment. The agreement provided that in the event an agency quoted space in the Curtis publications for less than the published rate, such a quotation would be considered a violation of the contract. The contract provided that upon a second violation, the agent would be dropped from the approved list of advertising agencies.

Gradually, all publishers and other media fell in line with the commission system which stabilized advertising rates and the income of the advertising agencies. Magazine publishers increased the commission basis first from ten to thirteen percent. In 1918, the American Association of Advertising Agencies sought to increase the commission basis of magazines from thirteen to fifteen percent, with an additional two percent cash discount for prompt payment. Today, the fifteen percent agency commission is standard with only inconsequential exceptions.

On various occasions from 1890 to the present time, publishers and advertisers have questioned both the commission system itself and the rate of commission paid; but since 1925, it has been more or less standard practice for the advertising agencies to receive a fifteen percent commission allowed by the publishers and other advertising media.

THE DEVELOPMENT OF THE MODERN AGENCY

The Space Buyer

The first service performed by the twentieth-century advertising agency was that of selecting the publications for the advertiser. Before the days of the open contract, there was considerable doubt whether this job was done to the best advantage of the advertiser; but certainly after the introduction of the open contract basis, it proved to be a valuable service to advertisers. The selection of advertising media, still a difficult job, was much more difficult around 1900. Before relatively recent times, there was not the information available concerning circulation, type of readers and geographical distribution which is published now.

In addition to the difficulty in selecting media, the early advertising agencies were faced with the question of the "best buy." Today, rates for advertising space are standardized and published. With the exception of a few small weekly papers and highly specialized publications, such as yearbooks and religious papers, the advertiser must pay the quoted price. There is no bargaining. The prices of printed advertising media today are based chiefly on the circulation of the media, so that in determining the best buy, the agency is mainly concerned with the type of readers as it relates to the advertisers' products. Even as late as the 1920, the space buyer was a key man in nearly every advertising agency. If he was a sharp buyer he secured some space at bargain prices. He studied markets and types of circulation. He had an intimate acquaintance with many of the publications and he could point out the advantages and disadvantages of most of them. Space buying, then, was a legitimate and important element of service in the early advertising agency, and still is, for proper selection can save substantial sums for the advertiser.

The Copywriter

Long before 1900, advertising agencies began to feel the need for the proper preparation and wording of advertisements. So long as advertising was confined to local announcements and classified ads, there was little importance attached to the preparation of advertising copy. It was not long before the agencies began to find that the advertising message could be something more than an announcement. Agencies recognized the importance of selling copy. About 1880, a few agencies announced that they would prepare advertisements for their clients. The preparation of copy began merely as an added service.

Not much importance was placed on it at the start. But with the rapid expansion of industry, manufacturers began to feel the need for wider distribution of their products, and advertising became an important tool for such added distribution. Advertising agencies quickly expanded and found themselves serving all sorts of businesses. Advertising copy took on great importance and the work of the copywriter soon began to vie with that of the space buyer in the importance of the services rendered by the agency to its clients. As an example of this, as early as 1905, Albert D. Lasker of Lord & Thomas employed John E. Kennedy as a copywriter, paying him $28,000 a year, and publicized this fact.

The Art Director

Art work played some part in ancient as well as in early modern advertising. The Roman signs we have mentioned often contained pictures. The tavern, for example, was represented by a suspended shield, indeed, the rate of literacy was then so low that the picture communicated more readily than the word. Care in lay-out, too, appeared in the earliest modern advertisements. One published in 1878 advertises compound oxygen as a new treatment for the cure of chronic diseases by the true process of revitalization. In this advertisement, Drs. Starkee and Palen claim that this treatment cures consumption, asthma, catarrh, bronchitis, dyspepsia, headache, rheumatism, neuralgia, etc. There was no picture in the advertisement of this elixir, but it did contain bold headlines and subheads.

In 1888, in an advertisement published by Ferris Bros., a number of drawings appear illustrating the use of corded corset waists. It was common in these early days of advertising to publish a picture of the founder of or some important personality in the business. An examination of these early lay-outs causes one to doubt whether the illustrations could really be called art work. However, the Uneeda Biscuit advertisement, published by the National Biscuit Company in 1899, clearly illustrates the function of planned art work in a printed advertising message. As the use of art work became more extensive in advertising, agencies developed certain methods and techniques to coordinate art work and advertising copy. Many advertising agencies in the early 1900's set up art departments or at least employed one or more persons whose job was to secure or produce the needed art work for the advertisements placed by the agency.

It was soon determined that no one agency could contain among its personnel a sufficient number of artists to produce the varied types of art work required in the advertisements produced for the different clients of the agency. For that reason, it has become more or less general practice for the agency itself to make the lay-out for the advertisement and perhaps to produce a very rough sketch of the art work required. After this has been done, the art director of the agency selects the artist who he feels can do the best job in producing the type of art work required. The art work is then purchased on the outside.

In certain specialized types of advertising agencies, it was necessary to expand the art service rendered; for this reason, some agencies actually employed artists to prepare the finished drawing or painting. Because it became a generally accepted fact that the illustration in an advertisement may be equally as important as the printed message, the art department of an advertising agency has become one of the important parts of the organization.

Research

In the very early days of the advertising agency, perhaps even before 1880, some agencies realized the importance of research. In the days before the open contract, when agencies were most interested in selling the space in the papers they represented, it became important to convince an advertiser that certain advertising media had greater value than others. For this reason, it was necessary to determine such things as circulation figures and the type of persons who read particular publications. In an effort to sell the space they had available, some of the agencies actually studied these things so as to convince the advertiser that he should place his advertisements in certain media. With the advent of modern types of outdoor advertising and car card advertising, it became necessary to determine the value of these new advertising media. This required statistics, which in turn required research. Consequently, many studies were made by newspapers, magazines and outdoor plants. While some research work was attempted by agencies before this century, it is doubtful if much really extensive research work, such as market analysis as we understand it today, was performed by agencies until about 1930.

By that time advertising had become recognized as a powerful and essential tool to modern business. Nearly every large manufacturer realized the need of distributing his products over a wide area. Millions of dollars were being spent to acquaint the public with the products available and the relative merits of each. The Federal Food, Drug and Cosmetic Act had done much to clean up the fantastic claims made by manufacturers of patent medicines.

As the science of marketing and merchandising developed, many questions presented themselves to advertisers, such as: What size package will sell best? Will the consumer prefer a liquid or a powder? What type of retail outlet can best distribute a certain product? Should a manufacturer push a low-priced, middle-priced or high-priced product? What is the best geographical area for the distribution of certain products?

Many advertisers came to their agents for the answers to these questions. It was logical, then, that the advertising agency began to feel the need to conduct studies in an effort to find the answers to the questions posed by the advertisers. Some agencies employed one or more persons to spend their full time conducting research studies for their clients. Others believed that they should consider their clients' problems and secure specialists on the outside to study the questions and resolve the answers. The quantity and quality of research work has varied, and still varies, between one agency and another. A fuller discussion of the problems of research will be found in a later chapter.

Another Measurement of Growth

It is not practicable to discuss the history of each of the other departments of an agency at this point. One additional subject however is interesting and indicative of the quick growth of the agency. How has the volume of the advertising agency business grown? Unfortunately, there is no reliable source from which to secure accurate figures to indicate the volume of advertising in the early years of the business. There are statistics which tend to indicate that the largest of the very early agencies prior to 1875 conducted a volume of business of from $5,000 to approximately $100,000 a year. By 1890 some of these agencies were doing a volume of nearly $1,000,000 a year and by 1900 a few were doing as much as double this. After the first World War the largest were doing a volume of about $10,000,000 a year. Today, there are two or three agencies that transact a business having an annual volume in excess of $50,000,000. Like any personal service business, most of the agencies deliver such a highly personalized service that their size is restricted. Out of about two thousand agencies today, approximately fifteen hundred handle a yearly volume of less than $500,000 each.

RECAPITULATION

We have found that although advertising is as old as civilization, the advertising agency is a product of modern times. It has gone through four stages:

1. Infancy: Before 1900, there were few in the business who even knew how they wanted to conduct the business, or whether they represented the advertiser or the publisher. Late in the nineteenth century, most agencies were space brokers, who bought space at wholesale and sold it at retail.
2. Adolescence: From 1900 to 1918 agencies were developing their organizations to become a positive force in business. A standard commission from publications was received by all recognized agencies, and the development of service departments was beginning. The techniques of media selection, copywriting and art work were being refined.

3. Early maturity: There was still considerable mystery in the business before 1930; thereafter the business settled down. Most of the functions to be performed by the advertising agency had been determined and competition between one agency and another was purely on the basis of who could best serve the client. The agency in its mature form has become, in some aspects, a profession.
4. Professional concept: The professional elements of the agency business are those related to the personal service offered to clients by the agency in connection with idea development, product analysis, the development of marketing techniques, the personal attention to writing, lay-out, art work, etc. In addition, there are the commercial elements of the business, those related to the purchase of advertising space and materials, the use of capital and routine functions such as checking copy, measuring ads, buying printing, billing, paying and accounting.

FUNCTIONS OF THE AGENCY AND PLANNING THE CAMPAIGN

The advertising agency business, having passed the period of adolescence, is now mature and in certain aspects it is achieving a professional level. In the earlier stages of agency development, the functions performed and the services rendered varied widely between one agency and another. Now, most agencies offer many of the same types of service. The modern agency, of course, still buys and sells advertising media as did the early agencies, but in addition it offers professional services in planning, developing and executing advertising campaigns.

General Outline of Functions

The following outline of some of the principal functions of the modern agency indicates both the maturity of the business and its claim to professional status.

1. *Campaigns*

It plans the actual advertising campaigns, and outlines many related activities to be carried on both within the agency and in the company whose product or service it is advertising, carefully integrating both.

2. *Copy Preparation*

It studies the product and the need for the product, and then determines selling points and makes the appeal.

3. *Copy Testing*

It endeavors to determine in advance, in so far as possible, how well comparative appeals will pull.

4. *Space or Time Buying*

It selects various advertising media and analyzes media according to coverage, costs and effectiveness. It orders, specifies and buys the advertising space or time planned for the campaign. It checks advertising as it appears, then audits quantity and quality and handles claims for shortages and substandard quality.

5. *Research and Counsel*

It conducts research regarding markets, copy, products, appeals, uses, etc.

6. *Radio*

It may have an entire department devoted to radio advertising, including programs and research.

7. *Production*

It specifies and purchases the production materials required for the campaign.

8. *Publicity*

It occasionally conducts or directs publicity campaigns in behalf of its client.

9. *Dealer Helps*

It may plan dealer helps, including displays.

10. Sales Helps

It prepares sales portfolios and manuals.

11. Design

It prepares packages and labels.

12. Retail Promotion

It plans retail promotion, including sales helps for retail clerks, local advertising tie-ins, etc.

I3. Miscellaneous

It performs numerous services of a miscellaneous nature related to the following:

- Sales and consumer films.
- Direct mail
- Contests
- Sales training
- Exhibits
- Premiums
- Instruction and recipe books
- Catalog planning
- House organ planning
- Planning sales policies
- Product design
- Sales meetings
- New product development
- Public relations
- Distribution channels
- Annual reports
- Working with salesmen in the field.

14. Billing

It bills advertising space and materials, and radio time, talent and mechanics, and furnishes the advertiser with statistics in relation to these.

In order to understand each of these functions, it is necessary to go into some detail to define what the usual practice and procedures are.

PLANNING THE CAMPAIGN

This is one of the creative services performed by advertising agencies. It includes such activities as:

1. Productt

Selecting the products to be advertised.

2. Markets

Determining where the advertising should appear.

3. Media

Deciding what general class of media should be used.

4. Copy

Conceiving and developing the "copy idea."

5. Visualization

Visualizing the advertising.

6. Imtegration

Cooperating with the manufacturer's advertising department on such matters as follow-through, dealer helps and the like.

It is not the purpose of this book to describe how an advertising campaign is conceived and developed. These services, which are acknowledged to be highly important in the agency business, are not directly connected with the subject of financial management except as the cost of performing these services affects finances. Usually owners of smaller agencies, and contact men in larger agencies, perform the important functions included in conceiving and developing the advertising campaign. In the larger agency, certain separate elements of work are delegated to departments or individuals within the agency. These would embrace copywriting and art work, including visualization.

It is customary for the contact men in the larger agency or the owner in the smaller agency to develop the advertising campaign and discuss it rather extensively with the advertiser.

Much of this work is called "client contact," and the contact man in an agency for this reason is an important factor in the success or failure of an advertising campaign. The contact man, therefore, has a great effect on the cost of performing all of the work for advertisers. If the contact man understands his job and issues careful instructions and orders to agency employees based on the actual needs of the advertiser, considerable waste will be eliminated. It is also important that a contact man have the courage of his convictions so that if a piece of work is completed satisfactorily he will avoid continual changes which are unnecessary and costly. Many books have been written on the subject of copywriting and others on the subject of advertising art. As stated previously, it is not the purpose of this volume to discuss the creative elements of the agency business.

RESEARCH

The research activities of the agency are currently the subject of much controversy and questioning. The main stream of belief is that where large sums of money are expended for advertising it pays handsome dividends to know as much about the product, the market and competition as it is possible to learn. This indicates rather extensive research activities. The question is whether the agency or the advertiser should initiate the research and, if the agency does, whether it should receive a special fee.

Few agencies are equipped to conduct extensive research operations, consequently there is considerable merit to the position that outside specialists should conduct them. However, at the outset it is necessary for the agency to know a good deal about the product it is going to advertise and the market in which the product is to be advertised. The implication is that in any event the agency must perform a certain amount of research.

When an agency first secures an account, it is standard practice to study the products to be advertised, the market for the products, and the competition, including advertising campaigns conducted in connection with the distribution and sale of competing products. Upon receiving a new account, the agency will often find that it has employees who have had experience with products similar to that of their new client. If not, provided that the size of the account warrants it, the agency often employs a person or persons with previous experience in advertising similar products.

Research by Agencies

It is difficult to generalize on the subject of research activities that are conducted as a preliminary to advertising, because the type and extent of research activities are largely dependent on the particular product to be advertised. Market and product analyses are specialties which would require a substantial number of highly trained and experienced persons in order to answer the questions that arise from time to time concerning the varied products with which an average agency is involved. The research activities generally conducted by an agency at its own expense are confined to a superficial analysis of:

1. The product to be advertised.
2. The market for the product.
3. The competition with other products.

Research by Outside Organizations

Often an agency recommends market analyses and other research activities. In such cases, the agency may suggest the research organization that is best equipped to make the studies. In all cases, the agency certainly should be furnished with a copy of any market studies or product analyses that are available. The U. S. Department of Commerce publishes numerous analytical reports that furnish considerable revealing information on products and markets. These statistics are available to the public and they are generally used by advertising agencies in planning advertising campaigns.

In addition, the various advertising media have made intensive market studies which are made available to advertising agencies. These reports are constantly referred to by agencies in their study and preparation for advertising campaigns.

Certain organizations have specialized in rating the effectiveness of advertising messages. Advertising agencies frequently contract for the services of these organizations to determine the effectiveness of their campaigns and of the campaigns conducted by other agencies for clients in competition with theirs. Research work as it affects advertising and regardless of who does it may be broadly divided into two classifications: product analysis and market analysis.

Product Analysis

Product analysis can involve many different subjects. Among these the most significant are:

1. Investigation of the company, including its capacity for production and for growth, and its sales set-up.
2. Engineering analysis to determine the quality of the product and its merit in relation to competing products.
3. Study to determine the kind of product needed in relation to its usefulness and some existing or potential need.

   This must be generally correlated to engineering analysis and market analysis.
4. Research to determine price and production scale. This too should be correlated with market analysis.
5. Analysis to determine methods of packaging, selling and distributing.

Generally, the product analyses are undertaken by advertisers rather than by advertising agencies. Of course, this type of research can have an important bearing on the effectiveness of the advertising campaign. Consequently the agency is always interested in these analyses and should always be consulted about them. Often the agency itself suggests a product analysis. This type of research is usually paid for by the advertiser. If the study is initiated by the agency, then the agency arranges for a fee on a cost plus basis or on a flat fee basis. Rarely does the agency undertake a product analysis without securing a special fee for the work.

Market Analysis

Market analysis may be undertaken to determine:

1. Size of the market or quantity of goods that the market can be expected to absorb.
2. Geographic location of the market.
3. Type of individual or company that is the logical prospective buyer of the product.
4. Seasonable factors which affect the sale of the goods.
5. Price level at which the product can be sold most effectively to produce a profitable result.
6. Most efficient methods of distribution.

Market analyses, like product analyses, vary considerably. Some analyses can be made through questionnaires sent to dealers or distributors to determine the best policies for the marketing of a product. Often the agencies themselves undertake this kind of study. In such cases, it is usual for the agency to charge a fee for conducting the study.

Dealer and Consumer Surveys

Occasionally an agency undertakes to make a dealer survey at its own expense but this is the exception rather than the rule. Consumer surveys are usually more costly than dealer surveys because to conduct a study among customers it is necessary to reach a large number of people.

Consumer surveys are made in four principal ways:

1. Personal interviews.
2. Questionnaires mailed or otherwise distributed.
3. Telephone interviews.
4. Consumer panels.

Before making a consumer survey, it is necessary to determine what information is needed and how it can be used. When this has been established, if the survey is to be made by method "1," "2," or "3," a questionnaire is generally prepared so that simple yes or no answers can be secured to a question or series of questions. The answers to the questions are secured and the results are tabulated. After interpreting these results, the advertiser or agency draws conclusions upon which future policies are based.

Consumer Panels

This fourth type of consumer research is an intricate procedure which may operate after the following pattern:

1. A number of typical consumers are selected in the geographical areas from which information is required.
2. These persons are furnished with daily, weekly or monthly questionnaires which when answered will indicate:
    a. Each of the items that the consumer purchased during a period of time.
    b. Who in the family made the purchase.
    c. What influenced the purchase.

The questionnaires used are often lengthy and sometimes require detailed answers to one hundred or more questions. Through a tabulation of the answers, the research organization can determine just what each person or family has purchased during the entire period covered. Several research companies operate research panels and at least one large advertising agency operates a panel. The tabulations made as a result of the questionnaires furnish statistics on many different articles and in many different geographic and economic areas. This has a much broader use than the tabulations made from a survey which is conducted for one specific purpose. Since the consumer study is far more costly than the distributor or dealer study, it is rare for an agency to undertake a consumer research study at its own cost. Often consumer research is conducted by the advertiser himself or through a research organization employed by the advertiser. As consumer research studies can have an important bearing on the advertising campaign, agencies prefer to have at least a part in supervising the studies.

Who Pays The Bills?

If any generalization can be made as to whether the agency or the advertiser pays the cost of research activities, it is this: Where the study is performed specifically in connection with the development of an advertising campaign, the cost is paid by the agency. Where the study is made for the general benefit of the advertiser, the cost is paid by the advertiser.

It is impossible to make satisfactory generalizations as to what research activities the advertiser should expect to receive from the agency. The advertising agency should not be expected to conduct market analyses and product research; rather, it should avail itself of existing information that will assist it in the preparation of the advertising campaign.

The agency executives, in addition, should help determine what additional facts are needed to develop the most effective advertising campaign. They should recommend that the advertiser secure that information by employing outside specialists to make the studies required, and should point out that where the agency directs the research activities, it is necessary for the agency to charge a special fee to cover the cost of such direction.

Certainly research studies, including product and market analyses, can be extremely important factors in the development of an advertising campaign. Such research activities are not an integral part of an advertising campaign any more than product engineering (which has an important bearing on salts) is a direct or integral part of an advertising campaign. For this reason, the agency can be expected only to express its opinion concerning the need for research; this in contrast to the job of actually performing the study.

Distribution and Sales

Since an advertising message is generally intended to reach the ultimate purchaser of a product, it is wasteful to advertise to persons who are not prospective customers; that is, to persons who cannot conveniently purchase the advertised article. A businessman would not advertise coal in an area which he did not serve; rather, he would concentrate his advertising in the area in which he distributed his product. The manner of distribution or type of retail outlet also becomes an important element to be considered in connection with the development of an advertising campaign. Often the manufacturer has a choice of the type of outlet through which he can distribute his product. For example, some manufacturers of phonograph records distribute records through jobbers, each jobber having the exclusive rights in a specific geographical area. Other manufacturers of phonograph records distribute their products directly to the retail stores.

The advertising agency should be in a position to advise the advertiser concerning the various available methods of distribution. One method of distribution may provide a much greater rate of gross profit than another. Obviously, where the profit margin is larger, there are more funds available for advertising. On the other hand, it can be assumed that a method of distribution which provides a smaller profit rate presupposes the need for less sales expense and probably smaller advertising appropriations. The advertising agency can be expected to be of valuable assistance in determining the most efficient method of distribution, but it cannot be expected to be of actual assistance in distributing the goods. This is a job for the advertiser and his salesmen.

In any event, the method of distribution must be determined before the advertising campaign can be successfully planned. The agency should be taken into the advertiser's confidence and should be fully informed of the distribution methods used by the advertiser and of any contemplated changes in the methods. The agency should be informed of the current sales rate in each territory and through each type of distributor, dealer or jobber. Such facts are helpful to the agency and will indicate where the advertising is successful and where it is not.

MEDIA SELECTION

It is pointed out that how the early advertising agencies performed the single function of buying advertising space and selling it to the advertiser. This phase of the agency business has continued to be one of its important functions, and this chapter, therefore deals with the problems and methods of selecting advertising media. This is a complex process which calls for wide knowledge and acute judgment.'

Types of Media

The types of media from which selection must be made according to their appropriateness for advertising a particular product are:

1. Daily newspapers; Sunday newspapers; weekly newspapers; farm papers; national magazines; trade papers and magazines; and various specialized or restricted publications.
2. Radio and television, including sponsored programmes or spot announcements, either local or network.
3. Outdoor advertising, including posted outdoor displays, painted outdoor display signs and spectaculars, and car cards as they appear in streetcars, busses, subways, elevated trains and other forms of commuter transportation.
4. Direct-mail materials, dealer displays, catalogs, etc.
5. Special advertising, including commercial moving picture productions, sky-writing, sales-convention materials, etc.

Procedure Followed

The agency executive in meetings with the advertiser develops a general plan for the campaign. When the plan has developed to a point that will permit a determination of the kinds of advertising media to be used, it is necessary to determine which publications, which radio stations and what outdoor locations or car cards are to be used. The space buyer in an advertising agency and the space-buying department until recent years specialized in analyzing, selecting and buying printed media, i.e., newspaper and magazine space. With the advent and popularity of radio advertising, it became necessary for the agencies to provide a means of analyzing the effectiveness of the various radio networks and independent stations in order to determine which stations and chains were best suited for each advertising problem. Today the selection of printed media is quite separate and apart from the selection of radio advertising media.

The selection of outdoor advertising space is a relatively simple matter; consequently an established media department is usually assigned the task of selecting this medium. The National Outdoor Advertising Bureau compiles statistics relative to the effectiveness of various outdoor advertising locations. In addition, each outdoor advertising plant has many available statistics showing the effectiveness of each of its various locations. When the agency and the client have tentatively determined the types of media to be used and the approximate advertising budget for each type, the problem of actual selection of the specific media is at hand.

The Contact Man

Usually, the contact man or account executive has a general idea of the type of coverage that would serve the advertiser best. He may suggest, for example, that morning newspapers be used in preference to evening papers, or that Sunday editions be used exclusively. He may suggest that the product be advertised only in cities having a population in excess of a certain minimum; or, conversely, that the product be advertised only in small weekly papers.

If the problem concerns magazine choice, he may recommend those magazines appealing to the quality buyer; or, conversely, those appealing to the larger group of popular-price brand buyers. The contact man may have a well-defined opinion concerning the type of radio network or independent station that should be used, or he may suggest at what time of day the programme would be most effective. (In any case, the contact man, with or without the media-selection department, will develop a general idea of the time or space to be used. The media-selection department will then analyze the available publications, radio stations, outdoor locations, etc. This analysis will consist of a detailed study of population, "circulation, type of circulation, comparative costs of equal quantities of space and comparative" costs of getting the advertising message before each reader or listener.

For example, one radio station may charge one hundred dollars for a two-minute announcement; another may charge only fifty dollars. However, the importance is not only in the length of time the message is on the air; it includes also the number of people who will hear the message. But the question is further complicated: It is also necessary to determine how many actual prospects may listen to the message. If an advertiser is selling dog food, it is important to know how many listeners own dogs and therefore would be prospective purchasers of dog food. A similar type of analysis is necessary in connection with printed advertising appearing in magazines, newspapers, yearbooks, theater programmes, classified telephone directories, etc.(it is necessary for the media-selection department to determine the cost per unit of space, the comparative cost of reaching each reader, and the comparative cost of reaching each prospective buyer.

Where to Get the Facts

Nearly every newspaper, magazine, radio station and outdoor plant has compiled statistics from which the media-selection department can secure many facts to assist in the selection of the proper media for each campaign. In addition, there are other sources for obtaining statistical information, such as Standard Rate & Data, a service of directories which lists each advertising medium with its advertising rates, circulation, population and like data. Ayer's Directory of

Newspapers and Periodicals, published annually, furnishes considerable information on nearly every publication in the United States. This book, along with Standard Rate k Data, will be found in every agency's media department.

The Media Recommendation

Upon completing the study to determine where the advertiser's product can be advertised most effectively, a media recommendation is prepared which consists of the following:

1. List of various advertising media to be used.
2. Dates and quantities of space to be used on each date.
3. Total quantity of space to be used during the advertising period.
4. Cost of each advertisement.
5. Total cost of the advertising in each medium.

The media recommendation is discussed in detail with the contact man, who may suggest revisions. When the recommendation is in its final form, the contact man presents it to the advertiser and discusses the merits of the recommendation in whatever detail is pertinent. It should be noted that the entire advertising appropriation cannot be spent for advertising space, since a substantial sum must be reserved for the cost of the various advertising materials required to produce the advertising. This refers mainly to print advertising in newspapers and magazines. Here art work in the form of lay-outs and finished art, engravings, typesetting, electros, mats, Photostats, etc., are required. In an advertising campaign running in newspapers or magazines, from eight to fifteen percent of the total advertising budget may be spent for advertising materials.)

The selection of radio advertising presents problems different from those connected with printed advertising. In radio advertising, it is necessary not only to select the network station and the time of day for the advertising, but it is also imperative that the type of show or announcement fit the product. Obviously, the soap operas which are currently popular would not be in keeping for an advertisement of Cadillac cars or Steinway pianos. Conversely, a symphony orchestra programme would not be suitable for advertising, say, bubble gum. In radio advertising, the selection of one station over another or one network over another is often not so important as the selection of the programme or type of programme.

The spot announcement or chain break is a form of advertisement that has paid nice dividends. This presents an additional problem for the agency. It is necessary to determine if the programme is to take the form of spot announcements and chain breaks or if it is to be a sponsored programme. After this determination has been made, if the decision is for the spot announcement or chain break, the procedure follows a pattern similar to that of printed advertising. A radio media recommendation would contain a list of the stations to be used, the hours during each date on which the programme would be broadcast, the cost of each broadcast, and the total cost of advertising on each station.

When the sponsored programme is decided upon, the agency encounters a more difficult job. Here it is necessary to determine first what type of programme is to be used; second, what kind of talent is available; and third, what radio time is available on each station or network. Sometimes the agency can buy a "package show," which means that one lump sum is paid for the talent and the radio time. In other cases, the agency secures the talent, which is paid for separately from the radio time.

The sponsored-programme form of radio advertising usually involves substantial expenditures. Generally, not only the media-selection department, but also the executives of the agency will give serious consideration to all of the elements involved in selecting a sponsored programme for an advertiser, fn presenting its recommendation to the advertiser, the agency will submit statistics showing the approximate audience for each programme suggested. There are various independent organizations which rate radio shows and indicate the approximate number of listeners. The services of these organizations are often purchased by agencies in an effort to determine the effectiveness and circulation of the programme. (Kledia selection, whether it is in connection with printed advertising, radio advertising or outdoor advertising, is an established service of the advertising agency. The function of media selection never ceases; and even though an adverstising campaign has been completely decided upon, the agency continually reviews the various media being used by a client in order to determine the comparative effectiveness of the advertising. This is a service which the advertising agency renders to its clients in consideration of the commissions received from the newspapers, magazines, radio stations, etc. No additional charge is customary for media-selection service.

SPACE BUYING

After the media recommendation has been approved, it is necessary to make arrangements for purchasing the publication space, radio time or outdoor displays. In small agencies, it is not practicable to have a separate department to carry out this function, in which case the space is purchased by one of the principals of the firm. In larger agencies, the space-buying job is assigned to a department consisting of one or more space buyers and the necessary assistants. Prior to the actual purchasing of space, a media recommendation may have been made as described in the preceding chapter.

Where no formal media recommendation has been prepared in advance of the space-buying operation, there is always at least an informal media recommendation.

Space in newspapers and magazines is generally contracted for in advance for a period of a year. The contracts with newspapers sometimes call for "space as required." Radio time is purchased in terms of weeks of broadcasting, thirteen weeks generally being the minimum contract period. Frequently, radio time is contracted for longer periods, contracts being commonly issued for twenty-six, thirty-nine, or fifty-two weeks.

The Space Buyer

With the media recommendation at hand, the space buyer refers to various statistical records such as Standard Rate & Data to secure the terms and conditions for purchasing space from each source. Sometimes when it is not possible to secure sufficient information from the published data, the buyer must contact representatives of the radio station, periodical or outdoor plant.

Most of the printed advertising media (newspapers and magazines) have either their own direct salesmen or a special representative located in each of the principal cities of the country. The appointed representatives are usually companies that make a business of representing newspapers or magazines. They are commonly called "space reps." The function of the space representative is much the same as was that of the advertising agency itself in the early days of the business. The space representative has a contract with each of a number of newspapers or other publications. He solicits business from the agencies and acts very much like a direct salesman for the paper. Often the space representative forwards the copy to the paper and collects from the advertising agency, in which case he furnishes bills for the space and proof of its insertion.

Contracts and Rates

After the space buyer has secured the necessary facts regarding the advertising media, he prepares and issues contracts. Each contract covers the space to be used by one client only. Although the advertising agency may use space in the same periodical or radio station for many clients, the space is contracted for each client separately.

It may be that the rate charged for the advertising space varies from one client to another. Such rate differences occur because of different total quantities of space contracted for and different times of placing contracts. It is important to note here that newspapers, magazines and radio stations offer different rates for advertising space depending on the conditions under which they serve the advertiser. The rate for a black-and-white advertisement is usually less than for a two-colour one; likewise, a two-colour advertisement is cheaper than a four-colour one.

Special positions take special charges; for example, an advertisement on the financial page or on the sports page will take a higher rate than one which can be inserted anywhere in the paper; likewise, magazines charge more for the inside front or back cover than for space elsewhere in the publication. In addition to these variances in rate, many newspapers offer combination rates for combination advertisements that are run both evening and morning, or that are run both daily and on Sunday. As a general rule, all newspapers charge higher rates for space in Sunday editions than in daily editions. Some newspapers offer "sliding-scale" rates; that is, the rate per line is set on a minimum amount of space, and if the advertiser uses more space, the rate is reduced. For example, a paper might offer a rate of thirty cents a line for the first two thousand lines, after which the rate is reduced to twenty-five cents a line until the total amount of space during the year has equaled five thousand lines, at which time the rate will be reduced to perhaps twenty cents. Often these rate reductions of sliding-scale papers are retroactive to the beginning of the contract year.

There are many small weekly newspapers published throughout the country. These weekly newspapers are excellent advertising media for certain advertisers, but buying space in these papers is more difficult than carrying on business with the larger daily papers. For this reason, several associations have been formed to represent groups of weekly papers. These associations offer space in a large number of weekly papers. Space contracts sometimes can be let for a group of papers through such associations. The associations then assume the responsibility for billing and for furnishing copies of the papers in which the advertising appears.

Contracts for advertising space in newspapers, whether small or large, and for all kinds of magazines will ordinarily include the following information:

1. The name of the advertising agency contracting for space.
2. The name of the client on whose account space is purchased.
3. The product to be advertised.
4. The kind of space purchased—whether daily, Sunday, combination daily and Sunday, combination morning and evening, etc.
5. The rates at which space is purchased.
6. The frequency of insertions (in reference to magazines).
7. The position requested (run-of-paper, back cover, front cover, financial page, etc.).
8. The period covered by the contract (this is usually one year).

The above list includes the major items; however, the contract often includes further specifications, such as to whom tear pages or proofs of insertion are to be sent, where bills for advertising are to be sent, how many copies of such bills are required, and the general terms and conditions of the contract.

STANDARD CONTRACTS

Standard conditions governing advertising contracts and orders were adopted in 1920 and revised in 1933 by the American Newspaper Publishers Association, Periodical Publishers Association, Agricultural Publishers Association, and the Associated Business Papers, in cooperation with the American Association of Advertising Agencies. Agencies that are members of the American Association of Advertising Agencies or that are "recognized" by one of the publishers' associations listed, usually print these terms and conditions on the reverse side of each contract. If the standard conditions are changed in any way, there is a possibility that such a change could affect the liability of the agency and any change in these conditions could result in confusion and delay. Contracts for radio time and outdoor advertising usually take a form that is different from contracts for newspaper and magazine space. When network radio shows are purchased, special contracts are drawn up to cover each situation. Spot radio broadcast contracts are much simpler in form and follow a pattern similar to the contract for printed advertising space in newspapers and magazines.

I. Terms of Payment

(a) The Agency agrees to pay and the publisher agrees to hold the agency solely liable for payment for the advertising covered by this contract.

The agency personally agrees to pay for advertising covered by this contract at the office of the publisher or his authorized representative on or before the last day of the month following that in which the advertising is published unless otherwise stipulated on publisher's rate card on which this contract was based, or when cash discount is deducted but payment date not specified on the publisher's rate card, on the 15th of the month following.

Bills must be rendered not less often than monthly but failure to do so shall not constitute breach of contract.

(b) The agency agrees to pay in the manner specified in paragraph (a) for all drawings, composition, cuts or mats if furnished by the publisher at the request of the agency provided it is the practice of the publisher to charge for such service.

(c) Cuts and mats shall be sent to the publisher prepaid. If they are not, the publisher may accept them, and pay transportation and import charges and the agency shall promptly reimburse the publisher.

(d) If at the end of the advertising period named in the contract or upon prior termination of the contract for any cause, the agency has not used the full amount of advertising contracted for, the agency shall pay to the publisher such additional sum on all advertising so published as shall be equal to the difference, if any, between the amount due at the rate named in the contract and the amount due at the rate applicable to the quantity of space used, according to that schedule of advertising rates of the publisher on which the contract was based, and upon such expiration or termination said additional sum shall become immediately due and payable. Short rate bills must be rendered within sixty days after the expiration of the contract period, otherwise the publisher agrees to a settlement at the rate named in the original contract. Unless otherwise expressed on the face hereof, this contract may be cancelled by the agency, or less space used, in accordance with the provisions of this paragraph.

(e) Any bill rendered to the agency by the publisher shall be conclusive as to the correctness of the items therein set forth and shall constitute an account stated unless written objection is made thereto by the publisher or the agency within sixty days from the rendering thereof.

(f) The publisher reserves the right to cancel the contract at any time upon default by the agency in the payment of bills, or other breach, or in the event of any material violation on the part of the agency of any of the conditions herein named; and upon such cancellation all advertising done hereunder, including short rates or other charges under this contract, and unpaid, shall become immediately due and payable. In case of delinquency in payment or impaired credit of the agency the publisher shall have the right at any time to change the requirements as to the terms of payment for further advertising under this contract as he may see fit.

(g) In all cases where date of payment is material, unless otherwise stipulated the postmark date on the envelope properly addressed to the publisher or to his representative shall be considered the date when payment was made.

2. Rates

(a) All rates shall be published. There shall be no secret rates, rebates, or agreements affecting rates. All rates shall be furnished agencies if requested.

(b) "Publisher's rate card" shall be understood to mean that" schedule of advertising rates of the publisher upon which this conlract is based.

(c) The rate stated in the contract is the minimum rate at which an equal or less amount of space, for the same class of advertising, to be published in a like position, under the same conditions, within the same period of time, can bo secured.

(d) If additional space is used within the period covered by the contract where the publisher has a schedule of graduated rates, any lower rate shall be given if earned, according to the publisher's rate card on which this contract is based.

3. Advertising Material

(a) The subject matter, form, size, wording, illustration and typography of the advertising shall be subject to the approval of the publisher but unless otherwise authorized in advance no change shall be made without the consent of the agency.

(b) If the publisher is unable to set any advertisement in the type or style requested, he may set such advertisement in such other type or style as in his opinion most nearly corresponds thereto, and the advertisement may be inserted without submission of proof unless proof before insertion is requested on the face of the order.

(c) Where cuts, electrotypes, or material furnished by the agency occupy more space than specified in the contract or insertion order, publisher should immediately communicate with the agency for definite instructions. If the publisher is unable to secure definite instructions from the agency, the advertising shall be omitted.

(d) If agency has contracted for a series of insertions in a publication, and before closing date insertion order and copy for next issue have not been received by publisher, publisher shall notify agency and follow agency's instructions.

(e) Advertisements ordered set in "space as required" shall be measured from office ad. rule to office ad. rule.

4. Proof of Insertion

(a) The page containing the advertising or, at the request of the agency a copy of each issue in which the advertising appears, shall be mailed or otherwise supplied to the agency, which shall be deemed to have received such copy or page unless the publisher is notified in writing of the non-receipt thereof within thirty days after the date of publication. The publisher may mail or otherwise supply an affidavit of publication in lieu of a second copy or page containing the advertisement. Failure to forward or furnish such copy, page or affidavit shall not constitute a breach of the contract.

5. Circulation

(a) Unless the publisher is a member of the Audit Bureau of Circulations, the agency shall be entitled, upon request, to a statement of net paid circulation verified by a certified public accountant, or in lieu thereof to the right to examine the publisher's circulation books.

6. Omission of Adverting

(a) Failure by the publisher to insert in any particular issue or issues invalidates the order for insertion in the missed issue but shall not constitute a breach of contract.

In newspapers the advertising must appear in all regular editions issued on the date for which the advertising is ordered. Advertisements omitted from any particular edition or editions must be reported to the agency and if received in time and omitted through fault of publisher must be made up or adjusted unless otherwise instructed.

Unless otherwise stipulated, the publisher shall have the right to omit any advertisement when the space allotted to advertising in the issue for which such advertisement is ordered has all been taken, and also to limit the amount of space an advertiser may use in any one issue.

7. General

(a) The agency agrees that it will not rebate to its client any part of the commission allowed by the publisher.

(b) In dealing with agencies, the publisher shall follow a uniform policy to avoid discrimination.

(c) Unless later date is specified in publisher's rate card, advertising in newspapers shall begin within thirty days from the date of this confract, or contract becomes null and void.

(d) A waiver by the publisher of any default or breach by the agency shall not be considered as a waiver of any subsequent default or breach of the same or any other provisions hereof.

Insertion Orders

After the space contracts have been issued and prior to the insertion of each advertisement in the printed media, it is necessary to issue what is commonly called an insertion order. The space contract has simply reserved the space and established the terms and conditions under which the purchase is to be made. The insertion order is a detailed description of the space to be used for each advertisement. When the agency has prepared an advertisement, the insertion order is issued by the space-buying department. The insertion order is often sent with copy instructions, mats, plates, etc. The insertion order should contain the following:

1. The name of the advertising agency.
2. The name of the advertiser.
3. The name of the product to be advertised.
4. The date for the insertion of the advertising. (This includes the edition, or editions if the publication has more than one edition.)
5. The amount of space to be occupied by the advertisement.
6. The position requested in the publication.
7. The number of colors to be used in printing the advertisement.

In addition, the agency often includes other information on the insertion order, such as to whom tear pages or copies of the publication are to be sent as proof of insertion; the number of copies of invoices requested and to whom they are to be sent; and special instructions regarding the printing of the advertisement. This usually refers to position and may include a statement that the advertisement is not to be printed next to competing copy, etc.

After the space-buying department has issued the insertion order, it has completed its function in connection with space buying with only one exception. It is the responsibility of the space-buying department to see that the agency fulfils its contract requirements with each vendor of advertising media. It is important to note that an advertising agency ordinarily does not act as an agent in the accepted legal sense. The advertising agency is itself financially responsible for carrying out its commitments. It is financially liable to pay for the space it buys. Whether or not the client pays is of no legal importance in the transaction between the agency and the publisher, radio station, etc.

Many newspapers, magazines, radio stations and outdoor advertising plants offer cash discounts in consideration of prompt payment of invoices. To secure this additional revenue, the agency must pay its bills in accordance with the vendors' terms. Therefore, it becomes important to set up a means by which the agency can collect from the advertiser before the cash discount payment date offered by the vendor. This subject will be discussed in a later chapter, but it should be emphasized here that the term "advertising agency" is misleading. The advertising agency, in the legal sense, is not an agent. It is responsible for whatever commitments for advertising space it makes.

CHECKING ADVERTISING

The purchaser of an article wants to be sure he receives it and wants to verify the quantity and quality before he pays for it. Printed advertising is purchased in accordance with definite terms and conditions as to quantity, quality and time of publication. Before the agency makes payment to the publisher, it is desirable to check the advertising to determine whether it meets the specifications in accordance with the contract and order. In most agencies one or more persons are assigned the job of checking the advertising. This is a routine job and usually follows a more or less standard pattern.

News Papers

A copy of each newspaper insertion order is sent to the checking department. Newspaper orders are filed by state and city in which the paper is published. Upon receipt of publications, agencies usually sort them in the same manner in which insertion orders are filed. Then, by referring to the insertion order bearing the same name as the publication, the checker is able to determine what advertising to look for. For example, if the checking department receives a copy of the Chicago *Sun,* the checker then looks in the file under "Illinois, Chicago, *Sun*" A copy of the insertion order covering the advertising should be filed there. If the title discloses an insertion order for "Illinois, Chicago, *Sun*" covering an insertion in a particular edition on a specified date, the checker then looks at the order further to find the name of the advertiser and the product, after which he runs through the paper to locate the advertisement. When this is located, the checker examines it for quality and correctness. Assuming that the correct advertisement has been published and that the quality of printing is acceptable, the checker then measures the advertisement to determine the amount of space occupied by it.

Newspaper space is usually sold in lines or inches. Daily papers usually sell space by lines; the small papers and weekly papers usually sell it by inches. An inch represents fourteen lines of "agate" type. The insertion order indicates whether the space is purchased by lines or inches. The checker is furnished with a rule calibrated in both. A line of space is the depth measure, a column is the width measure. In other words, if an advertisement occupies three columns in width and ten lines in depth, the space measurement would be thirty lines. The same rule holds true when the unit is inches instead of lines; that is, if an advertisement is three columns wide and three inches deep, the measurement would be nine inches.

Some agencies have established the practice of rating the various positions in which advertising appears in newspapers. The purpose of such a rating system is to determine whether or not a particular newspaper is giving the advertiser reasonably good positions in the paper. Generally, advertising which appears on the first few pages of a newspaper is considered to be more effective than that appearing far back in the paper. Advertising appearing in the upper right-hand corner of a page generally may be considered more effective than advertising appearing on the left bottom corner, etc.

After advertisement positions are rated, position reports are prepared to show the number of advertisements that secured the best position, the number that secured the second best position, etc. With these reports, the space buyer is in a position to determine which papers have been giving the advertiser reasonably good advertising positions and which have not. He can then call the representative of the paper that is not giving the advertiser reasonably good advertising positions and can demand greater consideration in the future.

Where the agency rates the positions of advertising, the key or code for such positions is noted on the insertion order at the time the checker examines and measures the advertisement. The position indication would be as follows:

Date of Insertion Ad Number Space Ordered Space Used Position.

Magazines and Trade Papers

Checking magazine and trade-paper space is considerably simpler than checking newspaper space. Space in magazines is usually purchased in units of pages or fractions thereof, although occasionally magazines arid trade papers sell space by columns or inches. The usual magazine advertisement occupying a page, half-page, quarter-page, etc. is not subject to shrinkage. This is because electrotypes and half-tones are used instead of mats. These are built to occupy the exact amount of space ordered. The checker, then, needs to inspect a magazine advertisement only for quality of print and position.

Some agencies, in addition to checking the appearance of advertising for quality and quantity, wish to determine the position secured in either a paper or a magazine. There are different methods of rating the comparative position of advertisements, but among the most important factors to be considered are:

1. The page number on which the advertisement appears.
2. The section in which the advertisement appears (such as buyer's guide, society section, financial section, etc.).
3. The position on the page.
4. Whether or not the advertisement appears adjacent to competitive copy.

Where the agency is interested in rating the position of the advertising, the checker usually is furnished with a code for this purpose. The code is entered on an accounting record from which the agency can prepare a report showing the various positions secured from the different publications.

Radio

The checking of radio advertising is, obviously, a different matter from checking printed advertising. Usually the broadcasting station sends the agency an affidavit certifying the fact that each message or programme was actually broadcast. Such affidavits are required by agencies before bills for broadcasting are paid. At times, advertising agencies have attempted to listen to each broadcast to check the message or programme, but this practice was never general. Most agencies rely on the honesty of the broadcasting stations and on other reports secured from the advertiser or his distributors in each town where a programme is broadcast. These distributors, of course, are acquainted with the facts concerning the advertiser's programme. Since the advertising is important to the distributor, it may be expected that the distributor would report any omissions or other defects in the radio advertising campaign.

In addition, there is a radio checking service available on both the East and West Coasts. Clients are furnished with actual recordings of what is said on the air waves on a particular programme, product or topic, or, occasionally, with programme scripts. There is available, also, a spot-checking service, with listeners or monitors in several hundred cities. Agencies and advertisers are advised whether the spots were actually used at the time they were scheduled; what the adjacencies were; the caliber of the presentation; and other pertinent data bearing on the effectiveness of the spot message.

Other Media

It is not a general practice for agencies to check the appearance of outdoor advertising and car cards. Lithographs or other material are sent to the outdoor advertising plants, which certify the actual placing and appearance of the advertising. It would be extremely difficult for an agency to check the posting date and the quality of the posting of each outdoor sign. The cost of such checking would not be warranted. For this reason, agencies do little or no checking of outdoor advertising space.

The National Outdoor Advertising Bureau does render a valuable service in this regard. In addition to checking the appearance of outdoor advertising, the Bureau furnishes other services.

One agency checked every outdoor location to determine the date on which each billboard was posted and the quality of the posting. In addition, for several years, this agency made intensive studies to determine the comparative value of the locations used. This practice was discontinued by the agency after a few years when it was found that the outdoor plants billed correctly for the space used and that the statistics furnished by the plant owners were reliable. This, they concluded, made independent checking and study of little value. Checking the appearance of advertising in the manner discussed is a service that the agency renders to the advertiser in consideration of the commissions received from the advertising media. No special or extra charge is made for such service.

Advertising Materials, Publicity and Miscellaneous

Certain materials are necessary to produce a printed advertisement. These are called mechanical production or advertising materials. They include art work, photography, typography, engravings, half-tones, electrotypes, mats, stereos, Photostats, etc.

WHY AGENCY SHOULD SPECIFY, ADVERTISING MATERIALS

It is highly desirable and almost essential for the agency to specify and purchase these materials, for only in this way can it control the final result or appearance of the advertising. Production work starts almost as soon as the contact man and the client have agreed on an advertising campaign, at which time it becomes necessary to visualize, at least roughly, the various advertisements as they are to appear. To do this, the agency prepares rough sketches of each advertisement. Sometimes these sketches merely take the form of rough lay-outs that are quickly penciled up by the agency's art department. In other cases, the visuals become more comprehensive and include an explanation of the final art work and a paste-up of the whole advertisement including the type, etc.

In any event, when the kind of advertisement has finally been approved by the client, the agency sets about procuring the necessary materials for printing it. The agency at the outset prepares a timetable showing on what dates each item of material is required, because it is necessary to secure the art work before plates can be made, etc., and all materials, including the final mats or half-tones, must be complete in time to send them to the publisher for printing the advertisement.

Production Orders

Orders are issued in the production department of an advertising agency for each of the materials as it is required; and, as the materials are received with bills from suppliers, all of the production elements for the advertisement are gathered together until the final piece of material is received.

The engraving, electrotype, mat or stereo is forwarded to the publication and the cost of all of the items is invoiced to the client. In some agencies, the art work required for the production of advertising is segregated from the other materials. In such cases, the securing of the needed art work becomes the function of the art director or art department and the securing of the other materials is delegated to the production manager or production department.

There is no standard of procedure in the operation of production and art departments of advertising agencies but there is some uniformity of operation among agencies in regard to certain parts of the art and production work. Most agencies prepare rough lay-outs and nearly all agencies undertake to secure the final art work required, either by creating the art work in their own department or by purchasing it on the outside. Nearly all agencies undertake to secure the other materials required, such as type, electros, half-tones and mats. The difference in the operation of production departments among agencies comes in the charges made for performing the functions. This subject will be discussed in the chapter "Basis of the Agency's Compensation."

Some agencies operate production departments in which the entire responsibility for securing all required mechanical elements rests within the department. This includes the scheduling of materials so that they are received when they are required. It also includes the responsibility of getting the final plates or mats to the publisher before a closing date. In other agencies, the production department is charged merely with the responsibility of purchasing the advertising materials required; the scheduling and expediting duties are delegated to a separate traffic department.

Publicity

Publicity, in the sense it is used here, may be defined as the dissemination of information regarding products or industries without the overt purpose of selling. It takes the form of news stories and feature articles in the press, in national magazines, in trade papers and in farm papers. Some publicity is also accomplished through the radio in connection with news and other programs. There is a growing feeling among agencies that publicity campaigns can be best conducted by publicity or public relations firms which specialize in this work. This feeling is emphasized by the attitude among publishers that advertising agencies, in attempting to secure publicity, are actually endeavoring to divert what should be paid advertising into free publicity.

Nevertheless there are a number of agencies that have completely organized publicity departments. These agencies plan, create, develop and place publicity as an extra service to certain clients. Unless the advertiser's account is very large and highly profitable, the agency cannot afford to provide a publicity service without arranging for a special fee to cover the cost of the work. On the other hand, most agencies do counsel and advise with their clients concerning publicity. They further assist the clients by cooperating with the publicity firms which handle that phase of service for the client.

Miscellaneous Functions

In addition to the principal services which have been discussed, agencies perform many diverse and incidental services, dependent on the need of the advertiser and the skill and elasticity of the agency. Some of these miscellaneous services are:

1. Making a study of competitive advertising.
2. Assisting the client in his own sales work in order to insure the greatest effectiveness from the advertising.

(This type of service often includes the attendance at sales conventions, and the preparation of material to be used for dealers' and distributors' conventions.)

3. Testing copy—an innovation in the agency service.
4. Preparing house organs, catalogs, and the like.
5. Testing recipes for making food products.
6. Securing personnel for the client's advertising department.
7. Preparing booklets to be distributed to dealers and jobbers.
8. Preparing sales manuals, etc.
9. Preparing exhibits for conventions and industry shows.
10. Supervising the production of commercial films.

Usually all of these special services involve expenditures on the part of the agency; therefore, since the average advertising account does not provide a sufficient margin of profit to allow for such expenditures, the agency usually arranges for a special fee for doing such work. These fees are generally on a cost-plus basis, but such jobs are sometimes undertaken on a flat fee basis as well.

Chapter 2

Billing and Budget

BILLING THE ADVERTISING

The advertising agency is semiprofessional, offering a combination of commercial and professional services. The agency attempts only to assist the advertiser by selecting the media to be used, by conceiving the advertising campaign and by developing it into the final advertising message. Today agencies do not compete with one another by offering different payment terms or by claiming that they can buy space below published rates.

AGENCY SHOULD NOT ACT AS A BANKER

The agency should not act as the banker for the advertiser, In fact, the average advertising agency has a smaller capital than most of its clients. The agency serves a useful professional function through the special skills of its employees. It renders inconsequential service to the advertiser in its financial dealings with media vendors.

For these reasons it is a cardinal principle of the advertising-agency business that all advertising space and radio time should be billed to the client sufficiently in advance to provide for payment to the agency prior to the date upon which the agency is obligated to pay the media.

Invoices for magazine and trade-paper space are usually prepared and sent to clients fifteen days before the date on which the agency is required to pay the publication. If the advertiser wishes to earn the cash discount, he must pay the agency prior to the date on which the agency must pay the publication. In practice, no well-run agency will continue to serve the advertiser who does not discount his bills. Magazines and trade papers have various payment terms, so no general rule can be established concerning the time of the month in which magazine and trade-paper advertising is billed. The billing time varies according to the terms of the publication.

Liability may be Substantial

It is very important to note that the agency's liability for magazine advertising may be much more substantial than is often realized. Frequently, the advertising agency takes a greater financial risk than any other creditor of the advertiser. This is because magazines often go to press months in advance of publication. After the magazine is once on the press, the agency's liability has been fixed. Thus it will be seen that an agency can be and often is liable to magazines for advertisements for a cumulative period covering two or three months. Magazines have established "closing dates" and "cancellation dates." The cancellation date is the last day upon which the advertiser can cancel the advertising. The closing date is the date on which the publication goes to press. Unless the advertising agency has convincing proof that the advertiser is fully capable of meeting its obligations, it is desirable to invoice advertising space so as to collect from the advertiser on or before the cancellation date for each magazine. After this date the liability of the agency is fixed regardless of whether the advertiser can pay the agency.

Newspaper advertising space, of course, can appear throughout an entire calendar month. Newspapers usually bill on a monthly basis, although some weeklies bill after each issue. Advertising agencies usually invoice newspaper space on a monthly basis. Since, as has been noted under the subject of checking newspaper advertising, newspaper space ordered is subject to shrinkage, it is impossible to complete accurate billing on a space-used basis until after all the newspaper advertising for the month has been measured.

It is common for advertisers to use newspapers that are published hundreds and thousands of miles distant from the place of business of the advertising agency. For this reason, copies of newspapers frequently reach the agency from five days to a week after the issuance of the paper. This means that checking of a month's newspaper advertising frequently cannot be completed until about the tenth of the subsequent month. If an agency were to defer billing until newspaper advertising for a calendar month was checked, frequently the bill could not be sent to the advertiser until after the tenth of the subsequent month. The standard payment terms of most newspapers call for payment by the agency to the newspaper on either the tenth, fifteenth, twentieth or twenty-fifth of the month subsequent to the advertising.

From this it is evident that final accurate billing for newspaper space cannot be accomplished early enough to permit the receipt of the funds by the agency before the date on which the agency must pay the newspaper. It is necessary for agencies to find a method by which they can secure payment from the advertiser in advance of the date upon which they must make payment to the newspapers.

Two different methods of billing for newspaper space have been developed to accomplish the desired result.

Billing on a Space-ordered Basis

One method is to bill all space ordered during a month on the basis of space ordered. Where this method is used, the agency sends its invoice to the client by the first or second day of each month to cover the advertising space ordered for the previous month. After all the advertising space has been checked, the agency sends the client a credit memo to cover omissions and shrinkage. This method, which is sometimes called "billing on a space-ordered basis," has the disadvantage of involving double work. First, a detailed invoice on a space-ordered basis must be prepared; second, a credit memo covering omissions and shrinkage is prepared. The method has the same disadvantages for the advertiser in that he must audit both the original bill and the credit memo.

Billing on a Prebill Basis

The more desirable method for billing newspaper space so that the agency secures payment before it must pay the publishers is to "prebill." A prebill is simply a commitment billing. It consists of an invoice, sent on the first of the month following advertising and containing one line only, something like this:

- Newspaper space for the month of June—$92,000

The amount of the monthly prebill can be secured by reference to the media recommendation, which is sometimes later refined and called an "estimate." On the twentieth or twenty-fifth of the month following advertising, the agency prepares a complete detailed invoice on a space-checked basis.

The advertiser's first reaction to the prebill method is, often, that he is paying the agency a large sum of money without any proof of the actual debt. This is without basis because: First, the advertiser knows what his advertising programme calls for and receives copies of the newspapers containing the advertising almost currently with its appearance; and second, by the time the advertiser pays the agency (the tenth of the month following insertion) the agency has already committed itself in substantial amounts for advertising that will appear prior to the payment of the previous month's invoice. Many of the largest advertisers in the country are paying their agencies on a prebill basis which has the distinct advantage of avoiding duplicate work, since only one detailed invoice is prepared by the agency and audited by the advertiser.

Radio time is often invoiced on a weekly basis, invoices being issued immediately following each week's broadcasting. It is a simple matter for the agency to prepare an invoice covering radio time. Such bills are mailed to advertisers either on the first day of each week covering the prior week's broadcasting, or on the first or second day of each month covering the broadcasting of the previous month. Radio talent is usually invoiced on a weekly basis, invoices being prepared by the agency and sent to advertisers on the first day of each week covering the talent costs of the prior week. Sometimes agencies prefer to invoice for radio talent on a monthly basis in which case the agency must meet current weekly payments and collect from the advertiser after the close of each month. Agencies usually add either 15 or 17.65 percent to the cost of radio talent. When the 15 percent is added, the commission is only 13 percent; whereas when 17.65 percent is added, the commission is the standard 15 percent which agencies also earn on printed space. Outdoor space is billed monthly and invoices cover posting for the current month. All bills are due ten days from the date of issuance.

Billing Advertising Materials

Advertising materials purchased by the agency for the advertiser include such items as art work, typography, engravings, electros, half-tones, mats, stereos, photostats, radio transuip-tions and lithography used for outdoor advertising.

It is more or less standard practice for the agency to group all of the advertising materials purchased for a particular advertisement and to bill them on one invoice. There are two methods: (i) billing monthly for all items purchased during the month, and (2) billing jobs for all materials for one advertisement when they have been secured. There is no standard method for fixing the price of the advertising materials billed by the agency to its clients. Perhaps the most common current method is for the agency to add 15 or 17.65 percent to the cost of the items purchased. Many agencies add 17.65 percent so that the selling price provides for a 15 percent commission. The subject of the agency's fee in connection with the purchase of advertising materials will be discussed in more detail later.

The same rule is not always followed in connection with the creation and preparation of catalogs, house organs, dealer helps and direct-mail advertising. Agencies usually provide for a special fee in connection with the preparation of these items which require the time and effort of the creative personnel of the advertising agency, since any commission based on a percentage of the cost of these items could not possibly compensate the agency for creative work. This creative work when it is used in connection with regular advertising media is compensated for by the commission received on the space used.

BASIS OF THE AGENCY'S COMPENSATION

The service that an advertising agency performs for a client is always tailored to fit the particular client's requirements. No two agencies deliver exactly the same services, and no one agency delivers exactly the same service to any two of its clients. The answer to the question of what an agency should charge its client for the work performed must of necessity be based on the quantity and quality of the work.

The commission system of compensation is a historical part of the agency business. Although attempts have been made to get away from the commission form of compensation for personal service in this business, such efforts have not been successful. Under the commission system, the agency's compensation (a commission paid by the advertising media to the agency based on a percentage of the advertising space or time purchased) is figured on the volume of advertising space and materials purchased rather than on the amount or quality of work required. To determine what services can be performed for the commission to be received from the advertising media, the agency must weigh the commission revenue against the estimated cost of performing the service. When this is done, it is found that many extensive services can be performed for one client, where only limited service can be performed for another.

THREE TYPES OF AGENCIES

It is necessary, then, to survey the several types of advertising agencies and the several types of advertising accounts before the elements of service performed and the basis of the agency's compensation for performing them can be discussed. For convenience, agencies may be classified as follows:

1. General advertising. In this category may be placed agencies whose accounts consist of those in which the client's product is advertised to the general public through the customary advertising media, including newspapers, magazines, trade papers, farm papers, radio, outdoor displays and car cards.
2. Industrial agencies. In this category may be included the advertising agencies that specialize in industrial accounts which advertise machinery, electrical devices, tools, equipment and other articles to the industrial consumer and not to the general public. In exceptional cases, articles that the agency is trying to sell to industrial consumers are actually advertised to the general public in order to secure a public demand for a product. An example of this type of advertising is the advertising of thermostatic controls which eventually become a part of heating systems.
5. Agency specialists. In this group may be placed agencies not included in groups one and two, such as, for instance, those specializing in foreign, retail store, financial, classified, fashion or theatrical advertising.

The differentiating factor in classifying the agencies into the three types has been the type of account handled. Each of the three types can be subdivided further according to the general character of services rendered. The agency whose most powerful selling appeal is created through art work may be typed as the art agency; the agency whose principal selling appeal is the advertising copy may be typed as the copy agency; the agency whose principal strength is in the field of radio advertising may be termed the radio agency, etc.

Effect of Size of Account

Before the basis of the agency's compensation can be intelligently discussed, it is necessary to classify advertising accounts by size of advertising appropriation. An account whose annual advertising appropriation is $50,000 or less may be considered a small account; one whose annual advertising appropriation is from $50,000 to $150,000 may be considered a medium-sized account; an account whose annual advertising appropriation is from $150,000 to $500,000 represents a large advertiser; an account whose annual advertising expenditure exceeds $500,000 is a very large account.

General advertising agencies in fixing the basis of their compensation on large or very large accounts usually find that they can perform all of the services listed in the chapter "Functions Performed by the Modern Advertising Agency" in consideration for the commissions received from the sale of advertising space and materials. The only exception would be research studies and publicity.

Services Rendered

General advertising agencies in determining the basis of their compensation in connection with handling medium-size accounts as a rule find that they are able to deliver the following services in consideration of the commissions received:

1. Developing the advertising campaign.
2. Writing the copy.
3. Selecting the art work and supervising its preparation.
4. Analyzing and selecting media.
5. Buying the advertising media.
6. Buying the production materials.
7. Checking the advertising.
8. Billing the advertising.

General agencies handling medium-size accounts bill production materials at cost, plus 17.65 or 15 percent. General agencies in fixing the fees for handling small accounts usually find that they cannot afford to perform the services required by the advertiser without securing a fee in addition to the commissions received. The cost of planning the campaign, writing the copy, etc., when added to the contact cost and the general overhead of the agency can, and does in many cases, exceed the commissions that an agency receives from the advertising.

When this condition occurs, the agency must arrange for a service fee or minimum charge per month or year. This fee is fixed by the agency after it determines the cost of the services required by the advertiser. Agencies make special arrangements with each client where service fees are required. The annual appropriations of industrial advertisers, by and large, are much smaller than are those of general advertisers. The cost of space in trade papers is relatively low and consequently the industrial agency's commission income per page of advertising is much less than that of the general agency whose clients advertise in national magazines or in large papers.

In addition, the industrial agency advertises specialized and technical products which require special skills and experiences to handle. Furthermore, the industrial account usually requires many collateral or miscellaneous services in connection with point-of-sale material, salesmen's manuals, descriptive folders, convention or business-show materials, etc. Because of these factors, it follows that the commission income from most industrial advertising accounts is insufficient to pay the cost of doing the needed work. The industrial account usually calls for a service fee or some other basis of compensation that will augment the commission received.

Agencies falling in the third, or specialists, classification differ so widely from one another that no generalization as to basis of compensation can be made. Each case will depend on the particulars. The agency often requires experience with an account before it can fix its compensation properly. All agencies have difficulty in determining the basis of compensation for research studies, but by far the larger number of agencies charges a special fee for conducting any but the most cursory investigation of markets or products. A few very large agencies maintain research departments and they offer certain services free to some larger clients. Because of the historic commission basis of compensation, an advertiser spends two or three million dollars a year in large costly space provides the agency with a large commission income allowing a sufficient margin for many "extras." Such accounts are rare. Research studies which have a direct bearing on advertising should be initiated and supervised by the agency. In most cases, these studies are billed to clients at cost plus a commission to cover the supervisory service.

Consultations with the advertiser concerning advertising, merchandising, selling and development of the advertising campaign are nearly always a part of the service the agency renders to its client for the media commissions and service fees received. It is in this area that the agency performs it's most vital and costly service. In the larger agency, one or more executives are assigned to an account. They are called contact men. These men are usually graduates from other departments, top men in the agency, and they carry the responsibility for planning and developing the campaign and coordinating the various services performed. In a small agency, the owners take on the responsibility for counseling and for planning and developing the campaign. This service is a free service in nearly every case.

The production activity of the agency, which includes the securing of the art work and advertising materials for the production of advertising, is one of the early functions of advertising agencies. Under the first open-contract arrangement, agencies purchased advertising space and materials for advertisers at cost plus a commission. Later, instead of adding a commission to the cost of the space, the various media allowed a commission to the agency. As long as advertising materials have been purchased by agencies, they have added a commission to compensate them for this service.

Different agencies use different commission rates in fixing the billing price of advertising materials. Many industrial and specialized agencies add 17.65 percent to the cost of advertising materials. Agencies dealing in low-cost space and agencies handling small accounts often add a higher percentage. Some general agencies handling medium-size and even large accounts add 17.65 per cent, but many of the general agencies add 15 percent to the cost of advertising materials.

This practice of adding a fifteen percent commission to the cost of advertising materials nets the agency only thirteen percent. Actual cost studies show that production departments cannot operate on a thirteen percent margin. Perhaps ten or fifteen years ago there was a sufficient margin of profit from space commissions to make up for a loss incurred in handling the advertising materials. This is not the case today. With the advertiser clamoring for more and more service, and the increasing cost of experienced personnel, the agency is facing the difficult job of making both ends meet. There is considerable current opinion that production departments must meet expenses. This has caused many agencies to add 17.65 percent to the cost of advertising materials purchased.

Agency Terms and Conditions

Many agencies carefully define the services that they offer for the fees that they charge. The functions performed, fees charged and other conditions are often incorporated by agencies into a booklet or other outline carrying a title such as "Standard Terms and Conditions." In the final analysis, what an agency has to sell is the accumulated experience of its personnel. The fees it receives from clients must be based on the amount and cost of services performed for them. In other professions, the services are first performed and then the fee is fixed based on the amount and cost of such service. In the agency, because of the "commission system," the fee is fixed first, after which the amount and quality of service must be determined. If the cost of the service exceeds the commission income, either the cost of the service must be reduced or an extra fee charged.

In the early days of the agency business, few services were performed and then the profit margin was large. But as each year passed, clients demanded additional services. Now an agency must analyze its business in order to determine the cost of performing the tailor-made service on each account. It must be in a position to tell the client what services can be performed for the commissions received and what must be compensated for by an extra charge.

CREDITS AND COLLECTIONS

Advertising agencies commit themselves to purchase advertising space, radio time and advertising materials that are to be used exclusively in connection with client's advertising. Regardless of whether the client discharges its debt to the agency, the agency, ethically and legally, is responsible for its commitments. An agency cannot hide behind a client's skirts.

Credit Angles

Magazine space is purchased many months in advance of publication. Magazines, trade papers and farm papers go to press weeks and months prior to distribution dates. Each publication fixes the date on which the agency's liability is fixed and non-cancellable.

Radio time is generally purchased in multiples of thirteen weeks of broadcasting. Non-cancellable contracts are entered into between the agency and the radio station or network. Expensive talent purchased for radio shows is contracted for long periods of time.

Contracts for outdoor advertising are often non-cancellable and cover periods of time up to a year. Newspaper advertising space cannot be billed until the last day of the month of advertising, at which time the agency is obligated to pay the newspapers for the advertising space used during the entire month. In addition, the advertising to run for the next few days probably could not be cancelled prior to the publication date. Art work and advertising materials are purchased and paid for in many cases weeks or months prior to the time the items are invoiced to the advertiser.

The agency, many times, is irrevocably committed to media and to suppliers of advertising materials for the payment of sums which will aggregate from one sixth to one third of the client's annual advertising appropriation. In other words, the credit extended to a client by an agency will equal from two to four months' billings. Manufacturers and distributors of cosmetics, pharmaceuticals, cigarettes and similar items frequently spend a large proportion of their total sales volume for advertising and it is possible for the agency's commitments in such cases to equal as much as the total capital of the client.

To approach the matter of credits from another angle, let us consider the credit risk in proportion to the profit received from handling an account; for after all, business risks to be sound must be in proportion to the possible gain. Advertising agencies these days do well to net from one and one-half to three percent of their total sales volume. From this, it will be seen that the agency's profit from handling the account of a client spending $100,000 would average between $1,500 and $3,000 a year. When it is realized that the agency risks as much as $30,000 or $40,000 to secure a net profit of perhaps $2,000, it will be seen that little further financial risk can be prudently accepted.

The usual credit terms of an agency provide that the client must pay the agency a few days prior to the date on which the agency must pay the media. For all non-media items, usual terms provide for payment ten days from the date of the agency's invoice. Unless the financial position and integrity of the advertiser are beyond question, these usual terms cannot be granted because the possible gain just isn't worth the risk.

Of course, one of the first considerations in connection with the solicitation or handling of agency business is the question of the credit of the prospect or client. To determine the volume of credit to be allowed to a client, it is necessary to study each case individually. Unfortunately, there are no hard and fast rules that can be applied in order to measure a credit risk.

Credit Guideposts

A few generalities may be stated, however, to serve as guide-posts in this difficult matter of investigating the credit of prospects and clients for the purpose of determining whether a credit risk should be accepted:

1. The client or prospect should have a credit rating which justifies the extension of the credit sought. For this rating, one refers to the commercial rating companies such as Dun & Brad street.
2. The prospect or client should willingly give factual information upon which credit is to be based.
3. The client or prospect should have an undisputed record in connection with meeting its obligations and discounting its bills.
4. The agency should be convinced that the advertising campaign is in line with the advertiser's ability to produce and finance. The amount of credit extended by the agency (the amount of the agency's maximum commitment at any one time, plus the amount currently due for bills rendered) represents the credit risk. This should not exceed the largest line of credit granted to the client by other creditors. The advertiser's financial statement should clearly indicate his ability to pay advertising bills. That is, cash on hand at any one time should be sufficient to pay the agency's invoices.
5. When the agency has any question concerning the credit risk, it might be advisable for the agency first to determine the largest amount for which it is liable at any one time on account of purchases made for the advertiser. If a bank would not be willing to make an unsecured loan to the advertiser for this amount, it could be assumed that the credit risk is a bad one. The best rule for granting credit in the agency business is: If there is a question, the risk isn't worth taking.

There are many ways of reducing an agency's credit risks. Some methods used to accomplish this are:

1. Billing. Changing the agency's terms so as to bill for all media in time to secure payment prior to the date

on which the agency is finally committed to the purchase of the space. In the case of national magazine advertising, this would require that the advertiser pay the agency before the magazine's cancellation date. If the advertiser fails to make payment on such date, the agency could still cancel the advertising. In connection with newspaper advertising, this would require that the advertiser pay for each month's advertising on the first day of the month. The amount to be paid would be based on the space ordered for the coming thirty-day period. It is more difficult for the agency to protect itself from credit loss in connection with radio time and talent. This would require an advance payment from the client. The same applies to outdoor advertising and advertising materials.

2. Guarantee. Another method used for minimizing credit risks is for the agency to secure a guarantee where the client has a financial sponsor or parent company whose credit is unquestionable. Occasionally, the media may be willing to accept a credit risk where the agency would not do so. In such cases, it is possible to arrange for the client to be responsible to the media, thereby relieving the agency of this liability.
3. Insurance. Certain insurance companies have developed credit insurance policies to protect agencies from financial loss. For a description and discussion of advertising agency credit insurance.

Credit insurance should be considered only as an additional safeguard, as a guide to the agency in connection with accepting credit risks and as an aid in the collection of accounts. A credit risk should not be accepted simply because the agency carries credit insurance to cover the risk. On the other hand, no agency can afford to accept a credit risk that a credit insurance company would not insure. The fact that a credit insurance company is willing to accept a credit risk may be taken as a favorable factor. It must be remembered that even with credit insurance, the agency could suffer substantial financial loss as the result of failure to collect from the advertiser.

Collections

Usual billing terms provide for payment within ten days from the date of the agency's invoice. Cash discounts allowed by media are passed on to the advertiser as an inducement for prompt payment. Agencies do not allow the same rate of cash discount as is allowed to them by the media. They pass along or allow the same amount of cash discount as they receive. This means that where a publication allows a two percent cash discount to the agency, the two percent applies to the agency's cost which is eighty-five percent of the amount charged to the advertiser (on the fifteen percent media). On an item billed to a client for $100, the cash discount would be two percent of $85 or $1.70. This cash discount of $1.70 is allowed the client if the agency's bill is paid within ten days.

Not all advertising media allow cash discounts. There is never any cash discount allowed on radio talent and seldom on art work or advertising materials. Nevertheless, these items are payable ten days from the date of the agency's invoice.

No agency can afford to do business with a client who does not pay his bills on time. Consider for a moment that the average agency's capital is not more than one tenth of its annual sales volume. From this capital, the agency must provide for fixtures and equipment, for the payment of salaries, services and overhead items and for materials purchased in connection with client's advertising campaigns. When an agency bills advertising materials only upon the completion of a production job, substantial funds may be tied up in unbilled advertising materials.

No agency can afford to finance a client. It is a cardinal principle in the agency business that clients must pay their bills on time. Perhaps the reader will begin to wonder why such extreme caution in connection with credits and collections is urged. It is because the advertising agency is virtually the only professional business that becomes financially liable for huge commitments from which only the client can benefit.

The agency that transacts an annual volume of a million dollars actually should be compared to the architect, accountant or lawyer who does an annual volume of $150,000. In one situation in which a small agency was serving a very large manufacturer, the agency's bill covering one month's advertising amounted to nearly $100,000. The funds were not received on the due date. The contact man urged that the advertiser not be contacted since its financial reputation was above question. The bill was two days past due, and the agency was dealing with an out-of-town client. A telegram was promptly dispatched, requesting immediate payment of the outstanding account. The telegram brought a telephone response and the invoice was paid, but it was discovered that the client was holding up the bill because of one or two small items that he could not check. Not only did the procedure result in the prompt payment of the invoice, but it straightened out the client's auditing procedure and cleared the way for the prompt payment of all future invoices.

No responsible client will object when the agency calls its attention to a past-due item. Good business dictates the prompt payment of obligations and good businessmen like to keep their record clean. They appreciate it when a creditor calls their attention to an oversight or faulty procedure that holds up payment.

Because agency invoices involve substantial sums, it becomes necessary to follow collections closely. Some systematic method for doing this should be used. One method is to have a threeby-five card prepared from each invoice sent to a client. These cards show the name of the client, the due date and amount of the invoice. They are filed in a simple box file in due-date order. As clients' checks are received, the cards representing the invoices which are covered by the remittance are taken from the file and destroyed. The remaining cards represent unpaid invoices. The treasurer or other executive of the agency needs only to refer to this file to determine what invoices are outstanding or past due. Agency's terms should provide that where one item on an invoice is questioned, the amount of that item should be deducted by the client and the balance of the invoice paid promptly.

The responsibility of following collections should be delegated, without reservation, to one individual in each agency. Where that individual is not given sufficient ^authority to take the steps outlined in a collection policy, past-due accounts should be reported to whomever in the agency has the necessary authority. In the event of a substantial delay without good cause, where payment cannot be secured by the agency even after communicating with the client, the agency is justified in cancelling future advertising space. When this is necessary, the agency should notify the client of its intention. After such notification, the agency should have no hesitation in going through with the cancellations.

Usually, magazines and other advertising media will protec t the agency in that they will refuse to accept advertising from an advertiser who has not paid past-due bills. But to secure such protection, it is necessary for the agency to report such past-due payments. In such a case, if the advertiser attempts to place advertising space through another agency, it could be difficult for him to do so without paying his past-due obligations.

BUDGET

The function of a budget or forecast is to present management with the estimated results from future operations. To be useful to management on a policy-making level, it is necessary for the budget to present factual information from which operating policies can be determined. No budget, operating statement or balance sheet is of value unless it can be used by management for the good of the business.

General Considerations

An agency, to serve well, can afford to deliver only the service that each client pays for. In actual practice, many agency services are performed for the commission received from the sale of advertising space and materials. Agencies which have no method by which to determine the cost of serving each account are likely to "rob Peter to pay Paul." In such cases, the policy-making executives see only an operating statement which indicates that the agency made or lost money. Such operating statements do not show what it has cost to serve each account or what the income from each account has been.

A budget which simply forecasts the total revenue by classes and the total costs and expenses by type is of little use in advertising agency management. Such a budget could be compared with the budget of a manufacturing concern that does not segregate the income from various products or the costs applying to the manufacture and sale of each product. There are those who suggest that the advertising agency budget be segregated so as to show departmental costs; however, departmental costs are of little importance compared with the cost of serving each client. In some businesses, the steps in the manufacturing processes can be segregated within the departments of the manufacturer's plant. Departmental costs become of value in such cases. In the advertising agency business, there is no standard for grouping costs within departments.

For example, the copy cost could be large on one account; on another, the art cost could exceed copy cost; and on a third, contact cost could easily be the largest element. There is no scientific method for allocating gross revenue to the various departments within the agency, but it is relatively simple to determine each element of cost entering into serving one particular client.

It is impossible to prepare accurate budgets without first having established a cost-accounting system. No forecast of future operations can be accurately drawn without a knowledge of past operations in connection with similar types of transactions. Budgeting and cost accounting, therefore, are inseparable partners and must be used together.

A properly established cost-accounting system will furnish periodic statements showing separately the results of the agency's operations with each client. Such cost-accounting statements will show each of the sources of income, including, for example, commission received from newspaper space, magazine and trade-paper space, outdoor advertising, radio time, radio talent, advertising materials, service fees and miscellaneous items. The statement will show the various costs incurred in serving each client.

These costs are broadly divided into direct and indirect costs. Included among the direct expenses are creative and other direct salaries. These salaries include the cost of the time devoted to the account by creative people and others who spend time directly on clients' accounts, performing such services as contacting, planning, copy preparation, art direction, research, media selection and buying, production and publicity. Other direct expenses comprise those expenses that are incurred directly in connection with serving a particular client's account. They include such items as traveling, research, enter-So training and advertising materials purchased to serve a particular client which cannot be billed to the client. In this last category might appear such an item as resetting type because of an error made by the agency.

Included among the indirect expenses are indirect salaries. These include salaries paid to agency employees who do not work directly on any one account. Work performed in the following categories is generally included in this classification: stenography, typing, ordering, billing, accounting and administrative work. Other indirect expenses include all of the expenses of the agency that are incurred in its general operation, but which are not specifically incurred in connection with servicing particular clients. This classification includes such items as rent, light, local telephone, general travel, general entertaining, dues and subscriptions, stationery and supplies and the like.

The proper cost-accounting system will enable the agency to segregate its costs and expenses by clients and to segregate the costs and expenses on each account in accordance with the preceding formula. Because the advertising agency business lends itself particularly well to cost accounting, costs and expenses can be segregated properly with a minimum of effort, provided that the accounting and cost-accounting system is designed with this in mind. The form of the cost-accounting statements, to be of greatest use, must be in exactly the same form as the budget. There is no one ideal form. The type of statement to be used will depend somewhat on the requirements of the people who are going to work with the statements. The statements should be in such form that management can clearly understand the figures. The budget and the cost-accounting statements are intended to accomplish two principal objectives:

1. To show management how its policies are expected to work out.
2. To indicate to management how well the organization is carrying out its policies.

In other words, the budget is intended to show what will happen if the organization does what management directs, and the cost-accounting statement is intended to show whether the organization was able to do these things. No agency should attempt to prepare a budget or forecast until it has first established an adequate cost-accounting system. A forecast is not simply a schedule showing what business an agency can expect to do in the future; rather, it is a detailed report showing not only what business the agency is expected to do for a period of time, but showing as well the cost of transacting that business. The means for preparing an agency budget are well established. Following is an analysis of them.

FORECASTING MEDIA COSTS AND COMMISSIONS

It is not difficult to forecast the advertising space and materials that will be used during the budget period if each individual client is considered separately. Advertisers must determine their advertising expenditures for a period well in advance so that the agency can plan and develop the advertising and reserve the advertising space. After a client's appropriations have been established, it is customary for agencies to plan the advertising campaign and then to allocate the advertising expenditure by determining the amount to be spent for each advertisement in each publication. These breakdowns of advertisers' expenditures frequently take the form of schedules or estimates. Schedules or estimates may be formal documents submitted by the agency to the advertiser for his approval and signature.

Where estimates or schedules are used, it is obvious that these should be used in establishing the forecast of the client's billing. Frequently, there are no schedules or estimates that can be used for establishing billing forecasts. Even where the formal estimate or schedule system is used, clients may have the habit of frequently revising schedules, or they may sign schedules covering only certain parts of the advertising campaign, leaving other items open for future consideration. It is not infrequent for advertisers to change plans without much advance notice. The agency, the client, or both may unexpectedly consider the purchase of a radio show; or they may decide to market a new product; or they may alter advertising expenditures, depending on seasonable factors, competition, etc. The agency executive who is in contact with his client will always have a reasonably accurate knowledge of the client's advertising plans for the coming few months, at least.

The first step in budgeting sales is to prepare a separate schedule for each client, showing in detail the advertising space and materials which that client is expected to use for the budget period. This schedule should list the name of each advertising medium, the date of each advertisement and the billing price and cost of each advertisement. The schedule should contain an estimate of the advertising materials required in connection with each advertisement and a list of special services to be rendered that are to be billed to the client, including the estimated price and cost of each item. The schedule should be prepared to show the total billing and cost figures for each month in the period.

In listing each item on the schedule, a notation should be made to indicate whether the item was scheduled on the basis of a signed estimate, on the basis of a contract already issued to the medium or on other information. These schedules are usually prepared by contact men who refer to media recommendations, estimates and other data. Properly completed billing schedules for each client will show the expected billings and costs by months and classification of media. In the larger agency, these individual client billing and cost schedules are reviewed by the administrative department. The accuracy of a billing forecast depends on who gathers the material and on the source of the figures.

Obviously, such figures as arc based on signed estimates or completed contracts with media are reasonably accurate, subject only to cancellations caused by unexpected events. Those items which are estimated on the basis of a contact man's guess cannot be so accurate. The degree of accuracy in such instances depends on the estimator. To check the accuracy of the billing forecast, the agency administrative executive must familiarize himself with facts. This can often be done by an examination of past activities on each account and by conferences with contact men and heads of space and production departments. Billing estimates should be in such form as to permit revisions. Additional copies of estimates should be held for such purposes. Since budgets are usually prepared for periods upwards of a month or two, it is necessary to revise these estimates as clients change their advertising plans.

Forecasting Direct-salary Costs

Direct-salary costs designate costs for the time devoted to clients' accounts by people who work directly on them. Often many people work on one client's advertising account. The number working on one account depends on the size and type of the account and the manner in which the agency is operated. It is common in large agencies to have a departmental organization which includes the following departments: contact men, copy, media selection and buying, art, production, research, radio, accounting, billing, checking and administrative. Some of the larger agencies have found that the departmental set-up in itself does not provide the necessary concentration of individual effort on individual accounts. They have further subdivided their activities by what is often called the "group system so that a certain group of people in each department works on one account, or on a series of accounts.

Even where the group system is not well defined, agencies have found it necessary to assign the various elements of work on one account to individuals within departments. Where an agency has had past experience in handling an advertiser's account, the individuals working on that account have formed a rather accurate idea of what service the account requires and how much time it will take them to perform that service. Where an agency has operated a cost-accounting system, the cost-accounting records will indicate who has devoted time to each account and the amount of time that has been required of each individual.

Some agencies have gone further than just to record the amount of time required by each employee to serve a particular account. First, they have evaluated advertisements so as to put them into several classes; then, they have rated each class of advertisement. For example, they decide that a four-colour full-page advertisement of a certain type falls into Class 1, which requires the greatest amount of time to develop; then other types of advertisements they rate as Class 2, Class 3, Class 4, etc., with the rating depending on the skill required and time involved to develop the advertising. The same types of classifications have been established by some agencies for radio programs and outdoor displays. While this is an organized method for estimating the time required to prepare an advertisement, it is usually unnecessary to go into such detail to prepare an estimate of the direct cost of serving a client's account.

To prepare the estimate of the direct-salary cost involved in servicing each client's account, the first step is the preparation of a separate schedule for each client. The name of each employee who works on the account is listed. Each employee is then requested to furnish an estimate of the amount of time that he will spend on the account for each month in the budget period. At the time of requesting this information, it may be helpful to give each employee a statement showing the time he devoted to each particular account during a similar prior period. In addition, it may be helpful to furnish each such employee with a schedule showing the advertising space to be used for the client during the budget period. In large agencies where the departmental or departmental and group system is used, each employee's time estimates should be submitted to the group head and to the department head for review.

On this time sheet the names of the various accounts handled are listed on the left-hand margin of the sheet from top to bottom. The months in the budget period are represented by columns running vertically and covering the space from the left- to the right-hand side of the sheet. The individual employee notes the amount of time he estimates will be required of him during each month in the budget period opposite each account he is to work on. By adding each column, the total time to be devoted by the individual employee for each month is secured. Sometimes, in order to assist the employee, a second time sheet exactly like the one described is furnished; but, in this case, the cost-accounting department has inserted figures to indicate the time devoted by the individual to each account during the prior year. This second time sheet showing the actual time devoted to the accounts by the employee for the prior year is used as a guide to estimate the time required during the budget period.

When individual employees have made their estimates showing the time required of them in connection with each account for the budget period, these estimates, like billing estimates, are reviewed by an agency administrative executive. Such a review may require conferences with individual employees, department heads and contact men. When the time estimates have been reviewed, the estimated time must be converted into dollars of cost. The best procedure for converting time estimates to cost estimates involves the accumulation first of the time estimates for each employee.

After the time estimates have been refined so far as possible, the number of working hours accounted for is divided into the compensation of the employee. This produces an hourly rate. For example, if the budget period is one month, and an individual employee receives one thousand dollars compensation, and the total hours he has estimated he will spend on all accounts for the period is one hundred, then obviously his rate is ten dollars per hour. Having established the hourly rate for each employee, the time estimates are converted to cost estimates. In making this conversion, no allowance is to be made for lost or idle time. By the method described, each account is charged proportionately for each employee's idle time.

Forecasting Direct Expenses

Direct expenses consist of those items of expense that are incurred specifically through handling a client's account. Past experience is usually a valuable guide in determining what direct expenses may be incurred in the future. The proper cost-accounting system will provide management with the amount of the direct expenses that have been incurred in serving each account during prior periods. It will also give the nature and detail of each item. An examination of these items will serve management well and, as stated, will be of great assistance in forecasting future costs.

In larger agencies where contact men are more or less responsible for incurring expenditures for such items as traveling and entertaining, these men should be held responsible for budgeting anticipated direct expenses and for keeping actual costs in line with the budgets. Adhering to this principle, to secure forecasts of such direct expenses it is advisable to take contact men into consideration. To estimate these expenses for the budget period in a small agency, where one of the principals contacts each account, it is necessary only to examine past direct expenses and to speculate on what items of expense may be recurring. Such things as client sales conventions, new types of advertising campaigns and the distance of the client's office from the agency's place of business must be taken into consideration.

Agencies operate differently: Some follow a policy of liberal entertaining and traveling; others restrict these expenses. Much, of course, is dependent on the type of account and the type of agency. In the larger agency, to secure accurate estimates, it is best to apprise the contact man on each account of figures and details of direct expenses for past periods. With the past experience as a guide, and the contact man's knowledge of present and future operations, he should be able to furnish management with a reliable estimate of future costs. These estimates, like billing and time estimates, are to be reviewed by an administrative executive and then incorporated in the budget. No specific form need be used to secure the figures from the various contact men.

Forecasting Indirect Salaries and Expenses

Indirect expenses include (a) salaries of people who do not work directly on clients' advertising and (b) all other expenses except those that are incurred specifically because of handling one or more clients' accounts. Both indirect salaries and other indirect expenses are sometimes referred to as overhead expenses.

It is necessary to do some research work within the agency to determine what part of indirect expenses should be allocated to each client's account. The first step in making the allocation of indirect expenses is to prepare a schedule to determine the total cost within each classification of work, such as bookkeeping department billing clerks, stenographers, file clerks, production department employees, etc. After the total salary costs in each classification have been determined, it is necessary to find a way to allocate these costs to the several clients served.

No one method of doing this may be applied to all classifications. For example, it may be practical to allocate billing clerks' time on the basis of the number of items billed. It may be possible to allocate production department employees' time on the basis of the number of items purchased. Each classification requires a separate investigation. The following are some of the methods that have been successfully used to determine how much indirect-expense cost should be allocated to each client:

1. Income Method. When allocating according to the income method, the ratio of income from each client to total income of the agency is established, and then the allocation is made by using the established ratio.

   Example: If the commission and fee income of the agency is $100,000 and the income received from one particular client is $5,000, then the ratio of the income from the one client to total income of the agency is five percent. When this method is used, five percent of the item to be allocated is charged to the particular account.

2. Direct-Salary Method. Costs and expenses are allocated on the basis of the direct time devoted to accounts, on the theory that indirect salaries and indirect expenses pertaining to an account are proportionate to the direct time devoted to the account. To allocate on this method, it is first necessary to determine the total direct time charged to all accounts.

   Next, the direct time applicable to each separate account is determined. Then the percentage of the total direct time that was used on each account is calculated. This percentage when established is used for allocating expenses.

   Example: Total direct time charged to all accounts, one thousand hours; time devoted to Account A, one hundred hours; the ratio is ten percent. Then ten percent of the item to be allocated is charged Client A.

3. Insertion-Order Basis. Certain indirect salaries and indirect expenses in an advertising agency may be allocated on the basis of the number of insertion orders issued to magazines, newspapers, trade papers, etc. This method is used in connection with those classifications of indirect salaries and indirect expenses where the work performed or the expense incurred results from the issuance of orders. This would be true in the checking department, the forwarding department (departments in which orders are issued and released), space-billing department, etc.

   To make an allocation under this method, first the total number of insertion orders issued by the agency is established. Next, the number of insertion orders issued on account of each client is established. The percentage of orders issued for each client to total orders issued by the agency is established. An allocation is made on this basis. Example: One thousand insertion orders issued; five hundred orders issued in connection with Client A. The allocation is made on the basis of fifty percent to Client A.

4. Purchase-Order Method. Certain work performed in agencies results from the issuance of purchase orders, particularly those issued in connection with the purchase of advertising materials. Indirect employees whose time could be allocated on the basis of the purchases of advertising materials might include those working in the production department and might also include those employees whose work consists of billing and accounting for advertising materials. This type of allocation is made in the same way that the insertion-order allocation is made, but the number of purchase orders is used in place of the number of insertion orders.

5. Contract Basis. A few indirect employees and some indirect expenses may be allocated on the basis of contracts issued to radio stations, magazines,

newspapers, etc. The type of employee whose time could be allocated on this basis would include employees in the media-selection and media-buying departments. It would also include the time of clerks who devote their time to the preparation of space contracts. The allocation is made in the same manner that the insertion-order allocation is made except, of course, the number of contracts issued is used in place of the number of insertion orders.

These are some of the methods that have been successfully used to allocate indirect salaries and indirect expenses. Other methods may be found for allocating particular types of salaries and expense items. It is important to note that no one method of allocation can be applied to all items. A study must be made to determine the basis for allocating each class of item. When the methods to be used have been established, probation should be based on these methods, and the methods used should not be disturbed for a period of at least six months. After this, the allocating methods should be restudied to determine whether they are still correct or if there is room for refinement or improvement.

A work sheet should be prepared to list each classification of indirect salaries and indirect expenses together with an explanation of how the allocation of the item is to be made to the various client's accounts. This work sheet will serve as a basis for making the allocation from month to month as the budget is revised. When the work sheet is completed, two schedules should be prepared: A schedule listing the indirect-salary classifications and a second schedule listing the other indirect expenses by class.

The schedule of indirect salaries should contain headings for each classification. Under each heading, the name of each employee falling in the classification should be listed together with the employee's salary for the period. Each classification total should then be allocated to the various clients' accounts. A fourteen-column work sheet is suggested. The classification headings and the names of the employees may be listed on the left-hand side of this sheet with each individual's salary listed in a column next to his name. The remainder of the columns may be used for distributing the salaries to the several accounts.

The same type of work sheet may be used as a schedule of other indirect expenses or overhead. In this case, the classifications of expense are listed on the left-hand side of the sheet from top to bottom, the estimated amount of expense is listed in the column directly to the right of the name of the classification of expenses, and the remaining columns from left to right are used for distributing each class of expense to the several clients' accounts.

GROSS PROFIT

The gross profit is the commissions and fees less the direct costs. Gross profit is the most significant figure in the advertising agency budget or cost-accounting statement. It is a true figure. The income received from an account must be sufficient to produce a gross profit that is large enough to allow for the payment of indirect costs (indirect salaries and overhead expenses) and still leave a reasonable margin of profit.

It is not unusual for an agency upon an analysis of budgets and cost-accounting statements to find that the revenue from one or several accounts is insufficient even to pay for the direct salary costs. When this condition occurs, the gross-profit figure is a negative amount, and this is a clear indication that the account is unprofitable.

The gross-profit margin must be sufficient to provide for indirect costs. It is important to know not only what the gross profit is on each account, but also what the rate of gross profit should be on the average. If the ratio of the total of the two items (indirect expenses and profit) to total commissions and fees earned is determined, this ratio would represent the average rate of gross profit required.

Example:

Total commissions and fees $100,000.00

Profit requirement 20,000.00
Indirect expenses (salaries and overhead) 25,000.00
Total $ 45,000.00

Forty-five thousand dollars is forty-five percent of the total commissions ($100,000). Therefore, the average gross-profit requirement in the example cited is forty-five percent. To secure the figures from which to determine the average rate of gross-profit requirement, two schedules should be prepared. One is a schedule of indirect-salary costs and the other a schedule of the other indirect expenses.

The schedule of indirect-salary costs consists of a list of all of the employees who do not keep time reports and who do not work specifically in connection with serving one or several accounts. The schedule consists merely of a list of these employees and their salaries. The total of the schedule represents the total salaries paid to employees who fall under the classification "indirect salaries." The schedule of other indirect expenses or overhead can be prepared merely by listing the classifications of expense with the estimated expenditure that will be made for such class of expense for the year or budget period. A total taken from this schedule represents the agency's indirect expenses or overhead for the period.

After the two schedules have been prepared, the totals that appear on these schedules may be compared with the total expected commissions and fees of the agency as previously established through the preparation of schedules of billings, media costs and commissions. Thus a ratio is determined. When the ratio, or percentage, of the indirect costs to income has been determined, such a ratio provides management with a means of measuring the adequacy of the gross-profit figure as shown by the individual client operating forecasts. Because the accounts served by an agency differ widely, it may be possible that one account which produces a relatively small gross profit could still be a profitable account; whereas another that produces a relatively large gross profit could be unprofitable. This emphasizes the fact that in addition to the gross-profit factor, it is necessary to determine what indirect costs are incurred in connection with handling each account.

Example: An advertiser who uses four-colour, full-page advertisements in national magazines presents quite a different problem for the agency from the advertiser who uses small space in hundreds or thousands of weekly newspapers. The magazine account requires the issuance of only a few contracts, a few insertion orders, the preparation of several invoices and the payment of several bills to magazines. Checking the quantity and quality of the space used in the advertisements is a relatively simple task. On the other hand, the mechanics involved in the newspaper account require the completion of a substantial amount of detail work.

Where newspaper advertisements appear weekly, it is sometimes necessary to issue separate insertion orders for each advertisement. For an advertiser who uses several hundred daily or weekly newspapers, it is necessary first to issue several hundred contracts, then as many as four times that number of insertion orders each month. Each advertisement must be checked and measured. Each advertisement must be billed and paid for. Because newspaper advertisements generally appear in less space than that ordered, it is necessary to go into quite some detail in order to bill the client properly.

These two examples are given merely to show that there can be a good deal more indirect cost in handling one account than in handling another. The very terms "direct cost" and "direct salary" indicate that these classifications of cost, as they apply to a particular account, can be determined with accuracy; but "indirect costs" do not lend themselves to so accurate or specific an allocation. It is not an easy matter to determine what part of a stenographer's time is devoted to work in connection with the handling of one account, and it is not simple to determine what part of the rent expense is incurred because the agency serves a particular advertiser.

THE MASTER BUDGET

The procedure for budgeting each item of income, cost and expense has been explained. In discussing billings, media costs, direct salaries and direct expenses, it has been suggested that separate schedules be prepared for each client's account. It is now necessary to consolidate the figures in order to prepare a budget for the agency as a whole. The individual schedules showing the billings and media costs by clients may be consolidated by the preparation of a schedule listing the names of the several clients on the left-hand side of the sheet, the total billings in a column directly to the right of the client's name, the total media costs in the next column and the resulting commissions in the third column. Service fees may be shown in the column to the right of the commissions with the total commission and fee income being developed by adding the sum of the commissions and the service fees for each account.

A master schedule of direct salaries is now prepared by listing the names of all the employees in this classification with their total salaries. The schedules of direct salaries which were prepared to show the amount of direct salaries applying to each client's account are to be summarized to produce an overall or master schedule.

The schedules of direct expenses for each individual account are consolidated by listing clients' accounts on the left side of a work sheet and providing a column for each class of expense. The total amount of expense in each class applying to each client is then inserted on the work sheet. This develops the total direct expenses for each client and the total of all the direct expenses for the agency by class of expense. These totals by class of direct expense for the agency as a whole should be compared with the expenses in each classification for a similar prior period. The budget for the agency as a whole is now prepared by reference to the schedules which have been described.

The advertising agency business may be less stable than some other types of business. The addition or loss of one account may have an important effect on the operations. Because the total volume of transactions may be affected by events beyond the control of the agency, it may be impossible to prepare an accurate budget for a period of time in excess of a few months. The first budget should be prepared for a period of one year; this budget should then be subdivided into periods of three months each so that, when completed, there will actually be five budgets —one for the entire year and a separate budget for each three-month period. At the end of the first three-month period, the budgets for the remaining three periods should be reviewed and an additional budget should be prepared for the three months following the year-period of the original budget.

By this method, the agency always has a budget for a period of one full year, because as each three-month budget period has been completed, an additional budget for three months is prepared. A quarterly review of budgets insures reasonably accurate budgeting for the immediate ensuing three-month period. It provides a yearly budget from which management can make decisions with knowledge of expected operations.

The quarterly review of budgets may seem like a big job, but it is not nearly so difficult as it would first appear. A review of each of the schedules is all that is required. An examination of the direct-salary schedule for each client together with a knowledge of direct-salary costs for the past three-month period, and other information relative to changes in the client's advertising plans, will indicate what corrections are required. An examination of indirect-salary costs and indirect expenses for the past three months will indicate whether these expenses as budgeted are accurate in total, or whether revision is required. The cost-accounting reports for the past three months will indicate whether the allocation of the expenses in the budget is in line with the actual costs.

Chapter 3

Cost Accounting of Advertising

The agency primary serves the advertiser by conceiving, developing and placing advertising, but the publisher pays the advertising agency for its work. It is true that the advertising agency is of great benefit to the publication, the radio station and the outdoor plant because, if it were not for the agency, publishers might have the tremendous job of trying to conceive and develop advertising campaigns. It would be difficult to correlate the advertising appearing in the various media.

If there were no advertising agencies, publications would have to collect from thousands of advertisers instead of from hundreds of agencies. Advertisers would have to be educated concerning the various technical requirements of the media. Yes, the advertising agency is of tremendous service to the publisher, and the publisher can well afford to pay for this service, not the least of which is the policing of advertising messages, for the agency has a responsibility for the kind of message it conceives.

The selling price of most services and products is in the final analysis based on the cost of producing them. If an advertising agency is to stay in business, it must make a profit from its operations. To do this, it must measure costs against selling prices. The selling price of the agency's service is represented by the commission received from publications and other media, plus service fees and special charges collected from clients. The cost of the service includes the salaries of agency employees and all other expenses incurred in the operation of the business. The total commissions and fees received by an agency, less the total salaries and expenses paid, produce a figure that represents the profit from operations. To be sure, this one figure (net profit) is the final result of all of the transactions that have been performed, but the prudent and progressive executive needs more information than this. He wants to know which operations were profitable and which were not, and why. Consequently, it is necessary to find a method of presenting facts so that they will express the result of management's policies and methods.

In a manufacturing business, it is common practice today to keep records that will show the cost of performing each important function in the business. The giant enterprises of the country could never have been built without such factual information from which management could determine the wisdom and profitableness of what they had done. In the agency business, service is rendered to clients and income is received as the result of that service. The way in which one account is served determines the profitableness of that operation. For this reason, it is of prime importance for the agency's management to know the income and costs that result from serving each client.

More than one type of service is performed for a client. In the well-organized advertising agency, budgets are prepared to show the anticipated costs of the agency's operations segregated by clients' accounts handled and types of services performed for each. These budgets express management's policies and enable the agency to plan for an operation that will produce a reasonable profit. The cost-accounting records of an agency should show the result of carrying out the policies and methods expressed in the budget.

It is necessary to segregate the income and costs so that each item can be compared with the budget. Before designing a cost-accounting system or, for that matter, any accounting system, it is necessary to determine exactly what end result is sought— what kind of cost-accounting statements can the management use best? To some extent, this depends on the previous experience of the people in the agency that are going to work with the figures. No one cost-accounting report could serve for all agencies.

The general accounting records described here provide for the accumulation of all cost-accounting information with the exception of the allocation of salary costs, which are also discussed in this chapter. The sources from which the cost-accounting information is secured are:

1. Each client's sales and costs of sales are secured from the Sales and Cost Journal where a separate page is used for recording each client's transactions.
2. The commissions and fees are secured by subtracting the costs from the billings.
3. Direct expenses:
   a. Salary costs applicable to each client's account are secured from Time Reports.
   b. Other direct expenses applying to each client's account are secured from the Expense Voucher Register.
4. Indirect expenses are allocated to clients' accounts by methods.

THE COST-ACCOUNTING STATEMENTS

The cost-accounting statements illustrated in this chapter are intended as guides. They show the general formats of reports that have been successfully used by modern advertising agencies. The individual client operating statement is a statement form on which the agency operations with one client are summarized.

The amount of billings, costs and commissions for each type of advertising medium is shown, and the total of each class of direct expense is recorded. The gross profit from the operations is the difference between the commissions and fees on the one hand, and the direct expense on the other. This is the most significant one on the statement form and will be discussed further. Next, the statement shows the share of the general and administrative expense prorated to the client which, when deducted from the gross profit, produces the net profit resulting from the transactions with the particular client.

The over-all operating or profit-and-loss statement for the agency as a whole shows what has happened, and the individual client operating statement shows why it has happened.

Since the individual client operating statement summarizes the result of the transactions with each client, it is necessary to support the statement with more detailed. Hie media billings and costs are self-explanatory and generally need no further analysis; however, when the actual figures for the period are at considerable variance with the budget or forecast, the detail of the actual figures can be secured by an examination of the Sales and Cost Journal. A separate page in the Sales and Cost Journal records the billings and costs from each client's business. The sheets contain separate columns for each medium so that the total billings or costs for any particular medium can be analyzed quickly by reference to the Sales and Cost Journal.

Time Records

The direct expenses include two classifications: salaries and expenses. The individual client operating statement shows the total cost of the time of each class of employee (executives, contact men, secretaries, copy, art, production, media selection, radio and other direct salaries). It is necessary to know how much of each employee's time was devoted to each client's work. No estimate allocating time be tween the various accounts served is reliable; and unless reliable figures are developed, the whole purpose of cost accounting vanishes.

It is necessary for each creative employee in an agency to keep reasonably accurate time records, so that an accurate allocation of time costs can be made. It is not practical for every employee of the agency to keep a time record to show how many hours were devoted daily to each client. Some employees perform tasks that cannot be directly attributed to any one client's business. Others devote a few minutes at a time to each of several client's affairs.

A cost-accounting system should not be so burdensome that it consumes substantial amounts of time of valuable employees. For this reason, it is not desirable for an employee who does not devote at least a half-hour at a time to a client's account to keep time records.

Employees who can keep reasonably accurate time records include contact men, research employees, copywriters, radio continuity writers, radio script writers, art directors and artists. Employees who may or may not be able to keep accurate time records without excessive effort include production-department employees, space buyers and checking-department employees.

Time records may be kept either on a daily, weekly or semimonthly basis. The shorter the interval, the more accurate the record is likely to be; for when weekly or semimonthly recording forms are used, the employee is likely to wait until the last day of the period before he fills out the record. The semimonthly form is usually the most convenient for accumulating the hours devoted to each client's account. If a daily or weekly form is used, it is suggested that the daily or weekly time reports be summarized onto a monthly schedule similar in form to the semimonthly time report.

This semimonthly time report, it will be noted, contains clients' names from top to bottom along the left-hand margin of the sheet. It provides columns for each day in the semimonthly period. Where this form is used, the names of all the clients of the agency are mimeographed and the forms are distributed to all agency employees who keep these time records. At the end of each day, the employee records the amount of time devoted to each client's account.

A daily allocation in hours and half-hours is thought to produce sufficiently accurate time records. For the purpose of discussing the recording of agency employees* time and the allocating of this time to the various accounts served, employees are first divided into two classes called direct and indirect. Direct employees consist of those who work directly on clients' accounts. Indirect employees are those whose time only indirectly benefits the agency's clients. People in this latter class include bookkeepers and clerks, stenographers, receptionists, sometimes production employees, space buyers, etc.

Usually the people in the first class keep time records allocating their time to the several accounts served, while the people in the second class usually do not. Direct employees sometimes devote part of their time to administrative work or to other duties that do not directly concern a particular client's business. In reporting the time devoted during the day, two methods are used. One method is to record only the hours devoted to clients' accounts, making no entry on the time sheet for the time devoted to work of a general or indirect character. When this method is followed, the total time reported by the employee, divided into the employee's compensation, produces a cost rate per hour. The costs applying to each client's account are then computed by multiplying the hourly cost rate by the number of hours reported as having been spent on each client's account.

Since under this method the individuals make no report on administrative or general time, the only time reported is that devoted directly to clients' business. By charging each client on this basis, the cost of unallocated time is automatically absorbed by charges to clients, the absorption being proportionate to the portion of time devoted to each client.

Example: If an employee reports one hundred hours for a monthly period divided as follows:

Client
A 40
B 50
G 10

and if the employee's monthly salary is $1,000, the hourly rate would be $10. Client A would be charged with $400, client

B with $500 and client C with $100. Since the total of these allocated costs equals the employee's compensation, the time that the employee devoted to administrative or other classifications of work has automatically been allocated to clients in the pro-ration shown.

The other method used is to provide for showing on the time report the time devoted to indirect work. When this is done, the employee indicates the type of work performed and notes the number of hours devoted to each class of work such as administrative, accounting, sales promotion. When an individual's time reports include time devoted to general classifications of work not directly involving clients, the salary costs of the individual are prorated both to each client and to other classifications. The costs in the other classifications are charged to overhead and the overhead expenses are then prorated to the clients' accounts as described later.

Agency employees who have not been in the habit of keeping time records usually are reluctant to do so, feeling that they should not be subject to this menial work or to such detailed scrutiny of their efforts. In this connection, it is interesting to note that physicians, surgeons, dentists, attorneys, architects and accountants keep accurate records of the time devoted and services rendered to each client. Agency employees will find that the keeping of time records is of great help in eliminating waste and inefficiency. Time records are essential to the success of any advertising agency cost-accounting system. To keep these records requires only a few minutes a day on the part of each employee. The high-priced executive sometimes can assign this duty to his secretary, but in any event, the recording of time should be daily.

Schedule of Direct Salaries

On the individual client operating statement, the total of each class of direct salaries is shown as it applies to each client's account. Obviously, if the cost of a particular class of direct salaries greatly exceeds the budgeted cost, management will want to know why. For this and other reasons, it is necessary that the total of each salary classification be broken down to show the items making up the total. A separate schedule supporting the individual client operating statement is used for this purpose; it is called "Schedule of Direct Salaries."

This schedule shows the cost of each employee's salary that applies to the particular account. The items are arranged so as to group employees by classes of work. This grouping automatically provides for securing the total cost of each class of direct salaries, which total is shown on the individual client operating statement. The Schedule of Direct Salaries includes both the actual salary costs as they apply to each client, and the budgeted cost.

For this reason, the schedule form provides columns for reporting the current month's costs, the budgeted amount for the current month, the year-to-date actual cost and the budgeted amount for the year to date. The cost figures shown on the Schedule of Direct Salaries are the costs computed on the basis of the time devoted to each account as they are found from an examination of time records.

Schedule of Direct Expenses

The individual client operating statement shows the total of each class of direct expenses incurred in handling the client's account. When the actual figures vary in any important degree from the anticipated costs as shown by the budget figures, alert management will want to know the reason for the difference. The cost-accounting system that is described here has been developed so that all needed figures can be secured with a minimum of effort.

The agency's expenses are recorded in a voucher register which is described in the chapter "General Books and Chart of Accounts." The Expense Voucher Register provides for recording expenses in such a manner that those items incurred directly because of one client's account are segregated. A recap of these items provides the detailed information for preparing the schedule of direct expenses. This schedule may include as much detail as management requires. Usually, it is set up in the manner shown in Figure 12, which provides for a heading covering each classification of expense, followed by a listing of the important items of expense incurred during the period, with the total of the expenses in each class. This total agrees with the amount reported for the item on the individual client operating statement. Where a classification of direct expense varies materially from the budget allowance for such items, management will examine the schedule of direct expenses.

Sometimes even the schedule is not in sufficient detail to provide the necessary information; in such cases, the data supporting the Expense Voucher Register of the agency are gathered together and submitted to management so as to show all of the details in connection with the particular item under scrutiny.

Allocation of Indirect Expenses

The overhead expenses of an advertising agency include the costs and expenses that do not directly result from the handling of one client's business. These expenses include indirect salaries. The indirect salaries include administrative, executive, accounting, secretaries, typists, bookkeepers, clerks. They may include production employees, media-department employees and part of the time of contact men or other creative people. Expense in this classification includes such items as rent, light, local telephone, stationery, dues and subscriptions, insurance, legal, auditing, etc. Various means have been employed to allocate general and administrative expenses as properly applying to the cost of serving each client.

In the cost-accounting system described, it is desirable to make an allocation of general and administrative expenses to the individual client operating statements, but it is not entirely essential. The choice of allocating or not allocating expenses in connection with the preparation of individual client operating statements must be management's choice and must be dependent on how management can best understand and interpret.

Where no allocation is made, the individual client operating statement ends with the gross-profit. In thinking of this figure, management must allow for both general and administrative expense and profit.

Where the expenses are allocated, the amount of such expense applying to each client is shown on the individual client operating statement, being deducted from the gross profit to produce the net operating profit resulting from handling each client's account. However, if an allocation of general and administrative expense is to be made, it is necessary to provide a basis for making such an allocation. In determining the basis for such allocation, the first question that must be answered is how scientific should the basis for allocation be? Ideally no one basis for allocation could apply to all items.

Example: The cost of preparing bills to clients and checks to publishers could be distributed on the basis of the number of transactions rather than on the relative dollar volume of the billing or payments. On the other hand, rent might be distributed in the same ratio as a distribution of salary costs of direct employees. A discussion of the various methods for distributing overhead or general and administrative expenses could fill a volume in itself. Here it will be limited merely to listing the various methods that have been used by agencies. These have been discussed in greater detail in the chapter on budgets.

1. Distribution of items on the basis of direct salaries.
2. Volume. (This distribution is made by first determining what part of the agency's commissions and fees was earned as the result of handling each individual client's business. The expenses are then allocated, using these ratios.)
3. Insertion orders. (Expenses may be allocated on the basis of the number of insertion orders issued.)
4. Purchase-order basis. (Expenses may be distributed on the basis of the number of purchase orders issued.)

What the Cost-accounting Reports Mean

One of the peculiarities of the agency business grows out of the fact that the income for work performed is usually recorded on the books months after the completion of the work. This is because clients must be contacted and advertising plans conceived and developed long before they can appear in magazines and newspapers, as outdoor posters or as radio shows. Perhaps the greatest lag between the time of doing the work and the time of recording the income is in connection with foreign advertising. Sometimes this lag is more than one year, but there is always a considerable time lapse between doing the work and recording the income; for this reason, cost-accounting statements must be interpreted with care.

Obviously, the cost of serving a new client would not be covered by the income received during the first few months. Costs applying to new clients' accounts are always likely to be distorted in proportion to the income shown on the cost-accounting statement. One month's cost-accounting figures are always likely to be misleading in themselves. Therefore, the accumulative for the year to date are much more important than the figures for the current month. No conclusions should be made based on one or two months' operations; so where a few months' figures indicate the need for action it is generally best to adopt a "wait and see" attitude until longer experience can prove or disprove the tentative conclusions.

The gross-profit on the individual client operating statement is perhaps the most significant one on the report. The gross profit is the difference between the commissions and fees and the direct expenses. If the records are accurately kept there can be little or no question as to the accuracy of the gross-profit. Agencies should expect to realize a net profit (before Federal tax) of about three percent of gross billings or twenty percent of the commissions and fees. The gross-profit figure must be sufficiently large to provide for general and administrative expenses and profit. If the three-percent profit on gross billings (twenty percent of commissions and fees) is accepted as a reasonable, then after deducting this amount from the gross profit there must still remain an allowance sufficiently large to pay the agency's general and administrative expenses.

While it is difficult to generalize about advertising-agency costs and expenses because agencies differ so widely from one another in size and type of service performed, perhaps a rough guide can be given. General and administrative expenses in an advertising agency could vary from a low of ten percent of commissions and fees to a high of thirty percent of commissions and fees.

For the purpose of discussing methods of interpreting individual client operating statements, the following ratios are given as an example:

Commissions and Fees	100%
Direct Expenses	55
Gross Profit	45%
Indirect Expenses	25
Net Profit	20%

In the case of this example, a minimum gross profit of twenty-five percent is needed to meet indirect expenses alone, while forty-five percent is needed to meet indirect expenses and provide for a profit of twenty percent of commissions and fees.

Cost accounting in the agency business furnishes management with facts on which intelligent decisions can be based. Just how each person uses these facts varies considerably. A few suggestions can be made, however.

After one determines which accounts are profitable and which are not, both the unusually profitable account and the unusually unprofitable account should be investigated; for if an account is unusually profitable, it could be that the agency is not performing all the services that it should. If an account is not a profitable one, this does not necessarily mean that the agency should resign the business; rather, the facts should be studied to determine what, if anything, can be done to turn the loss into a profit.

The first investigation should be directed to determining whether or not the agency is spending too much money in consideration of the services to be performed. Sometimes high-priced personnel are assigned to small accounts that cannot economically justify the assignment. In such cases, different employees could be assigned. In other cases, it may be that the employees assigned to certain accounts are devoting too much time to them. This can be determined by a study of the work performed in comparison with that on other accounts. It may be that the client is receiving services that he does not require, and perhaps whole areas of work can be eliminated.

If a careful investigation discloses that the cost on an account cannot be reduced, then it is time to determine whether or not the operation for the period under study is a typical operation with the particular client. Perhaps some unusual work was performed; or it could be that the income for the particular period was less than average. If it is determined that the period under study is typical, and that, based on past operations, a continued loss could be expected as a result of the operations with the particular client, then if there is no feasible way of reducing the cost of performing the service, it is entirely practicable to request a service fee from the client to augment the commission income.

Perhaps the most significant facts which can be secured from an examination of the cost-accounting statements are found by comparing the budget figures with the actual figures for the period.

Usually, where a budget is carefully prepared, the difference between the two figures is caused by the fact that the operations took a different turn from that anticipated. Such differences continually occurring indicate the lack of control over the operations of the business. Adequate steps should be taken to set up controls that will work. Many agencies provide incentive systems offering bonuses or other incentives to key men, department heads, contact men, etc. They then hold these department heads, contact men and others responsible for operating an account within the budget.

In the routine preparation of cost-accounting statements, the agency's accounting department should compare the budget figures with the actual figures. Where important differences exist between the two figures, an analysis should be made to find the cause, and an explanation of each difference should be submitted to management along with the statements. The above are a few of the ways in which the facts secured from a cost-accounting system can be profitably used, but each individual will develop his own techniques for interpreting and using these facts.

There are no hard and fast rules that can be applied to determine the cost ratios for such items as contact cost, copy cost, art cost, etc. Neither are there established ratios which one can use to compare an agency's costs in connection with indirect expenses for items such as rent, supplies, dues and subscriptions, etc., because agencies' operations differ widely from one another just as the character of the agencies differs. The cost to service one account will vary widely from the costs incurred to service another.

A few surveys have been made of the agency business in an effort to establish general over-all ratios, and some figures are available from these surveys. The American Association of Advertising Agencies makes an annual survey of agency costs and operations, but the survey is limited to a study of the operations of some of the Association's members, and the results of the study are made available only to members of the American Association of Advertising Agencies. *Printers' Ink* recently inaugurated a study of agency operations and costs. The figures are available and may serve as general guides and ratios. In comparing the figures of a particular agency with general operating ratios, caution must be used, for it is difficult to find an agency that is "average."

NEWSPAPERS: BILLING, PAYING AND ACCOUNTING

The principles of accounting discussed in this chapter are used also in connection with other media. The differences of methods are in the detail rather than in the principles. Here, the matters of principle are discussed at some length. These principles were established with the following objectives in mind:

1. To achieve complete internal control for protection against errors and defalcations.
2. To function with the greatest simplicity and efficiency possible.
3. To gain promptness in completing operations.

The methods discussed have been carefully developed and tested over long periods of time. They have provided the ultimate in flexibility and ease of operation and at the same time have provided adequate controls to assure the greatest accuracy. One of the cardinal principles used throughout these procedures is that once a document has been prepared, it is not to be copied or recopied. Instead, the original document is used for various purposes by filing either the original or carbon copies and adding information to the document to complete a transaction.

It is sufficient here to repeat that when an advertising campaign is developed, a detailed list is prepared to show the space to be used in each newspaper, the dates for each ad, the size of each ad, the rate per line or inch, and the cost of each ad. The media recommendation, or a more formal schedule sometimes referred to as an estimate, is presented to the client for approval since the agency wants the client to be responsible to the agency before it makes commitments with papers. After clients have approved schedules or media recommendations, they are referred to as approved schedules or approved estimates. The approved estimate, schedule or media recommendation—depending on the form used by the agency—is sent to the media department so that contracts can be issued to the various papers.

Contracts

It is customary for agencies to protect their clients by issuing contracts to papers so as to assure the advertiser the best rates available. Usually, contracts with newspapers cover a period of one year. When a space-buying department receives a copy of an approved schedule or estimate, the first job of the department is to check the files to see if a contract has already been issued to each of the publications listed. Bear in mind that to protect a client, the agency must issue a specific contract with each publication in behalf of the specific client. Publishers do not recognize blanket contracts. These conditions set up the terms under which the agency buys the space. The recommended contract form provides for mailing in window envelopes and for the insertion of all the pertinent information in convenient order for later reference.

The contract should include: The name of the publisher, the name of the client for whom the space is being contracted, the name of the client's product that is to be advertised in the publication, the contract period, the position requested in the publication such as financial page, sports page, etc., the rate Usually, a contract for newspaper space calls for space as required for a period of one year. In some cases, a minimum quantity of space may be specified, such as five thousand lines. This practice is followed where the paper has a sliding-scale rate structure so that it becomes necessary to contract for a minimum quantity of space in order to secure a desired per-line rate. For example, where a client is to use more than five thousand lines of space, and the paper has one rate for less than five thousand lines and a lower rate for more, the contract would be issued for "five thousand lines or more."

There is a box on the upper right-hand portion of the contract headed "Rates for This Contract." There is considerable space provided in three vertical columns. The one on the extreme left has no heading. The second one has a heading "Contract Rate," and the third has the heading "Next Lower Rate."

This entire box with its three columns is used to show the various rates for different kinds of space. It is not uncommon for a newspaper to have five or six different rates. Papers always have different daily and Sunday rates. Some publishers publish both morning and evening papers and offer a combination rate where both the morning and evening editions are used. An additional combination rate may be offered for morning, evening and Sunday combinations. There may be still another rate for special positions, such as financial page, sports page, etc. If a client contemplates using different types of space which call for different rates, this information is noted in the box headed "Rates for This Contract."

This acknowledgment when filled in and returned by the publication amounts to an acceptance of the contract and all of its terms. Usually the acknowledgment when received is pasted or clipped to one of the copies of the contract that is retained by the agency. The usual thing is to make at least four copies of the contract, although additional copies may be required depending on the client's requirements and the organization of the agency.

Sometimes clients request copies of all contracts issued by the agency. In this case, a copy of the contract of course must be made for the client. The space-buying department of the agency needs to retain one copy of each contract, and the accounting department of the agency requires one copy of the contract. These three carbon copies are in addition to the original copy that is sent to the publisher.

The question of rates demands special consideration. It has been stated that many publications offer special rates where large quantities of space are used. This type of rate structure is called a sliding-scale rate structure. A newspaper may offer one rate for space used up to five thousand lines during a contract year. A lower rate may be offered for five to ten thousand lines and still a lower rate for ten to twenty thousand lines, with the lowest rate being offered for space used in excess of twenty thousand lines in a contract year.

There are both advantages and disadvantages in using the lower rates. When it is known that a client is going to earn a rate lower than the highest rate offered by the paper, and if the contract is issued for the total quantity of space that the client is expected to use during the contract year, the publisher will sometimes bill the space at the lower rate.

Example: If a paper offers, say, a twenty-five-cents-per-line rate for space up to five thousand lines and a twenty-cent rate for space in excess of five thousand lines used in one year, then if a contract is issued for five thousand or more lines to be used during the contract year, the publication in many cases will bill the agency at the twenty-cent rate. If the contract were issued for space as required during the contract year without specifying a minimum of five thousand lines, then the publication would undoubtedly bill the agency at the twenty-five cents-per-line rate.

The advantage in using the low rate is that if the paper bills the agency at the low rate, the agency then bills the client at this rate, and if the client uses the space anticipated, no adjustment need be made. On the other hand, a disadvantage is involved if the client fails to use enough space to justify the low rate, in which case the paper will bill the agency for the additional five cents per line on all space used during the contract year. The agency must then bill the client for this additional charge. This additional charge may be difficult to explain to the client and may lead to disputes and difficulties that would never have arisen if the client had been billed for the high rate initially and then, if he qualified for it, had received a credit for the next lower rate.

INSERTION ORDERS

Prior to the date upon which an advertisement is to appear, an insertion order is issued to the newspaper to inform the newspaper of the details concerning the particular advertisement which is ordered. The contract that was issued to the paper merely reserves space in the publication and protects the client from the standpoint of rates and terms. Before any advertisement can appear, the agency must issue a specific order calling for the publication of that advertisement. Sometimes one order calls for the publication of several advertisements, but, in any event, an order must be issued before any advertisement is published. These orders are always referred to as insertion orders.

On the reverse side of the original or first copy of the insertion order, the standard conditions governing the advertising contracts and orders are usually printed. In addition to the insertion order that is sent to the publication, at least one carbon copy of the order is made for the agency's file; sometimes two or three carbons are made, depending on the organization of the agency and its requirements, but, in any case, at least one copy is required for billing and paying purposes which will be discussed later.

In addition to the order number and the date, space is provided for the name of the publication, the address, the rate per line, the cash-discount rate, the commission rate, the name of the advertiser, the name of the product and a description of the position requested. Even if the run-of-paper rate is used, often some specification is made as to position. For example, a special request such as the following is frequently used:

"Do not publish next to competing advertising. Second, third or fourth page urgently requested."

An indication is given if the copy is enclosed or forwarded separately; the same is true with regard to "cuts." The date of each insertion, the advertisement number and the space ordered for each date are shown under the appropriate column headings. If a series of advertisements is ordered on one insertion order, the information to identify each advertisement would read as follows:

Date of Insertion Ad Number Space Ordered
10/10 1345 120 lines
10/20 1479 160 lines
10/28 1571 180 lines

Considerable space is provided under the heading "Special Instructions," and under this heading agencies frequently insert particular instructions concerning the advertisements to be published. Often agencies give the publication optional dates on which the advertisement can be issued. Sometimes in connection with clothing advertising or other style material, instructions are issued indicating that the advertisement is not to be published unless the temperature on the preceding day is equal to seventy degrees, etc. Such instructions could be issued in connection with straw-hat advertising, for example.

While there is no guarantee that the publication will accept such an order, this is an example of the conditions that agencies often attempt to impose upon publications in the interest of their clients.

Each insertion order should cover one month's advertising only. This is because the insertion order is used as a basis for paying the publisher and billing the advertiser which is done monthly. Often advertisers advertise in the same papers month in and month out. When this is done, it is advisable to prepare the insertion orders by using addressograph plates rather than by typing each order individually.

The insertion order has been designed for use with addressograph plates. The addressograph plates insert the name and address of the paper, the line rate, the cash discount terms, the commission percentage, the name of the advertiser and the name of the product. The balance of the order is filled in by multigraph, mimeograph, hectograph duplicating process or spirit duplicator.

Checking Newspaper Space

Where any considerable volume of newspaper advertising is transacted, the agency operates a checking department, or at least one or two persons are assigned to the job of checking the newspaper advertising. The checking of this advertising consists of three operations:

1. Examining the advertisement to determine that it meets the quality requirements specified on the order.
2. Measuring the advertisement to determine the quantity of space occupied.
3. Determining the position of the advertisement as it appears in the paper.

The checking operation is usually performed in the following manner: Copies of insertion orders are filed alphabetically by state, city and newspaper name. These orders are either filed in a binder, a ledger tray, a vertical file or some visible filing device. The contract that is sent to the publication and the insertion order that is sent to the publisher both specify that copies of the advertisement are to be sent to the advertiser and to the agency. It is customary for the publication to send the agency (purchaser) one or two copies of the page in which the advertising appears, or of the entire publication itself. Upon receipt of these, the agency's checking department files the tear sheets alphabetically by state of issue, city and name of publication.

The first job of the checker is to locate the insertion order covering the advertising. When this is done, the checker determines what the advertising specifications were. If the agency is paying a premium for insertion on the financial page or the sports page, it is important to determine that the advertisement actually appeared on such a page in the paper. If the agency has specified that the advertising must not be inserted next to competitive copy, then it is important that the checker determine whether or not this qualification has been met. The checker must also examine the advertising to determine that the correct copy has been inserted.

It is not infrequent for agencies to run daily or weekly advertisements in the same paper for the same client. In such cases, the agency may forward the copy for three or four advertisements to the publication at one time. Newspapers have been known to repeat the same advertisement, or to change the order of the advertising. Usually, a copy of each advertisement that is currently appearing is furnished to the checking department so that it can refer to the correct copy when examining the tear sheets received from the paper. The checker must also note the quality of the printing. After the checker has examined the advertisement to determine that it meets the specifications established by the insertion order, the next job is to measure the advertising to determine the amount of space occupied.

It is general practice for advertising agencies to pay only for the space occupied by the advertisement, and not to include any white space allowed above or below it. This kind of measurement is called "type to type" measurement. Checking-department employees are furnished with rules calibrated in both lines and inches. This type of rule expedites the measuring job. The checker measures the advertisement and notes the measurement on the copy of the insertion order opposite the date of the insertion:

Date of Insertion Ad Number Space Ordered Space Used
10/20 1234 180 lines 178 lines

If for any reason the advertising does not meet the specifications contained on the insertion order, the checker notes such discrepancies on the insertion order before forwarding it to the bookkeeping department.

Billing the Advertising

Before the agency can accurately bill its client for newspaper advertising space, each advertisement must be checked and measured to determine that it was properly inserted to meet the specifications set up, and to determine the number of lines or inches used by the advertisement and therefore to be billed. In addition, it is an established practice for agencies to pay the newspaper and bill the client for the lesser of the amount of space computed, whether it be that measured by the agency's checking department or that billed the agency by the paper. It is not infrequent for the newspaper to measure the advertisement as one line more or less in depth than the measurement computed by the agency. Because the agency wishes to give its client the benefit of the doubt where two people measure differently, it is necessary to compare the linage billed by the newspaper with that measured by the agency.

It is a cardinal principle in agency finance that the advertiser must pay the agency for advertising space prior to the date upon which the agency is required to pay the publisher. Newspaper publishers require payment for advertising space on the tenth, fifteenth, twentieth or twenty-fifth of the months following the advertising. A large portion of the publishers require payment on the tenth or fifteenth of the month following publication.

In any sizable newspaper advertising campaign, advertisements will appear in newspapers that are published hundreds of miles distant from the agency's place of business. Where advertisements appear during the last few days of a month, the tear pages or checking copies of publications, which are frequently sent second- or third-class mail, may not be received for from five to fifteen days after the date of publication.

Newspapers send bills to agencies once a month. They usually submit a separate bill to cover the advertising of each client (although a few papers send one bill to cover all the advertising purchased by the agency). Newspapers usually require a few days after the first of the month in which to complete the invoicing. The reader will see that, because of this procedure agencies cannot receive bills from newspapers before the third fourth or fifth of the month following advertising. In some case invoices are not received until after the tenth of the following month.

Because it is impossible for agencies to send accurate invoice for newspaper advertising in time to secure payment from client before the agency must pay the publication, it is necessary to develop some procedure through the operation of which the agency can collect substantially all the money due for the news paper advertising before it has to pay the papers. Obviously, to accomplish this, it is necessary for the agency) to get an invoice of some kind to the advertiser on or about the first day of the month following the month of advertising. In other words, on June first an agency should send invoices to it, clients covering all of the newspaper advertising for the month of May. This invoice cannot represent the exact amount due for space used since the space has not yet been checked and audited with bills from newspapers. Several methods are commonly used to secure payment from the advertiser so that the money is received before the agency must pay the publication. They are:

1. Billing on a space-ordered basis.
2. Billing checked space as checked, and unchecked space as ordered.
3. Prebilling on an estimated basis.

Billing on a Space-ordered Basis

Where this method of billing is used, all of the insertion orders are secured from the checking department, and the total linage ordered is multiplied by the rate in order to compute the billing price, which is noted on the insertion order. An in voice is then typed by reference to the insertion orders. Insertion orders are returned to the checking department, and after they have been completely checked, they are routed to the accounting department for auditing against publishers' bills. When this procedure is completed, the difference between the linage ordered and the linage to be paid for (the linage measured by the have been completely checked, they are routed to the accounting department for auditing against publishers' bills. When this procedure is completed, the difference between the linage ordered and the linage to be paid for the linage measured by the are issued once a month and usually appear in a form.

While this method of billing provides a basis for securing payment from the client in time for the agency to pay the papers, it is a cumbersome procedure causing considerable duplicated work for the advertiser as well as for the agency, because, when the first invoice is prepared, all computations must be made to compute the billing price of the space ordered in each paper. If the advertiser uses precaution in checking invoices, he will want to check all the computations appearing on the invoice. The credit memo that will be issued later to show the amount of credit due to the advertiser will again require a series of calculations and a complete new typing job. Because of the method used by newspapers to print advertising, the great majority of advertisements will appear in less space than that ordered, and consequently there will be a credit due to the advertiser for almost every paper used in the advertising campaign during the month.

This means that the original invoice on a space-ordered basis will show the details of the advertising ordered in each paper and that the credit memo which is issued later will again show the details of the advertising ordered in each paper, as well as the amount of space that actually was used and the credit to which the advertiser is entitled. For the client to determine the net cost of the advertising in each paper, he must deduct the credit issued from the original billing for the same paper, and this is a cumbersome procedure.

Billing Checked Space as Checked, and Unchecked Space as Ordered

To accomplish this manner of billing, it is necessary for the accounting department to secure all of the previous month's insertion orders on about the first or second day of the month following the advertising. These insertion orders are taken from the checking department where advertisements have been checked with tear sheets as the tear sheets have been received.

Obviously, on the first or second day of the month following the advertising, all of the advertisements ordered for the previous month will not have been checked by the checking department; but where tear sheets have been received, the checkers will have checked the advertisements and measured the space used.

Based on the information contained on the insertion orders, a detailed invoice is now made up by the accounting department by billing the space that has been checked and measured on the basis of the number of lines measured by the checking department. Advertisements that have not yet been checked or measured are billed on the basis of the space ordered. Obviously, this form of hybrid billing is usually unsatisfactory to both the agency and the advertiser because, following such billing, it is necessary to review all of the work in order to issue credits or additional charges to adjust the final billing for the amount of space to be paid for.

To accomplish this final billing, it is necessary to return all of the insertion orders to the checking department where there are one or more items on an order that had not been previously checked. These orders must remain in the checking department until the tear sheets are received and the advertisements measured. They are then taken from the checking department and reviewed by the billing department to determine the difference between the space billed on the ordered basis and the space actually used (after auditing with publisher's bill).

When such differences are isolated and computed, an additional invoice or credit memo must be prepared to account for the differences. This operation is more complicated than it sounds, for it often occurs that two or more different advertisements are ordered for one client to appear within one month. At the time of the first billing, some of the advertisements will have been checked and measured, but others will not have been measured. In making up the bill to the client, the agency should indicate which of them have been measured and checked in, and which have not. Also, after paying the invoice, the client should hold the invoice aside and later verify the adjustment for the items that had not been measured and checked at the time the invoice was prepared. This type of billing—that is, billing some items on the basis of space ordered and others on a checked basis —is highly unsatisfactory. Newspaper billing should be performed on an estimated basis, which is next explained.

Prebilling on an Estimated Basis

The properly operated advertising agency secures an approved or signed estimate covering the newspaper space to be ordered before insertion orders are issued to papers. If, before the advertising appears, changes are made, each such change should be represented by an approved estimate revision.

Unless some form of authorization is received by the agency from its client, the agency may be in an embarrassing position. Since agencies make huge commitments at the special request and for the benefit of clients, it is important for both advertiser and agency that such expenditures are approved in writing. This point cannot be overemphasized, and such written approvals have served to eliminate many misunderstandings. Approved estimates form the basis for determining the amount of an advertiser's commitments for a period. If, in preparing such estimates, each estimate is limited to one type of advertising medium and one month of advertising, there will be a separate estimate to cover each month's newspaper advertising. These estimates will show the total commitment of each client. Prebilling is accomplished simply by preparing a one-line invoice which usually reads as follows:

> Newspaper advertising for the month of May, 1948, as per estimate #567.............................. $90,000.00
> Less 10% tentative allowances for shrinkage and omissions 9,000.00

An invoice similar to this is sent to the client on the first day of each month to cover the advertising of the prior month. The reader will note the arbitrary tentative allowance for shrinkage and omissions. By way of explanation, it should be noted that some shrinkage (about one and one-half percent) between the linage ordered and the linage used is expected. In addition, while it is expected that all the advertising ordered will appear, the agency should not ask the client for payment equal to one hundred percent of the expected advertising, since it is entirely possible that some papers may fail to publish.

Bear in mind that this billing on an estimated basis is merely so that the agency secures payment prior to the time it is necessary for it to pay the publishers. This prebill is not intended as an accurate invoice, but the client is asked to pay the prebill and is told that as soon as possible after the space is checked and the publishers' bills audited, a complete detailed invoice will be sent.

After the preliminary bill is sent to the client, the newspaper tear sheets are checked against insertion orders, and the newspaper bills are audited against the linage checked in by the agency's checking department. As soon as the publishers have been paid, the agency prepares a complete detailed invoice to each client. Each newspaper used in the advertising campaign is listed, and that after the newspaper name there are the details of the space used, including the total linage used during the month in each paper and, finally, there is the billing price of the space. After this detailed invoice is completed, it is totaled; and from the total of the invoice, the amount of the prebill or commitment invoice is deducted, the balance representing the amount due to the agency. This method of first sending a prebill on an estimated basis, followed by a detailed invoice on the basis of checked and audited space, is by far the simplest method that can be used to accomplish the desired objectives. The client has a copy of the estimates which were previous approved. These estimates show the amount of the client's commitments for newspaper space.

The detailed invoice, which is later prepared and sent to the client by the agency, shows the actual amount of space used in each paper for the month, thus eliminating the necessity of making any calculations to determine just how much space was used in a certain paper for a certain period of time. It is only necessary for the client to audit one document, the final invoice, since this is the only document that contains any detail. By the time the final detailed invoice is received by the advertiser, the advertiser should have received tear sheets covering each advertisement, and these tear sheets may be checked against the agency's invoice in order to prove that the advertiser is paying only for the advertising that he had actually secured.

Payments to Publications

The detail of the procedure to be followed to prepare the check for the publisher is given below on the assumption that first the agency prepares an estimated invoice as explained previously, and that later the detailed invoice is prepared after all of the space has been checked with tear sheets and the linage audited against that billed to the agency by the newspaper.

The steps in the procedure are numbered in the order of their normal sequence:

1. Copies of insertion orders are taken from the checking department as bills are received from newspapers. (It is assumed that advertisements have been measured and linage used noted on the insertion orders.)
2. Bills from newspapers are audited with copies of insertion orders, at which time the following is verified:
   - Rate charged per line or inch
   - Agency commission rate allowed
   - Cash discount rate allowed
   - Number of lines charged for on each insertion date.

   (If the newspaper charges for a lesser number of lines than that measured by the agency, the insertion order is corrected to show the linage charged for by the paper.)

   If the rate per line or inch as charged by the paper is different from that shown on the insertion order, the proper or correct rate is ascertained and is used in making further computations.
3. The total linage used is computed by adding the lines used on each date. This is multiplied by the rate per line to determine the gross billing price. The agency's cost, the cash discount and the net payable are then computed.
4. After the computations (listed in 3 preceding) have been made, all the insertion orders for one paper are gathered together and an adding-machine tape is taken of the net amount payable, to determine the amount of the check to be issued to the newspaper.

When this has been completed, the adding-machine tape is clipped to the copies of the insertion orders for each paper, and they are sent to a disbursing clerk together with the bills from the paper. Previously it has been stated that newspapers send separate bills for each client's advertising and, further, that they forward two copies of each bill to the agency. Even though these requests are made, occasionally a newspaper will fail to meet the agency's requirements. In such case, it is advisable to prepare separate dummy bills for each client by reference to the one bill sent to the agency by the paper, which bill covers the charges on account of all clients of the agency. In addition, if the paper fails to send bills in duplicate, a duplicate copy of the newspaper's bill should be made to be used in the procedure which is explained in the following.

5. When the disbursing clerk receives the copies of insertion orders with adding-machine tapes attached, representing the totals due to each paper, he receives also copies of bills from publications.

   Here it should be noted that where the agency's payment is going to differ from the publisher's bills, the difference should be noted on both copies of the publisher's bill. Such differences occur frequently because of different linage or different rates, and, as stated before, the differences should be shown on both copies of the publisher's bill, and the total of the publisher's bill should be corrected to agree with the computations as shown on the insertion orders.

6. A check is now typed in triplicate. The original copy is sent to the publisher together with one copy of the publisher's bill. Note that this check is designed for use in window envelopes. Under certain conditions, a different check is desirable.

7. Immediately after the preparation of the check, the paid insertion orders are stamped with a rubber

stamp to indicate the date on which each item was paid. One copy of the check is stapled to the copies of the publisher's bills, and the check and publisher's bills are filed alphabetically for future reference. The other copy of the check is filed in numerical sequence and constitutes the cash disbursement record of the agency. The third carbon is filed by medium.

8. Insertion orders that have now been paid are filed, awaiting the preparation of the final detailed client invoice. All insertion orders which have been paid, but which have not yet been billed, are lodged in one file.

Details of Billing Procedure

As soon as the payments for the month have been completed, all paid and unbilled insertion orders are taken from the file for the purpose of preparing the client invoice. Insertion orders are now sorted so as to gather all of the orders pertaining to one client. These stacks of orders are then re-sorted so as to bring the orders into alphabetical sequence by the name of the state, the city and the publication. The information contained on the insertion orders for the client is transcribed by the typist to the client invoice, which, when completed.

It is important to note that the copies of the client's invoice which are retained by the agency are wider than the copies which are sent to the client. These office copies, or carbon copies, of the invoice show the agency cost of each item, as well as the gross billing price. This information is needed for the bookkeeping entries which will be discussed later. Clients usually require two copies of each invoice. A third copy is needed for the agency's own records. Sometimes a copy of each invoice is made and it is filed by the treasurer in a tickler file under the date on which payment should be received by the agency. After the invoices have been typed and totaled, the original copies are mailed to clients in window envelopes and the office copies are filed.

The invoice number is now noted on each insertion order that has been billed, and the insertion orders are filed in a completed file containing paid and billed insertion orders. These files are usually segregated by clients and further segregated alphabetically by state, city and paper name. At the beginning of the description of these detailed billing and paying procedures, it was explained that the assumption was made that a preliminary or estimated bill had been sent to the client. Based on this assumption, the payments are usually made to the papers before the detailed invoice is prepared. Occasionally, for one reason or another, a paper is not paid prior to the time of preparing the detailed client invoice (approximately the twenty-fifth of the month following the advertising).

In exceptional cases payments to papers could be held up because of missing tear sheets, a dispute in rates, a question as to the quality of the printing or for various other reasons. Sometimes clients wish to have all of their billing for a month completed, so they request the agency to include charges for all advertising which has appeared, even though the agency has not yet finally satisfied itself as to the correctness of the charges. As stated previously, in such cases, the agency would not have paid for the item at the time the detailed invoice was prepared for transmission to the client. When this occurs, the insertion orders would have been taken from the checking department file, but at the time of payment they would have been held up because of the questioned items.

Such insertion orders would then be used in preparing the client invoice even though payment had not been made to papers. These insertion orders, which contain no indication of payment, cannot be placed in a paid-and-billed file after the client invoice has been prepared, but must be filed in a billed-but-unpaid file.

Thus there usually are four files of insertion orders:

1. The unpaid and unbilled orders which are kept in the checking department and then sent to the accounting department to be audited against publishers' bills.

2. The paid but unbilled insertion orders which are filed in the accounting department directly following the payment of publishers' bills.
3. The billed but unpaid insertion orders consisting of those items which have been invoiced to clients, but which have not been paid.
4. The paid and billed orders.

ACCOUNTING AND BOOKKEEPING ENTRIES

The bookkeeping and accounting entries that are required are limited to those listed below. No others are needed. The customary accounts-payable and accounts-receivable ledgers are eliminated entirely where the procedures outlined are followed. The preliminary invoice which is prepared on the first or second day following the month of advertising shows the estimated billing price of the newspaper space for the prior month.

At the outset, it is known that this is not an accurate invoice. It is sent to the client for the primary purpose of collecting the monies due with a minimum of effort on behalf of the agency and the client.

In addition to serving this function, the preliminary invoice serves as a basis for entering the sales of space and the cost thereof. As a matter of accounting principle, the client is indebted to the agency as soon as the advertising appears, and certainly the agency is indebted to the publisher at such time. Therefore, for proper accounting, newspaper-space billing should be entered on the agency's books on or before the last day of the month in which the advertising was published.

Usually, it is not feasible for an agency to send the preliminary estimated bill to its client until the first or second day of the month following the advertising because it is desirable that all advertising ordered during the month be included. There is no objection to giving this invoice the date of the last day of the month of advertising, even though it is actually prepared on the first or second day of the following month. By dating the preliminary estimated invoice as of the last day of the month of advertising, it can be properly entered in the agency's books and records as of the month of advertising. The estimated invoices are usually prepared from approved estimates, media recommendations or signed schedules, since such records form a basis for securing the needed information without the necessity of again calculating the billing price of the space ordered in each newspaper.

These figures were already developed in preparing the estimate, schedule or media recommendation. To determine the cost of the space billed to the client on the preliminary estimated invoice, it is usual to multiply the billing price by eighty-five percent, since by far the majority of newspapers allow a fifteen percent agency commission. A cost figure which equals eighty-five percent of the billing price as shown on the estimated invoice is sufficiently accurate for recording this invoice and the cost of the space billed. A Sales and Cost Journal is one of the principal books of original entry of an advertising agency. All invoices sent to clients are entered in this record. A preliminary invoice would be entered in a Sales and Cost Journal. Note that the sale'is recorded under newspaper billings, and the cost of the space is recorded under newspaper costs.

The final accounting entries will be made from totals taken from this Sales and Cost Journal at the end of each month and they will be discussed later. When the final detailed invoice is prepared, after all space has been measured and the insertion orders audited against publishers' bills, the totals as shown on this final invoice are entered in the Sales and Cost Journal. Note that from the gross totals on this invoice there has been subtracted the amount of the preliminary invoice, leaving a balance in both the billing-price column and the cost column. The balance in the billing-price column represents the amount still due to the agency by the client, and the balance in the cost column represents the adjustment of the estimated cost as orīginally shown on the preliminary invoice.

At the end of the month, each column in the Sales and Cost Journal is totaled, and the total of the column headed "costs, newspapers" represents a charge to "cost of newspaper sales" and a credit to "accounts payable" control account. The total of the column "sales, newspapers" represents a charge to "accounts receivable" control and a credit to "newspaper sales."

In examining these accounting entries, it is important to note that "accounts payable" control account is never credited until the client is billed. The "accounts payable" control account is supported in detail by the files of insertion orders and the preliminary invoices which have not been finally billed. In other words, the total cost of the space as billed on preliminary invoices for which no final billing has been completed, plus all insertion orders which have been billed but have not been paid, minus all insertion orders which have been paid but which have not been billed, represents the detail of the control account "accounts payable, space".

MAGAZINES AND TRADE PAPERS: BILLING, PAYING AND ACCOUNTING

The methods used to bill, pay and account for magazine space are similar to those used for performing the same functions in connection with newspaper space. For that reason, only the differences in the two procedures will be discussed in this chapter.

Contracts

Contracts for magazine space specify the amount of space to be used and in many cases specify the dates on which advertisements are to appear. They specify the type of space contracted for, such as inside front or back cover, the number of colors in which the advertisement is to be printed, etc. This is because magazines go to press so far in advance of publication date that they require this information in order to make up the magazine properly and reserve the required space for the advertiser. The contract issued to cover magazine space then, unlike the contract for newspaper space, completely describes the space contracted for, and for many purposes could be considered as a definite order.

Insertion Orders

An insertion order is issued by the agency to cover each month's advertising in a magazine. The magazine insertion orders are similar to the newspaper insertion orders except that it is unnecessary to provide for recording the amount of space used to publish the advertisement, since magazine advertisements are printed from plates and the advertisements always require the entire amount of space ordered by the agency.

Checking the Space

Many magazines' terms provide that the agency make payment for the space prior to the publication date. For this reason, it is not possible to verify the appearance of the advertising before paying the magazine's bill; and since the agency collects from its clients on or before the date that it is required to pay the publisher, the client must be billed before the advertising has actually appeared.

Two carbon copies of magazine insertion orders are required in the bookkeeping process. One copy is sent to the checking department where it remains until after the magazine has been received and the advertisement checked. The bookkeeping copy of the insertion order is sent to the accounting department immediately after it is issued. This copy of the insertion order is filed in a tickler file under the date on which the client should be billed (about fifteen days prior to the date on which the agency must pay the publisher). After the advertisement has been billed to the client and perhaps after the agency has paid the publisher, a copy of the magazine is received in the checking department and the advertisement is checked. The checking copy of the insertion order is then initialed by the checker to indicate that the advertisement appeared in proper form in the magazine, after which it is sent to the accounting department.

Billing the Advertising

Weekly magazines usually require payment from the agency on the tenth, fifteenth or thirtieth of the month of issue. Some monthly magazines require payment during the month preceding issue; others require payment during the month of issue. On the billing date, the bookkeeping copy of the insertion order is taken from the tickler file and an invoice is typed by reference to the insertion order which contains all the particulars required for billing. The date on which the invoice was prepared is noted on the insertion order and it is filed in a billed-and-unpaid file. No adjustment of the original billing is required in connection with magazine space for, unlike newspaper space, the advertisements in magazines always require the amount of space ordered by the agency.

Payments to Publications

When the bills are received from magazine publishers, the insertion orders covering the space are located in the billed-and-unpaid file. The publisher's bill is audited against the insertion order and the check is prepared. The date of the payment is entered on the insertion order which is then filed in a paid-and-billed file. In some instances, agencies pay magazine publishers before they bill clients. This condition occurs where the agency does not have sufficient credit with the publisher. The publisher may require in such cases that the agency pay for space on closing date (the date that the magazine goes to press).

Since under normal terms the agency cannot bill its client until ten or fifteen days prior to the date, on which the magazine would normally require the agency to pay for the space, it becomes imprudent for the agency to bill the client in time to receive the money to make the payment to the magazine publisher on closing date. When this condition occurs, the copy of the insertion order is taken from the unpaid-and-unbilled file, the payment is made and the date of the payment is indicated on the insertion order, which is then filed in a paid-but-unbilled file under the proper billing date. On the proper billing date the invoice is prepared and sent to the client. The billing date is noted on the insertion order which is then filed in the billed-and-paid file.

RADIO TIME: BILLING, PAYING AND ACCOUNTING

Radio advertising requires "time on the air," radio performers and, in some cases, scripts, sound effects, recording, etc. Time on the air is purchased from either independent stations or networks, that is, groups of stations such as the National Broadcasting Company, American Broadcasting Company, Mutual Broadcasting System or Columbia Broadcasting System.

Advertising agencies, in some cases, purchase only the time on the air from the radio station or network; and they purchase the talent, sound effects and other required items separately. In other instances, the advertising agency purchases time on the air, the required talent, sound effects and production materials directly from the radio station or network. When this is done, it is called a "package," and the broadcast is referred to as a "package show."

The advertising agency receives a fifteen percent commission from the radio station on all charges for time on the air. Where package shows are purchased, or in other cases where either talent or production materials are purchased by advertising agencies from radio stations or networks, the radio station or network allows no commission to the agency on either talent or production materials; but it is usual for the agency to add 17.65 or 15 percent to the cost of talent and production materials purchased from networks or stations when computing the billing price of these items. (When 17.65 percent is added to

the cost, the commission realized on the selling price—117.65 percent of the cost—is fifteen percent of the selling price.)

Contracts

Contracts for radio time or for package shows are prepared by the radio station or network that is selling the time to the agency. Note the difference between this and the procedure followed in publication advertising where the contract is prepared by the agency and sent to the publication.

Radio time and radio package shows are sold in units of weeks of broadcasting and regularly cover thirteen-week periods, or multiples thereof. In many cases, the cost of the "time on the air" is reduced as the volume of time used increases; thus, the rate for each week's broadcasting is less per broadcast when twenty-six weeks' time is contracted for than when only thirteen weeks* time is used.

Usually, where better rates are offered for longer periods of time, contracts between stations and agencies provide that, if the contract period is extended, then the rate per broadcast will be retroactively adjusted. If, for example, the station has better rates for a twenty-six-week period than for a thirteen-week period, and only a thirteen-week commitment is entered into originally, and the contract is renewed for an additional thirteen weeks, then there will be a retroactive rate adjustment to the first thirteen weeks of broadcasting, and the next thirteen weeks of broadcasting will be at the twenty-six-week rate.

Where talent is purchased separately by the agency, of course a separate contract is entered into between the agency and the talent. The contract for live talent, when it is made separately, must cover a period running concurrently with that covering the radio time on the air; for obviously the talent is useless without the time on the air. Just as obviously, time on the air is planned with specific talent which is purchased for a particular programme.

The contract between the station or network and the agency will be specific even as to small detail. It will cover the time that the radio show will be broadcast each day, on what day or days of the week the show will be broadcast, and all of the contingencies that could be anticipated, such as interruptions in the programme, omissions of broadcasts, etc.

Often the contracts between radio stations or networks and advertising agencies are non-cancellable contracts. This suggests the enormous contingent liability or commitment that an agency can have in connection with a radio show covered by a fifty-two-week contract. Before an agency signs a contract with a radio station or network, it is of course necessary that the agencies have a firm commitment from its client.

It is suggested that the client be required to sign a contract with the agency containing exactly the same terms and conditions as the contract that the agency is required to sign with the radio station or network. This is for the station's benefit as much as for the agency's. It also benefits the client, since it is certainly desirable that the client understand just what his commitment is—particularly in the case of radio advertising where the non-cancellable commitments can run into vast sums even in short periods of time.

In certain types of radio advertising, the agency is required to furnish the station or network with scripts, recordings or other materials for the show. Where this is the case, the agency is obligated to secure the needed items and furnish them to the radio station or network in advance of the broadcast date.

Usually, agencies have separate departments for the production of radio advertising, including scriptwriters and copywriters. The difference between the two titles is that scriptwriters write stories and copywriters write advertising copy. Some radio advertising of course requires no scriptwriting, sound effects, or other services or materials.

In the early days of radio advertising, advertisers and agencies attempted to verify the programs broadcast by each station by appointing individuals in each city to listen to the broadcast of the station located in that city and to file a report on the quality of broadcast, the content of the broadcast and the elapsed time required. This type of verification proved to be expensive and cumbersome. Some agencies and advertisers still check radio broadcasts through the advertisers' dealers or through separate third-party organizations of one type or another. But most advertisers and agencies rely on the honesty of the broadcasting station which furnishes affidavits certifying the fact that each broadcast charged for was actually performed.

Billing Work Sheets

After the agency has entered into a contract with a radio station or network, the essential information required for accounting purposes should be extracted from the contract so that it will be readily available from week to week and month to month as it becomes necessary to refer to such data for bookkeeping and accounting purposes. It is best to compile this information in an orderly fashion so that it can be more efficiently used by the agency's bookkeepers and clerks. A billing work sheet is a convenient form for extracting the needed information from radio contracts. Billing work sheets should clearly set forth all of the following information:

- Client name
- Station name.
- Station address.
- Name of the programme.
- Term of the contract.
- Commission rate.
- Cash discount terms.
- Times and days of the broadcasts.
- Rate per broadcast.

The billing work sheet should provide ample space for computing the amount due the station and the amount to be billed to the client for each week or month of the contract period. Some radio stations bill agencies on a weekly basis, others on a monthly one.

Where the agency is billed on a weekly basis, it sends invoices to clients each week; where it is billed on a monthly basis, it bills its client on the same basis. If weekly bills are sent, the computations and invoices are prepared on the last day of the week; monthly invoices are prepared on the last day of each month.

When the agency prepares the invoice to its client to cover either a week's or a month's broadcasting, those invoices are prepared on the basis of full performance, since on the last day of the week or month of broadcasting, the billing clerks have not yet received bills from radio stations and therefore cannot account for interruptions and omissions. The procedure for handling such omissions and interruptions will be described later. Billing work sheets should be arranged alphabetically by client, with each client's billing work sheets arranged alphabetically by station call letters.

Invoices to Clients

As was stated previously, invoices for clients are prepared by reference to the file of radio-billing work sheets. Invoices could be prepared by referring directly to contracts with radio stations, but these contracts are legalistic in form. Therefore, to excerpt the needed information would require considerable time.

It is for this reason that the billing work sheet is prepared as soon as the contract has been completed, so that then this work sheet can be referred to month in and month out until the contract has expired. A separate invoice should be prepared for each programme. This means that there could be two or more invoices covering broadcasting from the same radio station, since one client may purchase several programs from one station and each programme could be covered by a separate contract.

At least three copies of each radio-time invoice should be prepared by the advertising agency. The original is to be sent to the client; the file and bookkeeping copies are to be retained by the advertising agency. After the invoices have been prepared, all radio-time invoices for one client should be grouped together and attached to a summary invoice. Billing amount but the cost amount as well. In addition, space is provided on the bookkeeping copy of each invoice to record adjustments to the original invoice and payments to radio stations.

Payments to Radio Stations

When the agency first prepares the invoice that it sends to its client for the radio-time charges, that invoice is prepared on the basis of the number of broadcasts contracted for; at this time no adjustment is made for interruptions, omissions, etc. The bookkeeping copy of the client's invoice is designed to act in the same manner as a payment voucher.

In other words, it is used as the authorization for the payment to the radio station. This is because the agency, having billed its client for the radio time, can authorize payment in an amount not exceeding the legitimate cost of the items so billed. Of course it is necessary for the agency to verify the cost of these items by comparing the figures shown on the bookkeeping copy of the invoice with those shown on the radio station's bill to the agency. It is also necessary to examine the affidavit from the station to determine that all broadcasts scheduled actually were performed.

Bookkeeping copies of radio-time invoices to clients are filed by the agency in a file called "Billed but Unpaid Items." It is important to note that when an invoice is prepared, that invoice is entered in the Sales and Cost Journal and the cost of the radio time is thereby credited to accounts payable. Accounts-payable radio time is never credited until a client is billed, since this credit originates from entering clients' bills to the Sales and Cost Journal, as will be seen in greater detail by examination of the chapter "Chart of Accounts and Accounting Records." No radio station should be paid without a client's having been billed, as will be seen in the following:

When a bill is received from a radio station, affidavits verifying the broadcasts should accompany such bills. The bills from the radio stations are then audited against bookkeeping copies of invoices sent to clients (found in the "Billed-but-Unpaid" files). If no bill has been sent to a client for the item billed by the radio station, an invoice should be prepared before the radio station's bill is passed for payment. If the station's bill allows credits for interruptions or omissions, etc., then that information should be posted on the bookkeeping copy of the agency's invoice.

The check number and the amount paid to the radio station is to be noted on the bookkeeping copy of the client invoice, and the check is sent to the radio station. Duplicate copies of checks issued to radio stations are filed and the total of such duplicates at the end of the month is charged to "accounts payable, radio time." The bookkeeping copies of the original radio-time invoices sent to clients are now examined to determine if any billing adjustment is required.

Adjustments to Original Billing

After the radio stations have been paid, the bookkeeping copies of the original invoices sent to clients are used to prepare adjustment invoices. Usually these adjustment invoices are the equivalent of credit memos, for it is rare that a client would

FALSE ADVERTISING

Although your use of the latest hot marketing and sales strategies may improve the bottom line of your business, you may get into hot "legal waters" if you do not exercise the proper restraints. This article discusses the boundaries beyond which you do not want to stray lest you run afoul of the laws governing false advertising. Two conflicting principles are involved in advertising law. On the one hand, the First Amendment, which is part of the U.S. Constitution and grants us the right of free speech, protects all forms of communication, including advertising (referred to by lawyers as "commercial speech"). On the other hand, the U.S. Constitution gives the federal government the power to regulate interstate commerce. Most state constitutions similarly give state governments the power to regulate commerce conducted solely within that state.

In exercising its power over interstate commerce, the Congress has enacted two statutes that have the greatest effect on advertising. These are the Federal Trade Commission (FTC) Act and the Lanham Act. The FTC Act states that false advertising is a form of unfair and deceptive commerce. The term "false advertising" has been broadly construed. As you might expect, the term includes advertisements that are in fact untrue. However, the term false advertising extends well beyond untrue advertisements. It also includes advertisements that make representations that the advertiser has no reasonable basis to believe, even if the representations turn out to be true. An example would be an advertisement for a photocopier machine which stated that the machine used less toner than any comparable machine. The advertiser would have committed false advertising if it had no reasonable basis to believe the truth of this claim (such as through comparative tests), even if it turned out to be true.

The FTC Act gives the FTC broad authority to regulate advertising. Under this broad mandate, the FTC has issued regulations barring advertisements that could be misleading even if they are true. A famous example involves Anacin, a brand of aspirin. The maker of Anacin ran ads claiming that clinical tests showed that Anacin delivered the same headache relief as the leading pain relief prescription. The ad did not mention that aspirin itself is the leading pain medicine. The FTC determined that the ad was misleading. The ad implied that Anacin was more effective than aspirin, when in fact, Anacin is really just aspirin.

In addition to barring advertisements, the FTC also has the power to order corrective ads. Corrective advertising requires a business to run ads that alert future consumers to certain unfavorable facts about a product not revealed in past advertising campaigns. Another famous example involved Listerine mouthwash. For years, Listerine was touted as a cold and sore throat remedy. The FTC forced the manufacturer to run ads stating that Listerine would not cure colds or relieve sore throats. Surely, this is not part of a desirable marketing strategy.

The FTC has a further power, known as "fencing in." This enables the FTC to bar misleading ads with respect to a particular product and across all of a business's other unrelated product lines. For example a testimonial constituting false advertising regarding product A could lead purchasers to believe that products B and c must also be great. In that case, the FTC could bar use of the ad for products A, B, and C.

Only the FTC has the authority to enforce the FTC Act. Private parties, such as consumers or competitors, can bring a legal action regarding false advertising under the Lanham Act. To establish a violation under the Lanham Act, consumers and competitors must prove the following:

(1) The advertiser made false statements of fact about its product;

(2) The false advertisements actually deceived or had the capacity to deceive a substantial segment of the target population;

(3) The deception was material;

(4) the falsely advertised product was sold in interstate commerce; and

(5) The party bringing the lawsuit (known as the "plaintiff") was injured as a result of the deception.

Actual loss is not required to show an injury. All that is needed is a reasonable basis for the belief that the plaintiff is likely to be damaged as a result of the advertising. An example of such damage would include ads that deceive consumers who are the target population of both the advertiser and the plaintiff. The penalties for a Lanham Act violation include the plaintiff's lost profits, the additional profits to the advertiser resulting from the deceptive ad, treble damages, and attorneys' fees.

In addition to the FTC Act and the Lanham Act, which are federal statutes, most states, including Illinois, also have laws proscribing false advertising. Illinois is one of many states that has enacted the Uniform Deceptive Trade Practices Act. Under the Act, a "deceptive trade practice" includes such practices as "palming off," misrepresentation, product disparagement, and bait-and-switch advertising.

Palming off occurs when an advertiser creates the impression that its goods or services are those that are furnished by a competitor. For example, this could occur if you set up a hamburger stand that looked like a McDonalds restaurant. Misrepresentation occurs when an advertiser makes false or misleading claims about its goods or services, as under the FTC Act and the Lanham Act. Product disparagement occurs when an advertiser intentionally makes false or misleading negative remarks about competing goods or services, causing its competitor to lose sales. Bait-and-switch advertising occurs when the advertised goods or services are withdrawn from the market and substitute goods or services are instead offered for sale.

The laws regulating false advertising present many traps for the unwary. If you engage a marketing or advertising agent to assist you in your marketing and sales campaign, you might want to get your agent to guarantee that your ads are lawful. Of course, if you are in the business of preparing marketing or advertising campaigns, you might want to get your client to guarantee that the information he or she provides is true. In either case, when in doubt, you should consult with an attorney.

Chapter 4

Hotel Management and Advertisement

A hotel is an establishment that provides paid lodging, usually on a short-term basis. Hotels often provide a number of additional guest services such as a restaurant, a swimming pool or childcare. Some hotels have conference services and meeting rooms and encourage groups to hold conventions and meetings at their location. Hotels differ from motels in that most motels have drive-up, exterior entrances to the rooms, while hotels tend to have interior entrances to the rooms, which may increase guests' safety and present a more upmarket image. In Australia, a hotel may also be an establishment that serves alcoholic drinks, and usually meals in a casual setting but which does not necessarily provide accommodation. This type of establishment would more usually be called a pub or bar in other countries. In general use in Australia, the terms '"hotel" and pub are usually taken to be synonymous.

In India, the word may also refer to a restaurant since the best restaurants were always situated next to a good hotel. The word hotel derives from the French hotel, which referred to a French version of a townhouse, not a place offering accommodation (in contemporary usage, hotel has the meaning of "hotel", and hotel particular is used for the old meaning). The French spelling (with the circumflex) was once also used in English, but is now rare. The circumflex replaces the 's' once preceding the 't' in the earlier hostel spelling, which over time received a new, but closely related meaning.

Services and Facilities

Basic accommodation of a room with only a bed, a cupboard, a small table and a washstand has largely been replaced by rooms with en-suite bathrooms and climate control. Other features found may be a telephone, an alarm clock, a TV, and broadband Internet connectivity. Food and drink may be supplied by a mini-bar (which often includes a small refrigerator) containing snacks and drinks (to be paid for on departure), and tea and coffee making facilities (cups, spoons, an electric kettle and sachets containing instant coffee, tea bags, sugar, and creamer or milk).

In the United Kingdom a hotel is required by law to serve food and drinks to all comers within certain stated hours; to avoid this requirement it is not uncommon to come across "private hotels" which are not subject to this requirement. However, in Japan the capsule hotel supplies minimal facilities and room space. The cost and quality of hotels are usually indicative of the range and type of services available. Due to the enormous increase in tourism worldwide during the last decades of the 20th century, standards, especially those of smaller establishments, have improved considerably. For the sake of greater comparability, rating systems have been introduced, with the one to five stars classification being most common.

Types of Hotels

Boutique Hotels

Boutique hotel is a term originating in North America to describe intimate, usually luxurious or quirky hotel environments. Boutique hotels differentiate themselves from larger chain/branded hotels and motels by providing personalized level accommodation and services / facilities. Sometimes known as "design hotels" or "lifestyle hotels," boutique hotels began in the 1980s in major cities like New York, London, and San Francisco. Very often it is the Morgans Hotel in Murray Hill of New York, that is awarded with the title of first boutique hotel in the world. It was opened by Ian Schrager in 1984 according to a design by Andree Putman.

Typically boutique hotels are furnished in a themed, stylish and/or aspirational manner. Although usually considerably smaller than a mainstream hotel (often ranging from 3 to 100 guest rooms), boutique hotels can often have hundreds of rooms in major cities. Guest rooms and suites are fitted with telephony and Wi-Fi Internet, air-conditioning, honesty bars and often cable/pay TV. Guest services are attended to by 24 hour hotel staff. Many boutique hotels have on-site dining facilities, and the majority offer bars and lounges which may also be open to the general public.

Despite this definition, the popularity of the boutique term and concept has lead to some confusion about the term. Boutique hotels have typically been unique properties operated by individials or companies with a small collection. However, their successes have prompted established multi-national hotel companies to establish their own brands. The most notable is Starwood Hotels and Resorts' W Hotels.

Currently, there is one publication dedicated to the boutique hotel, boutique DESIGN magazine, which is published quarterly. Boutique hotel resources are more commonly available online. One such site dedicated to boutique hotels is Tablet Hotels. There are also a number of sytlized design and coffee table books highlighting various properties throughout the world.

Apartment Hotel

An Apartment Hotel is a type of accommodation, described as "a serviced apartment complex that uses a hotel style booking system". It is similar to renting an apartment, but with no fixed contracts and occupants can 'check-out' whenever they wish. Apartment hotels are flexible types of accommodation; instead of the rigid format of a hotel room an apartment hotel complex usually offers a complete fully fitted apartment. These complexes are usually custom built, and similar to a hotel complex contain a varied amount of apartments. The length of stay in these apartment hotels are very varied with anywhere from a few days to months or even years. Prices tend to be cheaper than hotels. The people that stay in apartment hotels use them as a home from home therefore they are usually fitted with everything the average home would require.

Apartment hotels were first created in holiday destinations as accommodation for families that needed to 'live' in an apartment rather than 'stay' as they would in a hotel. The apartments would provide a 'holiday home' but generally be serviced. Later on these apartments evolved to be complete homes, allowing occupants to do everything they would at home, such as cleaning, washing and cooking.

Essentially the apartment hotel combines the flexibility of apartment living with the service of a hotel. Many of the apartments take advantage of prime locations with panoramic views of cities seen through wall to ceiling windows. Suites usually include high quality finishes, broadband connection & interactive TV, servicing and integrated kitchen and bathroom. High quality leather sofas in the living area and king size beds bring the hotel experience to a whole new level. Those are the luxuries, they also come with the basics: satellite or cable TV, washer, dryer, dishwasher, cooker, oven, fridge, freezer, sink, shower, bath, wardrobes, all the furnishings to be expected in a luxury home.

Bed and Breakfast

A Bed and Breakfast often referred to as a B&B is a type of boarding house typically operating out of a large single family residence. Guests are accommodated at night in private bedrooms and breakfast is served in the morning - either in the bedroom or, more commonly, in a dining room or the host's kitchen. Bathrooms can be private or shared (with other guests or with the family in smaller establishments) or en-suite (where the ablutions are directly accessed from the guest's bedroom).

B&Bs may be operated either as a primary occupation or as a secondary source of income. Staff often consists of the house's owners and members of their family who live there. Guests are usually expected to pay for their stay upon arrival and leave before noon (or earlier) on the day of departure. A big advantage of this type of hosted accommodation is the local knowledge of the host.

When guests stay more than one night, in some smaller B&Bs they will be expected to be away from the B&B during the main part of the day. This arrangement, however, may not be inconvenient since many popular B&Bs are located in beach and mountain areas, such as Hawaii, New England, and Colorado where daytime recreation and tourism activities are popular. One advantage of staying at a B&B is readier access to popular locations "off the beaten path" which may not be convenient to the city center.

Because most B&Bs are small, rarely with room for more than about 2-12 guests, it is advisable for anyone wanting to stay at a bed and breakfast to make reservations well in advance of their travel date. Consultation with a qualified travel agent knowledgeable in this type of accommodation may be helpful; However, many B&Bs belong to associations and have a web presence. Be aware that prices and tariffs described in various books and travel guides are often obsolete by the time they are published.

The B&B arrangement is actually a very old one; before the 20th century, it was quite normal for country travellers to spend the night at a private house rather than an inn, and the custom persists in many parts of the world. However, prior to the 19th century, this was strictly an informal arrangement constrained by acquaintance and social rank; a doctor might stay with a doctor or pharmacist, while a nobleman would only stay with the local gentry. The abbreviation of 'B&B' on roadside signs first became popular in the British Isles.

In the British Isles, breakfast is usually cooked on demand for the guest and usually features bacon, eggs, sausages, tomatoes, mushrooms, baked beans, etc but increasingly, because of either a desire of owners to economise or guests to minimise their calorie intake, a 'continental breakfast' is becoming more common. In the British Isles where hotel prices are often outrageous, B&B's are a budget option and this tradition continues in many parts of the world.

However, many B&Bs in North America and New Zealand often consciously seek to recall earlier days; they are frequently established in attractive older houses that have been renovated and filled with antique furniture. In some cases in North America an existing inn will relabel itself as a "B&B" to improve business and move itself `up-market'.

In Ireland, most B&Bs serve a traditional Irish breakfast as a point of pride. In Cuba, which opened up to tourism in the 1990s after the financial support of the Soviet Union ended, a form of B&B called casa particular ("private home") became the main form of accommodation outside the tourist resorts. The term "bed and breakfast" is also used to refer to a meal plan where breakfast is the only meal provided, commonly in package holidays, in a major hotel that may provide other meals to only some customers.

As they are often run by amateurs, with little lodge management experience, strict laws should govern the operation of B&Bs. However, regulations vary in each jurisdiction both in content and extent and in enforcement. The most common regulations B&Bs must follow pertain to safety. They are required to have fire resistance, a sufficient fire escape plan in place, and smoke detectors in each guest room.

Capsule Hotel

A capsule hotel, is a hotel system of extremely dense occupancy. Guest space is reduced in size to a modular plastic or fibreglass block roughly 2 m by 1 m by 1.25 m, providing room to sleep and little more, although facilities usually include a television and other electronic entertainment. These capsules are then grouped and stacked, two units high. Luggage is usually stored in a locker away from the capsule. Privacy is maintained by a curtain at the open end of the capsule but noise pollution can be high. Washing facilities are communal and there are often restaurants, or at least vending machines, and other entertainment facilities.

This style of hotel accommodation was developed in Japan and has not gained acceptance outside of the country. The

Japanese capsule hotels vary widely in size, some having only fifty or so capsules and others over 700. They are often male-only. There are also capsule hotels with separate male and female sleeping quarters. Clothes and shoes are sometimes exchanged for a yukata and slippers on entry. A towel may also be provided. The benefit of these hotels is convenience and price, usually around ¥2000-4000 a night 21-29, $25–34, £15–20). Such hotels are not necessarily regarded as only an option for those with lower incomes—a typical customer would be the business salaryman after a night of drinking who has missed the last train home. Some capsule hotels offer low daytime discounts for those needing an afternoon nap.

The first capsule hotel was the Capsule Inn Osaka, designed by Kisho Kurokawa and located in the Umeda district of Osaka. It opened on February 1, 1979 and the initial room rate was ¥1,600. These rooms can be seen in the movie The Fast and the Furious: Tokyo Drift. They were also used as a basis for sets in the film The Fifth Element. They also appear in the cyberpunk novel Neuromancer under the name of "coffin hotel."

Casa Particular

Casa particular is a phrase meaning private accommodation or private homestays in Cuba, very similar to bed and breakfast although it can also take the form of vacation rental. When the meaning is clear the term is often shortened to simply casa. A casa particular is basically a private family establishment that provides paid lodging, usually on a short-term basis. In general under this term you can find full apartment and houses, rooms inside people homes, mini-apartments or rooms with separate entrance (studio or efficiency type rooms).

It is also considered a type of boarding house typically operated out of a single family residence where guests can be accommodated at night in private bedrooms (which may or may not be equipped with private baths) and where breakfast, sometimes continental and sometimes the full English variety, is served in the morning. The business may be operated either as a primary occupation or as a secondary source of income, and the staff often consists of the house's owner(s) and members of their family who live there.

Because they are usually small, rarely with room for more than about 5-6 guests, it is advisable for anyone wanting to stay at a particular casa particular during high season to make advance reservations. However, outside the season there is no need because there are often many such casas, causing competition and opening opportunities to strike a deal. Prices can then drop to 15 euro or even less for longer stays. During high season they can rise to over 30 euro. Many belong to associations, have a web presence, and are described in various books and travel guides. Casas particulares can be recognised by a small sign on the door, with two blue triangles ('roofs') against a white background, which the owners obtain after paying a fixed per-room annual tax.

In some Cuban cities and tourist resorts, like Varadero, Playa Santa Lucia and Guardalavaca, local authorities determined that casas particulars would represent a threat to the hotel industry, and passed some legislation placing regulations and limits on the industry forbidding the operation of these establishments. "Casa particular" literally means "private house" but it started to be used to mean "private accommodation" in 1997, when the Cuban government finally allowed Cubans to rent out rooms in their houses or apartments to tourists, providing Cuban families with new sources of income. As any other type of accommodation in Cuba such as hotels, camping and motels were owned by the government, the term "casa particular" stated that this kind of paid lodging was privately operated.

Services and Facilities

All rooms are clean, safe and upgraded to tourist standards. It ranges from basic accommodation of a room with a bed, a closet, a small table to full furnished independent apartments upgraded to western standards. Other features found may be a telephone, an alarm clock, and a TV. Food and drink may be supplied by a mini-bar (which often includes a small refrigerator) containing snacks and drinks (to be paid for on departure).

It is possible to have breakfast/ dinner in the casa for price. Often breakfasts/dinners sold will decide if case owner will break even or not. So if it becomes clear that one plans to generally eat out, the price may go up because this is an important source of income.

Casas particulares have several advantages over other types of lodgings:

- The guest can quickly develop genuine Cuban relationships and become deeply involved in the culture of the country. Before he/she knows it, the guest will be part of the family. In a big resort one may only meet hotel workers and other tourists.
- The guest will enjoy the free and easy atmosphere, feel completely at home in the casa particular and will be able to invite friends over. The current regulations for state-run hotels don't allow to have Cuban guests invited to hotel rooms.
- It is almost always cheaper to stay in a private room than in a hotel.
- "Guests" are not usually allowed into the hotels. Usually one can take one local "guest" into his rented casa-particular.
- By renting a casa particular, the guest will be directly contributing to a person or family's standard of living. This is often obvious through the fact that casas particulares are freshly painted.

The cost and quality of casas particulars are usually indicative of the accommodation type and type of services available. Most of the casas particulars are rented for short term to travellers. Long term accommodation is also provided by some casas, especially for foreign students. In Havana, the casas particulares are usually family apartments and a smaller number of them are houses. In other cities, private accommodation is provided mainly in family houses.

Types of Casas Particulares rentals:

- Private Room: a room is rented out most of the times with private bathroom and a key to the apartment/ house is usually given to the guest.
- Private Room with independent entrance. Sometimes the house/apartment is split in order to allow this.
- Apartment: the guest can enjoy the privacy and independency of a full furnished apartment for his/ her vacations. Sometimes this apartment is part of house being split by a wall usually with a connecting door.
- Studio-type or mini-apartment: it is not an apartment with several rooms but just the bedroom, a kitchen-living-dining room and a bathroom.

Condo-hotel

A condo-hotel or a hotel-condo is a building used as both a condominium and a hotel. This type of residential building meets several needs that make it attractive. As development costs increase, the cost of hotel development can make developing new hotels difficult, especially in major cities. By selling the units as condos, the developer moves much of the development cost to the condo owners. By owning units that can be rented as hotel rooms, the owners are able to get a return on their investment allowing them the ability to own a residence in a resort or major city.

It should be noted that the U.S. Government is very strict about the type of advertising that can be done vis a vis Condo Hotel projects. Some condo projects have advertised themselves as "Real Estate Investments" - since the value of these condos as a real estate investment is not entirely clear - the U.S. Government currently disallows use of this reference when advertising condo hotels.

Condo hotels have been criticized in California for allowing developers to skirt laws designed to protect public access to beaches. Because such a facility has hotel rooms, it can be classified as a public accommodation, even though the majority of the units are privately held, and the facility does little to accommodate the public.

Destination Hotel

A destination hotel is a place of lodging whose inherent location and amenities attract visitors regardless of the route needed to arrive or the areawide features of interest. The destination hotel concept has existed at least since the 19th century and occupies a significant market share of all lodging in the world as of 2006. From the late 1980s to the present the extent of amenities and conference facilities has greatly expanded for many destination hotels. Destination hotels are also called destination lodgings and destination resorts. Considerable academic and business analysis has been conducted in the field of destination hotels. In the Arnold Encyclopedia of Real Estate a destination hotel is characterized as a place of lodging not chosen for convenience and not chosen for people in transit to other areas.

The following typically are characteristics of a destination hotel:

- Amenities which are quite complete and self-contained
- Upscale nature of the lodging operation
- Distinctive characteristics of the building, gardens or adjacent natural feature
- Activity set which makes leaving the property unnecessary

Since the 1800s, the traditional concept of a destination hotel has been based upon a venue which is typically remote and has a natural feature as its attraction. For example, the Kviknes Hotel in Norway is a difficult to reach remote location which provides visitors access to the scenic fjord at Balestrand. Historically there were certain built-in amenities such as gourmet cuisine, music recitals and shoreline trails; however, the amenities of modern destination hotels dwarf the scale of these earlier models. Many of the Las Vegas and Carribbean resort hotels have complete shopping malls, conference centers and large entertainment halls on site; thus, the contemporary version of a destination often features large on-site capital investment in activities, although the access to a local natural feature is still retained by many newer destination hotels.

Luxury Resorts

A luxury resort, sometimes referred to as an exclusive resort, is a very expensive vacation facility which is fully staffed and has been rated with five stars. Luxury resorts often boast many visitor activities and attractions such as golf, watersports, spa and beauty facilities, skiing, natural ecology and tranquility. Because of the extent of amenities offered, a luxury resort is also considered a destination resort. A luxury resort is an elite luxury property which exhibits an exceptionally high degree of customer service and hospitality. A flawless execution of guest services will be the resort staff's and managements main concern. A luxury resort will commonly also feature a superb architectural interior and exterior design as well as an interesting physical location.

The interior design will normally be elegant with stylish bedroom decor, exceptional dining facilities, and manicured landscaping and meticulous grounds. Luxury resorts will often also be in based in exceptionally desirable and strategic worldwide locations, from beautiful tropical islands, to snow caked mountains, to scenic lakes and rivers, to exhilarating cities. The locations will often be famous for featured activities from skiing to golf, water spots, diving, fishing, sailing and nature walks to glamorous shopping and nightlife entertainment.

A luxury resort may vary greatly in character, style and theme from resort to resort. A luxury resort will, however, normally be characterized by a high level of luxury, sophistication and off course price. Accommodations are first class, whether they follow a classic and traditional nature or a more minimalist and modern styling. An unmatched level of comfort will be available at a luxury resort, as well as many personalized services and amenities.

Extended Stay Hotel

Extended stay hotels are a type of lodging with features unavailable at standard hotels. These features are intended to provide more home-like amenities. There are currently 27 extended stay chains in North America with at least 7 hotels, representing over 2,000 properties. There is substantial variation among extended stay hotels with respect to quality and the amenities that are available. Some of the economy chains attract clientele who use the hotels as semi-permanent lodging. Occasionally, these budget establishments can be the scene of criminal activity.

Extended-stay hotels typically have self-serve laundry facilities and offer discounts for extended stays, beginning at 5 or 7 days. They also have guestrooms (or "suites") with kitchens. The kitchens include at a minimum usually: a sink, a refrigerator (usually full size), a microwave oven, and a stovetop. Some kitchens also have dishwashers and conventional ovens.

Extended stay hotels are popular with business travelers on extended assignments, families in the midst of a relocation, and anyone else in need of temporary housing. Extended stay hotels are also used by travelers who appreciate the larger space a typical suite provides. Residence Inn is credited with popularizing the "extended stay" concept. The chain was launched in 1975 in Wichita, Kansas by Jack DeBoer, and acquired by Marriott Corporation in 1987. As of April 2005, there were over 450 Residence Inn hotels in the United States, Canada and Mexico. Some extended stay hotels are coming up in United Kingdom and Ireland as well.

One of today's most popular long term lodging brands came from the merger of Extended Stay America and Homestead Hotels. Both these chains were already well established when they combined in 2004 to become Extended Stay Hotels with over 670 owned and operated properties nationwide. Another worldwide hotel chain, Choice Hotels International, franchisor for name brands such as Comfort Inn, Comfort Suites, Sleep Inn and Quality Inn, entered the extended stay market with their MainStay Suites brand. They proceeded to acquire the Suburban Extended Stay hotel chain in 2005, making them a sizeable extended stay system with over 150 hotels open and under development.

Flophouse

A flophouse or dosshouse is a place that offers very cheap lodging, generally by providing only minimal services. Occupants of flophouses generally share bathroom facilities and reside in very cramped quarters. The people who make use of these places are often transients, although some people will stay in flophouses for long periods of time—years or decades. Some people who live in flophouses may be just a step above homelessness. In the late 20th century, typical cost might be about US$6 per night. A typical flophouse might advertise its services with a sign such as "Hotel for Men; Transients Welcome".

Quarters in flophouses are very small, and may resemble office cubicles more than a regular room in a hotel or apartment building. A cubicle might only have wire mesh for a ceiling. In the past, flophouses were sometimes called "workingmen's hotels" and catered to hobos and transient workers such as seasonal railroad and agriculture workers, or migrant lumberjacks who would travel west during the summer to work and then return to an eastern or midwestern city such as Chicago to stay in a flophouse during the winter. This is described in the 1930 novel The Rambling Kid by Charles Ashleigh and the 1976 book The Human Cougar by Lloyd Morain. Another theme in Morain's book is the gentrification which was then beginning and which has led cities to pressure flophouses to close.

George Orwell also discussed flophouses in the UK in his book Down and Out in Paris and London. He described them as having rather poor cleanliness standards, often issuing unwashed and badly stained blankets, and sometimes renting beds in a large common room resembling barracks more than private rooms. He noted that at the time he wrote the book (1933) the term "dosshouse" was already falling out of use.

Some city districts that currently have or once had flophouses in abundance became well-known in their own right, such as the Bowery in New York, New York. The movies The Blues Brothers (1980) and Staying Alive (1983) both feature their lead characters living in flophouses. Another slang term for flophouses was mentioned in the movie Kids. This variation of the definition is a house or apartment (usually apartment) where substance abusers stay to party and abuse drugs and/ or alcohol. Such people, whether employed or unemployed, lead a hedonist self-destructive lifestyle. If they are employed, their money usually goes to drugs and/or alcohol. Other bums and partygoers can also temporarily stay for parties.

Some low-end flophouses have graffiti sprayed on the walls and lack beds, instead just have matresses on the floor. Some of the characters in the film Trainspotting lived in these conditions. Michael Dominic's documentary film Sunshine Hotel (2001) follows the lives of the denizens of one of the few remaining Bowery flophouses.

ORGANIZATION WITHIN HOTELS

Hotel Manager

The Hotel manager oversees all of a hotel's daily operations, from staffing to coordinating fresh-cut flowers for the lobby. Many, over time, are given long-term responsibility for negotiating contracts with vendors (such as maintenance supplies), negotiating leases with on-site shops, and physically upgrading the hotel. Hotel managers usually relish "the ability to put your own distinctive style on the [hotel] experience." While managing a hotel and giving it your unique flair are wonderful, they come with full responsibility for failure. "The better you are at what you do, the more responsibilities you are given, the more chances you have to fail," mentioned one hotel manager. When things fall apart, "no one is a hotel manager's friend."

Hotel managers can feel great about their positions, create strong relationships with regular customers, and maintain an amicable working environment. But should the bottom line waver and financial woes occur, the first neck on the chopping block is the hotel manager's. Those in the hotel management industry say that sometimes it seems that you need "to be born on the planet Krypton" to be a good hotel manager because only Superman could juggle the administrative, aesthetic, and financial decisions which constitute daily life on the job. Over 70 percent of the respondents said that tired was an understatement about how they felt at the end of the day or night.

A hotel manager's position as a liaison between the ownership and the staff can be difficult and isolating. But those who can put up with the long hours, the high degree of responsibility, and the variety of tasks emerge with a solid degree of satisfaction and a desire to continue in the profession. The average tenure of a hotel manager is 6.7 years, though this figure doesn't represent the number of managers who work for two years and those who work for decades. Many work at a variety of hotels, build up their resumes, and then find positions that allow them the freedom to operate their own establishments.

Aspiring hotel managers used to begin at the reception desk, as part of the wait staff, or as members of the cleaning staff, then work their way up the ladder. As hotels have become more commercial properties and the duties of hotel managers have expanded, this avenue of advancement has closed off. Now hotel manager hopefuls go to hotel management school, and those who don't should garner as much practical hotel experience as possible. Each chain or specific hotel puts new employees through their own training programmes, so those applying for jobs should learn all they can about the scope and functioning of the specific hotels where they wish to work. Part of life as a hotel manager can be similar to the life of a doctor, as managers can be called to duty at any time of the day or night. Hotel managers must handle any and all emergencies, and those who wish to remain in the profession and maintain respect must be quick-thinking and decisive. Candidates should have a good organizational and financial background, excellent communication and interpersonal skills, and strong self-discipline. They should also be extremely detail-oriented; when running a hotel, there is no such thing as an unimportant detail. The good manager drives himself to improve and upgrade the hotel at every available opportunity.

A hotel manager is responsible for the day-to-day management of a hotel and its staff and has commercial accountability for planning, organising and directing all hotel services, including front-of-house (reception, concierge, reservation), banqueting and housekeeping. In larger hotels, managers often have a specific remit (guest services, accounting, marketing) and make up a general management team.

Financial management - preparing budgets and marketing strategies and achieving targets for the business - plays a major role. The manager must strike a balance between customer satisfaction and effective business management, ensuring financial viability, and facilitate a smooth-running customer service, whilst ensuring staff work together as a team.

Typical Work Activities

Typical work activities vary depending on the size and type of hotel, but may include:

- Planning and organising accommodation, catering and other hotel services;
- Promoting and marketing the business;
- Managing budgets and financial plans;
- Maintaining statistical and financial records;
- Achieving profit targets;
- Recruiting, training and monitoring staff;
- Planning work schedules;
- Meeting and greeting customers;
- Dealing with customer complaints and comments;
- Addressing problems and troubleshooting;
- Ensuring events and conferences run smoothly;

- Supervising maintenance, supplies and furnishings;
- Dealing with contractors and suppliers;
- Ensuring security is effective;
- Carrying out inspections of property and services;
- Ensuring compliance with licensing laws, health and safety and other statutory regulations.

The manager of a large hotel may have less contact with guests but will spend time meeting heads of department and planning and monitoring the progress of business strategies. In a smaller establishment, the manager is much more involved in the hands-on day-to-day running of the hotel, which may include carrying out reception duties or serving meals if the need arises.

A significant number of hotel managers are self-employed and this can lead to a more general management experience, from greeting guests to managing finances.

How to Become a Hotel Manager

- Ask yourself if you have excellent interpersonal, communication and organizational skills. They are necessary for a successful hotel management career.
- Obtain a college degree in hotel management or restaurant management. Remember that a food services department contributes greatly to the profits of a hotel; a successful restaurant manager can see his or her career advance quickly.
- Take advantage of work-study programmes offered by many colleges so that you will gain solid experience working in hotels.
- Expect to go through a hotel's training programme once you are hired after college. During the first couple of years you will be handling only relatively mundane duties, instead of providing your input on issues such as staffing, hotel decor or conventions.
- Understand that you might be offered a position as a front office manager, a food and beverage manager, a

convention services manager, or any of a number of administrative positions after your training period. If you are successful at different managerial positions, your career will benefit in the long run.

- Be aware that a promotion might require you to relocate for a few years if you work for a hotel chain that has properties throughout the country.
- You will need to quickly become proficient with computers because of their widespread use in hotel reservations, billing and overall management operations.
- Consider working for hotels in warm tourist destinations or snowy mountains, depending on your preferred lifestyle.
- Be prepared for long hours, night and weekend work, and the occasional unhappy guest.

Different managerial personnel working as hotel managers –

Catering managers plan, organise and manage the food and beverage services of organisations and businesses, both inside and outside the hospitality industry, with the aim of achieving good quality at low cost and maintaining high standards of hygiene and customer satisfaction.

There is a range of jobs in catering management, along with a number of different routes into the industry. Roles include: managing restaurants, bars and other outlets in hotels, resorts or liners; providing catering services at events; and running catering operations at hospitals, schools and other organisations.

With ongoing growth in the service industry, opportunities in this demanding but rewarding area continue to grow.

The role varies according to the size and nature of the establishment: in a small operation, the catering manager has more of a 'hands on' role and will be involved in the day-today running of the operation; in contract catering, the catering manager will spend time negotiating with the client organisation, assessing its requirements and ensuring that it is satisfied with the service delivered.

Typical tasks will include:

- Recruiting and training permanent and casual staff;
- Organising, leading and motivating the catering team;
- Planning menus in consultation with chefs;
- Ensuring health and safety regulations are strictly observed;
- Budgeting and establishing financial targets;
- Monitoring the quality of the product and service provided;
- Keeping financial and administrative records;
- Managing the payroll and monitoring spending levels;
- Maintaining stock levels and ordering new supplies as required;
- Interacting with customers if involved with 'front of house' work;
- Liaising with suppliers and clients;
- Negotiating contracts with customers (in contract catering).

In more senior posts, principal tasks will involve:

- Setting and agreeing budgets;
- Monitoring quality standards;
- Overseeing the management of the facilities, for example checking events bookings and the allocation of resources and staff;
- Planning new promotions and initiatives, and contributing to business development;
- Dealing with staffing and client issues, as they arise.

Food and Restaurant Manager

Fast food restaurant managers are responsible for the provision of standardised food and customer service in outlets based in the high street, motor service areas, stations, airports or multiplexes.

Drawing on all the operational functions of a business, the work involves applying financial, marketing and operational know-how, and supervising and training staff.

Managers plan, organise, and co-ordinate all resources and activities in a store. The work involves: setting targets, planning budgets, and controlling stock; recruiting, training and inspiring restaurant teams; creating and driving marketing campaigns; and building bridges with the local community.

Ultimately, it is the manager's ideas, initiative and personality that shape the restaurant.

Tasks typically involve:

- Organising the store in terms of products, equipment and people;
- Planning and checking work schedules;
- Carrying out audits to check health safety, food safety and quality of service in the restaurant;
- Making sure the fast-track audit is completed daily to check the safety of equipment and that food is properly cooked, only in-date stock is used, and all other products are discarded;
- Carrying out work outside the restaurant, including 'mystery shopping' at other restaurants within the chain;
- Attending weekly meetings with senior managers;
- Dealing with problems, queries, complaints, staff and customers in the store;
- Monitoring and maintaining high standards of food, service and hygiene;
- Ensuring the company's required standards of customer care are met;
- Administering payrolls;

- Checking and securing cash receipts;
- Budgeting to ensure maximum profitability;
- Achieving set profit and loss targets;
- Maintaining and securing equipment and buildings and all company assets contained within the unit;
- Publicising and marketing restaurants in the locality;
- Motivating restaurant teams;
- Recruiting, selecting and training new staff and fully inducting the restaurant team in accordance with company policy;
- Developing all team members to their fullest potential using the performance management/review system and identifying individual training needs;
- Ensuring the implementation and maintenance of legislation, company standards and procedures;
- Recognising new trends and implementing action plans accordingly;
- Acting as a communication link between senior teams and the restaurant team;
- Leading by example, acting as a role model for the restaurant team.

A successful manager will strike the right balance between creating both a good service for restaurant customers and a fun work environment for members of staff.

Catering Manager

Catering managers plan, organise and manage the food and beverage services of organisations and businesses, both inside and outside the hospitality industry, with the aim of achieving good quality at low cost and maintaining high standards of hygiene and customer satisfaction.

There is a range of jobs in catering management, along with a number of different routes into the industry. Roles include: managing restaurants, bars and other outlets in hotels, resorts or liners; providing catering services at events; and running catering operations at hospitals, schools and other organisations.

With ongoing growth in the service industry, opportunities in this demanding but rewarding area continue to grow.

Typical Work Activities

The role varies according to the size and nature of the establishment: in a small operation, the catering manager has more of a 'hands on' role and will be involved in the day-to-day running of the operation; in contract catering, the catering manager will spend time negotiating with the client organisation, assessing its requirements and ensuring that it is satisfied with the service delivered.

Typical tasks will include:

- Recruiting and training permanent and casual staff;
- Organising, leading and motivating the catering team;
- Planning menus in consultation with chefs;
- Ensuring health and safety regulations are strictly observed;
- Budgeting and establishing financial targets;
- Monitoring the quality of the product and service provided;
- Keeping financial and administrative records;
- Managing the payroll and monitoring spending levels;
- Maintaining stock levels and ordering new supplies as required;
- Interacting with customers if involved with 'front of house' work;
- Liaising with suppliers and clients;
- Negotiating contracts with customers (in contract catering).

In more senior posts, principal tasks will involve:

- Setting and agreeing budgets;
- Monitoring quality standards;

- Overseeing the management of the facilities, for example checking events bookings and the allocation of resources and staff;
- Planning new promotions and initiatives, and contributing to business development;
- Dealing with staffing and client issues, as they arise.

Human Resources

Human resources has at least two meanings depending on context. The original usage derives from political economy and economics, where it was traditionally called labour, one of three factors of production. The more common usage within corporations and businesses refers to the individuals within the firm, and to the portion of the firm's organization that deals with hiring, firing, training, and other personnel issues.

Modern analysis emphasizes that human beings are not predictable commodity "resources" with definitions totally controlled by contract, but are creative and social beings that make contributions beyond "labour" to a society and to civilization. The broad term human capital has evolved to contain the complexity of this term, and in macro-economics the term "firm-specific human capital" has evolved to represent the original meaning of term "human resources".

Advocating the central role of "human resources" or human capital in enterprises and societies has been a traditional role of socialist parties, who claim that value is primarily created by their activity, and accordingly justify a larger claim of profits or relief from these enterprises or societies. Critics say this is just a bargaining tactic which grew out of various practices of medieval European guilds into the modern trade union and collective bargaining unit. A contrary view, common to capitalist parties, is that it is the infrastructural capital and (what they call) intellectual capital owned and fused by "management" that provides most value in financial capital terms. This likewise justifies a bargaining position and a general view that "human resources" are interchangeable.

A significant sign of consensus on this latter point is the ISO 9000 series of standards which requires a "job description" of every participant in a productive enterprise. In general, heavily unionized nations such as France and Germany have adopted and encouraged such descriptions especially within trade unions. One view of this trend is that a strong social consensus on political economy and a good social welfare system facilitates labour mobility and tends to make the entire economy more productive, as labour can move from one enterprise to another with little controversy or difficulty in adapting.

An important controversy regarding labour mobility illustrates the broader philosophical issue with usage of the phrase "human resources": governments of developing nations often regard developed nations that encourage immigration or "guest workers" as appropriating human capital that is rightfully part of the developing nation and required to further its growth as a civilization. They argue that this appropriation is similar to colonial commodity fiat wherein a colonizing European power would define an arbitrary price for natural resources, extracting which diminished national natural capital.

The debate regarding "human resources" versus human capital thus in many ways echoes the debate regarding natural resources versus natural capital. Over time the United Nations have come to more generally support the developing nations' point of view, and have requested significant offsetting "foreign aid" contributions so that a developing nation losing human capital does not lose the capacity to continue to train new people in trades, professions, and the arts.

An extreme version of this view is that historical inequities such as African slavery must be compensated by current developed nations, which benefitted from stolen "human resources" as they were developing. This is an extremely controversial view, but it echoes the general theme of converting human capital to "human resources" and thus greatly diminishing its value to the host society, i.e. "Africa", as it is put to narrow imitative use as "labour" in the using society.

In the very narrow context of corporate "human resources", there is a contrasting pull to reflect and require workplace diversity that echoes the diversity of a global customer base. Foreign language and culture skills, ingenuity, humor, and careful listening, are examples of traits that such programmes typically require. It would appear that these evidence a general shift to the human capital point of view, and an acknowledgement that human beings do contribute much more to a productive enterprise than "work": they bring their character, their ethics, their creativity, their social connections, and in some cases even their pets and children, and alter the character of a workplace. The term corporate culture is used to characterize such processes.

The traditional but extremely narrow context of hiring, firing, and job description is considered a 20th century anachronism. Most corporate organizations that compete in the modern global economy have adopted a view of human capital that mirrors the modern consensus as above. Some of these, in turn, deprecate the term "human resources" as useless.

As the term refers to predictable exploitations of human capital in one context or another, it can still be said to apply to manual labour, mass agriculture, low skill "McJobs" in service industries, military and other work that has clear job descriptions, and which generally do not encourage creative or social contributions.

In general the abstractions of macro-economics treat it this way - as it characterizes no mechanisms to represent choice or ingenuity. So one interpretation is that "firm-specific human capital" as defined in macro-economics is the modern and correct definition of "human resources" - and that this is inadequate to represent the contributions of "human resources" in any modern theory of political economy.

In terms of recruitment and selection it is important to consider carrying out a thorough job analysis to determine the level of skills/technical abilities, competencies, flexibility of the employee required etc. At this point it is important to consider both the internal and external factors that can have an impact on the recruitment of employees. The external factors are those out-with the powers of the organization and include issues such as current and future trends of the labour market e.g. skills, education level, government investment into industries etc. On the other hand internal influences are easier to control, predict and monitor, for example management styles or even the organizational culture.

In order to know the business environment in which any organization operates, three major trends should be considered:

- Demographics – the characteristics of a population/ workforce, for example, age, gender or social class. This type of trend may have an effect in relation to pension offerings, insurance packages etc.
- Diversity – the variation within the population/ workplace. Changes in society now mean that a larger proportion of organizations are made up of female employees in comparison to thirty years ago. Also over recent years organizations have become more culturally diverse and have increased the number of working patterns (part-time, casual, seasonal positions) to cope with the changes in both society and the global market. It is important to note here that an organisation must consider the ethic and legal implications of their decisions in relation to the HRM policies they enact to protect employees. Employers have to be acutely aware of the rise in discrimination, unfair dismissal and sexual/racial harassment cases in recent years and the detrimental effects this can have on the employees and the organisation. Anti-discrimination legislation over the past 30 years has provided a foundation for an increasing interest in diversity at work which is "about creating a working culture that seeks respects and values difference."

- Skills and qualifications - as industries move from manual to a more managerial professions so does the need for more highly skilled graduates. If the market is 'tight' i.e. not enough staff for the jobs, employers will have to compete for employees by offering financial rewards, community investment etc.also the political issues

In regards to how individuals respond to the changes in a labour market the following should be understood:

- Geographical spread - how far is the job from the individual? The distance to travel to work should be in line with the pay offered by the organization and the transportation and infrastructure of the area will also be an influencing factor in deciding who will apply for a post.
- Occupational structure - the norms and values of the different careers within an organization. Mahoney 1989 developed 3 different types of occupational structure namely craft (loyalty to the profession), organization career (promotion through the firm) and unstructured (lower/unskilled workers who work when needed).
- Generational difference -different age categories of employees have certain characteristics, for example their behaviour and their expectations of the organisation.

Recruitment methods are wide and varied, it is important that the job is described correctly and any personal specifications stated. Job recruitment methods can be through job centres, employment agencies/consultants, headhunting, and local/national newspapers. It is important that the correct media is chosen to ensure an appropriate response to the advertised post.

Human Resources within Firms

Though human resources have been part of business and organizations since the first days of agriculture, the modern concept of human resources began in reaction to the efficiency focus of Taylorism in the early 1900s. By 1920, psychologists and employment experts in the United States started the human relations movement, which viewed workers in terms of their psychology and fit with companies, rather than as interchangeable parts. This movement grew throughout the middle of the 20th century, placing emphasis on how leadership, cohesion, and loyalty played important roles in organizational success. Although this view was increasingly challenged by more quantitatively rigorous and less "soft" management techniques in the 1960s and beyond, human resources had gained a permanent role within the firm.

Facing mankind's problems it is opportune to mobilize as many intellectual resources as possible in order to resolve the emerging troubles. The students have to be trained to construct pertinent knowledge together (for example using the method Learning by teaching). Students can be trained in constructing knowledge outside the classroom too. They have to adopt following attitudes:

- Be aware that they are bearing resources
- Be aware that they have to increase their own resources in order to be more attractive inside the community
- Be aware that they can increase their own resources if they communicate
- Be aware that they can increase their own resources if they share their knowledge with other people
- Ability to identify resource from other community members and to make this resource available for all the group
- Ability to search for pertinent resources outside the group
- Ability to connect people looking for proposing resources
- Ability to organize collective thinking in networks

Employee Engagement

Employee engagement is a concept that is generally viewed in terms of employees feeling a strong emotional bond to the organization that employs them. (Robinson) This is associated with people demonstrating a willingness to recommend the organization to others and commit time and effort to help the organization succeed. (Harter) It suggests that people are motivated by intrinsic factors (e.g. personal growth, working to a common purpose, being part of a larger process) rather than simply focusing on extrinsic factors (e.g. pay / reward). (Ryan) The concept has gained popularity as various studies have demonstrated links with productivity.

In 1999, The Gallup Organization published research that showed that engaged employees are more productive, more profitable, more customer-focused, safer, and less likely to leave their employer. The review stated that "engagement with employees within a firm has shown to motivate the employee to work beyond personal factors and work more for the success of the firm." (Harter) Watson Wyatt found that high-commitment organizations (one with loyal and dedicated employees) out-performed those with low commitment by 47% in the 2000 study and by 200% in the 2002 study. (Wyatt) In a study of professional service firms, the Hay Group found that offices with engaged employees were up to 43% more productive, based on a comparison of revenue generation.

Recent research has focused on developing a better understanding of how variables such as quality of work relationships and values of the organization interact and their link to important work outcomes. From the perspective of the employee, "outcomes" range from strong commitment to the isolation of oneself from the organization. The study done by the Gallup Management Journal has shown that only 29 percent of employees are actively engaged in their jobs. Those "engaged" employees work with passion and feel a strong connection to their company. Moreover, 54 percent of employees are not engaged meaning that they go through each workday putting time but no passion into their work. Also,

Seventeen percent of employees are actively disengaged, meaning that they are busy acting out of their own personal unhappiness, which undermines what their engaged co-workers are trying to accomplish.

Access to a reliable model enables organizations to conduct validation studies to establish the relationship of employee engagement to productivity/performance and other measures linked to effectiveness.

It is an important principle of occupational psychology (i.e. the application of psychological theories, research methods, and intervention strategies involving workplace issues) that validation studies should be anchored in reliable scales (i.e. organized and related groups of items) and not simply focus on individual elements in isolation. To understand how high levels of employee engagement affect organizational performance/productivity it is important to have an a priori model that demonstrates how the scales interact. (Konrad) There is also overlap between this concept and those relating to well-being at work and the psychological contract.

As employee productivity is clearly connected with employee engagement, creating an environment that encourages employee engagement is considered to be essential in the effective management of human capital.

Employee engagement will be influenced by:

1. Employee perceptions of job importance. This study has found that "...an employees attitude toward the job['s importance] and the company had the greatest impact on loyalty and customer service then all other employee factors combined."
2. Employee clarity of job expectations. "If expectations are not clear and basic materials and equipment not provided, negative emotions such as boredom or resentment may result, and the employee may then become focused on surviving more then thinking about how he can help the organization succeed."

3. Career advancement/improvement opportunities. "Plant supervisors and managers indicated that many plant improvements were being made outside the suggestion system, where employees initiated changes in order to reap the bonuses generated by the subsequent cost savings."
4. Regular feedback and dialogue with superiors. "Feedback is the key to giving employees a sense of where they're going, but many organizations are remarkably bad at giving it." (Hay Group) "'What I really wanted to hear was 'Thanks. You did a good job.' But all my boss did was hand me a check."
5. Quality of working relationships with peers, superiors, and subordinates. "...if employee's relationship with their managers is fractured, then no amount of perks will persuade the employees to perform at top levels. Employee engagement is a direct reflection of how employees feel about their relationship with the boss."
6. Perceptions of the ethos and values of the organization. "'Inspiration and values' is the most important of the six drivers in our Engaged Performance model. Inspirational leadership is the ultimate perk. In its absence, [it] is unlikely to engage employees."

As additional research becomes available, the significance of the various factors will become more evident.

Human Interaction Management

Human Interaction Management (HIM) is the set of principles and patterns for structuring, supporting and controlling human work practices proposed by Keith Harrison-Broninski in his 2005 book "Human Interactions".

Current mainstream techniques and tools for work support, whether categorized as Workflow or as Business Process Management (BPM), deal only with "mechanistic" business processes. In such business processes, human involvement is limited to key data entry and decision points. Workflow/BPM techniques and tools deal with only the externally-observable aspects of work - tasks, that are visible from outside.

HIM extends this to include support for "human-driven" processes focused on human creativity and collaboration. To achieve this, HIM deals not only with tasks, but also with those aspects of work visible from inside - information, interaction and innovation.

In HIM, a business process requiring human knowledge, judgement and experience is divided into Roles, which are then assigned to the appropriate members of an organization via a Human Interaction Management System (HIMS). A HIMS is also used to manage the work and integrate it with organizational strategy/tactics, via separation into "levels of control".

The main focus of HIM is currently on the integration of organizational objectives with human work practices, in order to implement strategy/tactics and fulfil requirements for compliance. However, HIM has application beyond the improvement of organizational efficiency, since it provides a rich set of patterns for structuring and managing collaborative work that are also finding application in spheres such as social/political negotiation, law enforcement and healthcare.

Accounting Management (Business) is the practical application of management techniques to control and report on the financial health of the organization. This involves the analysis, planning, implementation, and control of programmes designed to provide financial data reporting for managerial decision making. This includes the maintenance of bank accounts, developing financial statements, cash flow and financial performance analysis. Accounting management is a mandatory knowledge module of any MBA programme. Cost management is the process whereby companies use cost accounting to report or control the various costs of doing business. The term CM is widely used in business today. Unfortunately there is no uniform definition. We use CM to describe the approaches and activities of managers in short run and long run planning and control decisions that increase value for customers and lower costs of products and services. For example, managers make decisions regarding the amount and kind of material being used, changes of plant processes, and changes in product designs. Information from accounting systems helps managers make such decisions, but the information and the accounting systems themselves are not cost management.

Cost management has a broad focus. It includes - but is not confined to - the continuous reduction of costs. The planning and control of costs is usually inextricably linked with revenue and profit planning. For instance, to enhance revenues and profits, managers often deliberately incur additional costs for advertising and product modifications. Cost management is not practiced in isolation. It's an integral part of general management strategies and their implementation. Examples include programme that enhance customer satisfaction and quality as well as programmes that promote blockbuster new product development.

Customer Relationship

Customer relationship management (CRM) covers methods and technologies used by companies to manage their relationships with clients. Information stored on existing customers (and potential customers) is analyzed and used to this end. Automated CRM processes are often used to generate automatic personalized marketing based on the customer information stored in the system.

Customer relationship management is a corporate level strategy, focusing on creating and maintaining relationships with customers. Several commercial CRM software packages are available which vary in their approach to CRM. However, CRM is not a technology itself, but rather a holistic approach to an organisation's philosophy, placing the emphasis firmly on the customer.

CRM governs an organization's philosophy at all levels, including policies and processes, front-of-house customer service, employee training, marketing, systems and information management. CRM systems are integrated end-to-end across marketing, sales, and customer service.

A CRM system should:

- Identify factors important to clients.
- Promote a customer-oriented philosophy
- Adopt customer-based measures
- Develop end-to-end processes to serve customers
- Provide successful customer support
- Handle customer complaints
- Track all aspects of sales
- Create a holistic view of customers' sales and services information

There are three fundamental components in CRM:

- Operational - automation of basic business processes (marketing, sales, service)
- Analytical - analysis of customer data and behaviour using business intelligence
- Collaborative - communicating with clients

Operational CRM provides automated support to "front office" business processes (sales, marketing and service). Each interaction with a customer is generally added to a customer's history, and staff can retrieve information on customers from the database as necessary.

According to Gartner Group operational CRM typically involves three general areas:

Sales force automation (SFA): SFA automates some of a company's critical sales and sales force management tasks, such as forecasting, sales administration, tracking customer preferences and demographics, performance management, lead management, account management, contact management and quote management.

Customer service and support (CSS): CSS automates certain service requests, complaints, product returns and enquiries.

Enterprise marketing automation (EMA) : EMA provides information about the business environment, including information on competitors, industry trends, and macroenvironmental variables. EMA applications are used to improve marketing efficiency.

Integrated CRM software is often known as a "front office solution", as it deals directly with customers. Many call centers use CRM software to store customer information. When a call is received, the system displays the associated customer information (determined from the number of the caller). During and following the call, the call center agent dealing with the customer can add further information. Some customer services can be fully automated, such as allowing customers to access their bank account details online or via a WAP phone.

Analytical CRM

Analytical CRM analyses data (gathered as part of operational CRM, or from other sources) in an attempt to identify means to enhance a company's relationship with its clients. The results of an analysis can be used to design targeted marketing campaigns, for example:

- Acquisition: Cross-selling, up-selling
- Retention: Retaining existing customers (antonym: customer attrition)
- Information: Providing timely and regular information to customers

Other examples of the applications of analyses include:

- Contact optimization
- Evaluating and improving customer satisfaction
- Optimizing sales coverage
- Fraud detection
- Financial forecasts
- Price optimization
- Product development

- Programme evaluation
- Risk assessment and management
- Strategic Marketing
- Operational marketing

Data collection and analysis is viewed as a continuing and iterative process. Ideally, business decisions are refined over time, based on feedback from earlier analyses and decisions. Most analytical CRM projects use a data warehouse to manage data.

Collaborative CRM

Collaborative CRM focuses on the interaction with customers (personal interaction, letter, fax, phone, Internet, e-mail etc.)

Collaborative CRM includes:

- Providing efficient communication with customers across a variety of communications channels
- Providing online services to reduce customer service costs
- Providing access to customer information while interacting with customers

Driven by authors from the Harvard Business School (Kracklauer/Mills/Seifert), Collaborative CRM also seems to be the new paradigma to succeed the leading Efficient Consumer Response and Category Management concept in the industry/ trade relationship.

In its broadest sense, CRM covers all interaction and business with customers. A good CRM programme allows a business to acquire customers, provide customer services and retain valued customers.

Customer services can be improved by:

- Providing online access to product information and technical assistance around the clock
- Identifying what customers value and devising appropriate service strategies for each customer

- Providing mechanisms for managing and scheduling follow-up sales calls
- Tracking all contacts with a customer
- Identifying potential problems before they occur
- Providing a user-friendly mechanism for registering customer complaints
- Providing a mechanism for handling problems and complaints
- Providing a mechanism for correcting service deficiencies
- Storing customer interests in order to target customers selectively
- Providing mechanisms for managing and scheduling maintenance, repair, and on-going support
- Scalability: the system should be highly scalable, as the volume of data stored in the system grows over time
- Communication channels: CRM can interface with a variety of different channels (phone, WAP, Internet etc.)
- Workflow - a company's business processes need to be represented by the system with the ability to track the individual stages and transfer information between steps
- Assignment - the ability to assign requests, such as service requests, to a person or group.
- Database - the means of storing customer data and histories (in a data warehouse)
- Customer privacy considerations, such as data encryption and legislation.

Improving Customer Relationships

CRM applications often track customer interests and requirements, as well as their buying habits. This information can be used to target customers selectively. Furthermore, the products a customer has purchased can be tracked throughout the product's life cycle, allowing customers to receive information concerning a product or to target customers with information on alternative products once a product begins to be phased out.

Repeat purchases rely on customer satisfaction, which in turn comes from a deeper understanding of each customer and their individual needs. CRM is an alternative to the "one size fits all" approach. In industrial markets, the technology can be used to coordinate the conflicting and changing purchase criteria of the sector.

The data gathered as part of CRM raises concerns over customer privacy and enables persuasive sales techniques. However, CRM does not necessarily involve gathering new data, but also includes making better use of customer information gathered as a result of routine customer interaction.

The privacy debate generally focuses on the customer information stored in the centralized database itself, and fears over a company's handling of this information. For example, there is virtually no way a consumer can determine if the company shares private (personally identifiable) data with third parties. Furthermore, companies may not always accurately declare to the consumer the types of information collected by CRM systems and the specific purposes for which the information is used.

CRM is also important to non-profit organizations, which sometimes use the terms "constituent relationship management", "contact relationship management" or "community relationship management" to describe their information systems for managing donors, volunteers and other supporters. salesforce.com, a popular CRM service that is on demand, offers its products for free to nonprofit organizations

Financial Management

New business leaders and managers have to develop at least basic skills in financial management. Expecting others in the organization to manage finances is clearly asking for trouble. Basic skills in financial management start in the critical areas of cash management and bookkeeping, which should be done according to certain financial controls to ensure integrity in the bookkeeping process. New leaders and managers should soon go on to learn how to generate financial statements (from bookkeeping journals) and analyze those statements to really understand the financial condition of the business. Financial analysis shows the "reality" of the situation of a business – seen as such, financial management is one of the most important practices in management. This topic will help you understand basic practices in financial management, and build the basic systems and practices needed in a healthy business.

If your small business is a corporation, you would do well to find someone experienced in financial management and encourage them to be your board treasurer (your board chair has this responsibility to find someone suitable, as well). Therefore, it's important to understand the role of the board treasurer.

New, more "organic" forms or organizations (self-organizing organizations, self-managed teams, network organizations, etc.) allow organizations to be more responsive and adaptable in today's rapidly changing world. These forms also cultivate empowerment among employees, much more than the hierarchical, rigidly structured organizations of the past.

Many people assert that as the nature of organizations has changed, so must the nature of management control. Some people go so far as to claim that management shouldn't exercise any form of control whatsoever. They claim that management should exist to support employee's efforts to be fully productive members of organizations and communities – therefore, any form of control is completely counterproductive to management and employees.

Some people even react strongly against the phrase "management control". The word itself can have a negative connotation, e.g., it can sound dominating, coercive and heavy-handed. It seems that writers of management literature now prefer use of the term "coordinating" rather than "controlling".

Regardless of the negative connotation of the word "control", it must exist or there is no organization at all. In its most basic form, an organization is two or more people working together to reach a goal. Whether an organization is highly bureaucratic or changing and self-organizing, the organization must exist for some reason, some purpose, some mission (implicit or explicit) – or it isn't an organization at all. The organization must have some goal. Identifying this goal requires some form of planning, informal or formal. Reaching the goal means identifying some strategies, formal or informal. These strategies are agreed upon by members of the organization through some form of communication, formal or informal. Then members set about to act in accordance with what they agreed to do. They may change their minds, fine. But they need to recognize and acknowledge that they're changing their minds.

This form of ongoing communication to reach a goal, tracking activities toward the goal and then subsequent decisions about what to do is the essence of management coordination. It needs to exist in some manner – formal or informal. The following are rather typical methods of coordination in organizations. They are used as means to communicate direction and guide behaviours in that direction. The function of the following methods is not to "control", but rather to guide. If, from ongoing communications among management and employees, the direction changes, then fine. The following methods are changed accordingly.

Note that many of the following methods are so common that we often don't think of them as having anything to do with coordination at all. No matter what one calls the following methods – coordination or control – they're important to the success of any organization.

Administrative Controls

Organizations often use standardized documents to ensure complete and consistent information is gathered. Documents include titles and dates to detect different versions of the document. Computers have revolutionized administrative controls through use of integrated management information systems, project management software, human resource information systems, office automation software, etc. Organizations typically require a wide range of reports, e.g., financial reports, status reports, project reports, etc. to monitor what's being done, by when and how.

Delegation is an approach to get things done, in conjunction with other employees. Delegation is often viewed as a major means of influence and therefore is categorized as an activity in leading (rather than controlling/coordinating). Delegation generally includes assigning responsibility to an employee to complete a task, granting the employee sufficient authority to gain the resources to do the task and letting the employee decide how that task will be carried out. Typically, the person assigning the task shares accountability with the employee for ensuring the task is completed. Evaluation is carefully collecting and analyzing information in order to make decisions. There are many types of evaluations in organizations, for example, evaluation of marketing efforts, evaluation of employee performance, programme evaluations, etc. Evaluations can focus on many aspects of an organization and its processes, for example, its goals and processes, outcomes.

Financial Statements

Once the organization has establish goals and associated strategies (or ways to reach the goals), funds are set aside for the resources and labour to the accomplish goals and tasks. As the money is spent, statements are changed to reflect what was spent, how it was spent and what it obtained. Review of financial statements is one of the more common methods to monitor the progress of programmes and plans. The most common financial statements include the balance sheet, income statement and cash flow statement. Financial audits are regularly conducted to ensure that financial management practices follow generally accepted standards, as well.

Performance management focuses on the performance of the total organization, including its processes, critical subsystems (departments, programmes, projects, etc.) and employees. Most of us have some basic impression of employee performance management, including the role of performance reviews. Performance reviews provide an opportunity for supervisors and their employees to regularly communicate about goals, how well those goals should be met, how well the goals are being met and what must be done to continue to meet (or change) those goals. The employee is rewarded in some form for meeting performance standards, or embarks on a development plan with the supervisor in order to improve performance.

Policies help ensure that behaviours in the workplace conform to federal and state laws, and also to expectations of the organization. Often, policies are applied to specified situations in the form of procedures. Personnel policies and procedures help ensure that employee laws are followed (e.g., laws such as the Americans with Disabilities Act, Occupational Health and Safety Act, etc.) and minimize the likelihood of costly litigation. A procedure is a step-by-step list of activities required to conduct a certain task. Procedures ensure that routine tasks are carried out in an effective and efficient fashion.

Quality Control and Operations Management

The concept of quality control has received a great deal of attention over the past twenty years. Many people recognize phrases such as "do it right the first time, "zero defects", "Total Quality Management", etc. Very broadly, quality includes specifying a performance standard (often by benchmarking, or comparing to a well-accepted standard), monitoring and measuring results, comparing the results to the standard and then making adjusts as necessary. Recently, the concept of quality management has expanded to include organization-wide programmes, such as Total Quality Management, ISO9000, Balanced Scorecard, etc. Operations management includes the overall activities involved in developing, producing and distributing products and services.

Risk, Safety and Liabilities

For a variety of reasons (including the increasing number of lawsuits), organizations are focusing a great deal of attention to activities that minimize risk, avoid liabilities and ensure safety of employees. Several decades ago, it was rare to hear of an organization undertaking contingency planning, disaster recovery planning or critical incident analysis. Now those activities are becoming commonplace.

Evaluation Activities

Evaluation, in the context of management activities, is carefully collecting information about something in order to make necessary decisions about it. There are a large number and wide variety of evaluations that can occur in businesses, whether for-profit or nonprofit. Evaluation is closely related to performance management (whether about organizations, groups, processes or individuals), which includes identifying measures to indicate results. Evaluation often includes collecting information around these measures to conclude the extent of performance.

Advertising and Promotions

Before you learn more about advertising, you should get a basic impression of what advertising is. Advertising is a major "phase" of overall product or service development and management. Advertising is specifically part of the "outbound" marketing activities, or activities geared to communicate to the market, eg, advertising, promotions, public relations, etc. Inbound" marketing activities are geared to communicate from the market, and include, eg, market research about the market.

Although your use of the latest hot marketing and sales strategies may improve the bottom line of your business, you may get into hot "legal waters" if you do not exercise the proper restraints. This article discusses the boundaries beyond which you do not want to stray lest you run afoul of the laws governing false advertising.

Two conflicting principles are involved in advertising law. On the one hand, the First Amendment, which is part of the U.S. Constitution and grants us the right of free speech, protects all forms of communication, including advertising (referred to by lawyers as "commercial speech"). On the other hand, the U.S. Constitution gives the federal government the power to regulate interstate commerce. Most state constitutions similarly give state governments the power to regulate commerce conducted solely within that state.

In exercising its power over interstate commerce, the Congress has enacted two statutes that have the greatest effect on advertising. These are the Federal Trade Commission (FTC) Act and the Lanham Act.

Employees

Your employees of usually the people who interact the most with your customers. Ask them about products and services that customers are asking for. Ask employees about what the customers complain about.

Comment Cards

Provide brief, half-page comment cards on which they can answer basic questions such as: Were you satisfied with our services? How could we provide the perfect services? Are there any services you'd like to see that don't exist yet?

Competition

What is your competition selling? Ask people who shop there. Many people don't notice sales or major items in stores. Start coaching those around you to notice what's going on with your competition.

Customers

One of the best ways to find out what customers want is to ask them. Talk to them when they visit your facility or you visit theirs.

Documentation and Records

Notice what customers are buying and not buying from you. If you already know what customers are buying, etc., then is this written down somewhere? It should be so that you don't forget, particularly during times of stress or when trying to train personnel to help you out.

Focus Groups

Focus groups are usually 8-10 people that you gather to get their impressions of a product or service or an idea.

Surveys by Mail

You might hate answering these things, but plenty of people don't – and will fill our surveys especially if they get something in return. Promise them a discount if they return the completed form to your facility.

Competitive Analysis

Marketing should include competitor analysis. Who are your competitors? What customer needs and preferences are you competing to meet? What are the similarities and differences between their products/services and yours? What are the strengths and weaknesses of each of their products and services? How do their prices compare to yours? How are they doing overall? How do you plan to compete? Offer better quality services? Lower prices? More support? Easier access to services? How are you uniquely suited to compete with them?

Competitive Intelligence for Business Success

Some businesses think it is best to get on with their own plans and ignore the competition. Others become obsessed with tracking the actions of competitors (often using underhand or illegal methods). Many businesses are happy simply to track the competition, copying their moves and reacting to changes.

Competitor analysis has several important roles in strategic planning:

- To help management understand their competitive advantages/disadvantages relative to competitors
- To generate understanding of competitors' past, present (and most importantly) future strategies
- To provide an informed basis to develop strategies to achieve competitive advantage in the future
- To help forecast the returns that may be made from future investments (e.g. how will competitors respond to a new product or pricing strategy?

Questions to Ask

What questions should be asked when undertaking competitor analysis? The following is a useful list to bear in mind:

- Who are our competitors?
- What threats do they pose?
- What is the profile of our competitors?
- What are the objectives of our competitors?
- What strategies are our competitors pursuing and how successful are these strategies?
- What are the strengths and weaknesses of our competitors?
- How are our competitors likely to respond to any changes to the way we do business?

Sources of Information for Competitor Analysis

Davidson describes how the sources of competitor information can be neatly grouped into three categories:

- Recorded data: this is easily available in published form either internally or externally. Good examples include competitor annual reports and product brochures;
- Observable data: this has to be actively sought and often assembled from several sources. A good example is competitor pricing;
- Opportunistic data: to get hold of this kind of data requires a lot of planning and organisation. Much of it is "anecdotal", coming from discussions with suppliers, customers and, perhaps, previous management of competitors.

The table below lists possible sources of competitor data using Davidson's categorisation:

Recorded Data	Observable Data	Opportunistic Data
Annual report and accounts	Pricing / price lists	Meetings with suppliers
Press releases	Advertising campaigns	Trade shows
Newspaper articles	Promotions	Sales force meetings
Analysts reports	Tenders	Seminars / conferences
Regulatory reports	Patent applications	Recruiting ex-employees
Government reports		Discussion with shared distributors
Presentations / speeches		Social contacts with competitors

In his excellent book Even More Offensive Marketing, Davidson likens the process of gathering competitive data to a jigsaw puzzle. Each individual piece of data does not have much value. The important skill is to collect as many of the pieces as possible and to assemble them into an overall picture of the competitor. This enables you to identify any missing pieces and to take the necessary steps to collect them.

What Businesses Need to Know about their Competitors

The tables below lists the kinds of competitor information that would help businesses complete some good quality competitor analysis.

You can probably think of many more pieces of information about a competitor that would be useful. However, an important challenge in competitor analysis is working out how to obtain competitor information that is reliable, up-to-date and available legally.

What businesses probably already know their competitors
Overall sales and profits
Sales and profits by market
Sales by main brand
Cost structure
Market shares (revenues and volumes)
Organisation structure
Distribution system
Identity / profile of senior management
Advertising strategy and spending
Customer / consumer profile and attitudes
Customer retention levels
What businesses would really like to know about competitors
Sales and profits by product
Relative costs
Customer satisfaction and service levels
Customer retention levels
Distribution costs
New product strategies
Size and quality of customer databases
Advertising effectiveness
Future investment strategy
Contractual terms with key suppliers
Terms of strategic partnerships
Competitor array

One common and useful technique is constructing a competitor array. The steps include:

- Define your industry - scope and nature of the industry
- Determine who your competitors are
- Determine who your customers are and what benefits they expect
- Determine what the key success factors are in your industry
- Rank the key success factors by giving each one a weighting - The sum of all the weightings must add up to one.
- Rate each competitor on each of the key success factors - this can best be displayed on a two dimensional matrix - competitors along the top and key success factors down the side.
- Multiply each cell in the matrix by the factor weighting.
- Sum columns for a weighted assessment of the overall strength of each competitor relative to each other.

Based on material presented in "Beat the Competition: How to Use Competitive Intelligence to Develop Winning Business Strategies", Ian Gordon, Basil Blackwell Publishers, Oxford, UK, 1989.

Competitor Profiling

Another common technique is to create detailed profiles on each of your major competitors. These profiles give an in-depth description of the competitor's background, finances, products, markets, facilities, personnel, and strategies. This involves:

- Background
  - – Location of offices, plants, and online presences
  - – History - key personalities, dates, events, and trends
  - – Ownership, corporate governance, and organizational structure

- Financials
  - P-E ratios, dividend policy, and profitability** various financial ratios, liquidity, and cash flow
  - Profit growth profile; method of growth (organic or acquisitive)
- Products
  - Products offered, depth and breadth of product line, and product portfolio balance
  - New products developed, new product success rate, and R&D strengths
  - Brands, strength of brand portfolio, brand loyalty and brand awareness
  - Patents and licenses
  - Quality control conformance
  - Reverse engineering
- Marketing
  - Segments served, market shares, customer base, growth rate, and customer loyalty
  - Promotional mix, promotional budgets, advertising themes, ad agency used, sales force success rate, online promotional strategy
  - Distribution channels used (direct and indirect), exclusivity agreements, alliances, and geographical coverage
  - Pricing, discounts,and allowances
- Facilities
  - Plant capacity, capacity utilization rate, age of plant, plant efficiency, capital investment
  - Location, shipping logistics, and product mix by plant
- Personnel
  - Number of employees, key employees, and skill sets
  - Strength of management, and management style
  - Compensation, benefits, and employee morale and retention rates

- Corporate and marketing strategies
  - Objectives, mission statement, growth plans, acquisitions, and divestitures
  - Marketing strategies

Media Scanning

We can learn a lot about the competitive environment by scanning our competitors' ads. Changes in a competitor's advertising message can reveal new product offerings, new production processes, a new branding strategy, a new positioning strategy, a new segmentation strategy, line extensions and contractions, problems with previous positions, insights from recent marketing or product research, a new strategic direction, a new source of sustainable competitive advantage, or value migrations within the industry. It might also indicate a new pricing strategy such as penetration, price discrimination, price skimming, product bundling, joint product pricing, discounts, or loss leaders. It may also indicate a new promotion strategy such as push, pull, balanced, short term sales generation, long term image creation, informational, comparative, affective, reminder, new creative objectives, new unique selling proposition, new creative concepts, appeals, tone, and themes, or a new advertising agency. It might also indicate a new distribution strategy, new distribution partners, more extensive distribution, more intensive distribution, a change in geographical focus, or exclusive distribution. Little of this intelligence is definitive : additional information is needed before conclusions should be drawn.

A competitor's media strategy reveals budget allocation, segmentation and targeting strategy, and selectivity and focus. From a tactical perspective, it can also be used to help a manager implement his/her own media plan. By knowing the competitor's media buy, media selection, frequency, reach, continuity, schedules, and flights, the manager can arrange his/her own media plan so that they do not coincide.

Other sources of corporate intelligence include trade shows, patent filings, mutual customers, annual reports, and trade associations.

Some firms hire competitor intelligence professionals to obtain this information.

New Competitors

In addition to analysing current competitors, it is necessary to estimate future competitive threats. The most common sources of new competitors are:

- Companies competing in a related product/market
- Companies using related technologies
- Companies already targeting your prime market segment but with unrelated products
- Companies from other geographical areas and with similar products
- New start-up companies organised by former employees and/or managers of existing companies

The entrance of new competitors is likely when:

- There are high profit margins in the industry
- There is unmet demand (insufficient supply) in the industry
- There are no major barriers to entry
- There is future growth potential
- Competitive rivalry is not intense
- Gaining a competitive advantage over existing firms is feasible

MARKETING THROUGH ADVERTISING

Marketing is a social and managerial function that attempts to create, expand and maintain a collection of customers. It attempts to deliver demand satisfying output through profitable exchanges.

- Marketing, as suggested by the American Marketing Association, is "an organizational function and a set of processes for creating, communicating and delivering value to customers and for managing customer relationships in ways that benefit the organization and its stakeholders".

- Philip Kotler, in his earlier books, defines marketing as: "human activity directed at satisfying needs and wants through exchange processes". Still another marketing definition, coined by Brian Norris: "The process of repeatedly moving people closer to making a decision to purchase, use, follow, refer, upload, download, obey, reject, conform, become complacent to another person's, society's or organization's value. Simply, if it doesn't facilitate a "sale" then it's not marketing."
- Identifying needs/wants and finding and implimenting solutions that satisfy those needs and wants.
- Add to Kotler's and Norris' definitions, a response from the Chartered Institute of Marketing (CIM). The association's definition claims marketing to be the "management process of anticipating, identifying and satisfying customer requirements profitably". Thus, operative marketing involves the processes of market research, market segmentation, new product development, product life cycle management, pricing, channel management as well as promotion.
- Marketing-"taking actions to define, create, grow, develop, maintain, defend and own markets".
- An approach to business that seeks to identify, anticipate and satisfy customers needs.
- Al Ries and Jack Trout defined marketing as simply "war" between competitors.
- Any activity that connects producers with consumers.
- At a macro level, marketing is the process of raising the standards of living, by identifying the existing problems and unsatisfied needs of people and then satisfying that need with a product/service that delivers value to the customer.

The practice of marketing is almost as old as humanity itself. Whenever a person has an item or is capable of performing a service, and he or she seeks another person who might want that item or service, that person is involved in marketing. A Market was originally simply a gathering place where people with a supply of items or capacity to perform a service could meet with those who might desire the items or services, perhaps at a pre-arranged time.

Such meetings embodied all the aspects of today's marketing methods, although in an informal way. Sellers and buyers sought to understand each other's needs, capacities, and psychology, all with the goal of getting the exchange of items or services to take place. Open air markets throughout the world, with buyers and sellers freely mingling, are today's example of this basic activity. Today's New York Stock Exchange had its humble beginnings as an open air market located at Wall Street in New York City.

The rise of Agriculture undoubtedly influenced markets as the earliest means of 'mass production' of an item, namely foodstuffs. As agriculture allowed one to grow more food than could be eaten by the grower alone, and most food is perishable, there was likely motivation to seek out others who could use the excess food, before it spoiled, in exchange for other items.

Prior to the advent of market research, most companies were product-focused, employing teams of salespeople to push their products into or onto the market, regardless of market desire. A market-focused, or customer-focused, organization instead first determines what its potential customers desire, and then builds the product or service. Marketing theory and practice is justified on the belief that customers use a product/ service because they have a need, or because a product/service has a perceived benefit. Two major factors of marketing are the recruitment of new customers (acquisition) and the retention and expansion of relationships with existing customers (base management).

Once a marketer has converted the prospective buyer, base management marketing takes over. The process for base management shifts the marketer to building a relationship, nurturing the links, enhancing the benefits that sold the buyer in the first place, and improving the product/service continuously to protect her business from competitive encroachments. Marketing methods are informed by many of the social sciences, particularly psychology, sociology, and economics. Anthropology is also a small, but growing, influence. Market research underpins these activities. Through advertising, it is also related to many of the creative arts.

For a marketing plan to be successful, the mix of the four "Ps" must reflect the wants and desires of the consumers in the target market. Trying to convince a market segment to buy something they don't want is extremely expensive and seldom successful. Marketers depend on marketing research, both formal and informal, to determine what consumers want and what they are willing to pay for. Marketers hope that this process will give them a sustainable competitive advantage. Marketing management is the practical application of this process. The offer is also an important addition to the 4P's theory. Within most organizations the activities encompassed by the marketing function are led by a Chief Marketing Officer, or an equivalent executive. Most often the CMO position reports to the Chief Executive Officer.

The big debate in the marketing discipline is whether marketing is an art or a science. Marketing is a technology or set of technologies. Marketing can be neither an art nor a science because arts and sciences only seek to explain natural phenomena. The objective of marketing is to manipulate and influence natural phenomena to create practical unnatural outcomes, specifically to manufacture, grow, sustain and defend markets. Marketers use their knowledge of economics, psychology, sociology, anthropology and strategy to arrange and control the external environment to their advantage and lock in profit. To understand what marketing is one must understand that marketing operates on three different levels.

Corporate Level Marketing

Marketing at the corporate levels asks this question as 'What business should we be in and what opportunities should we pursue?' This is marketing before we even have a business, idea or product. This is what is known as entreprenuership. This level of marketing strategy is where the Ted Turners, Bill Gates' and Michael Dells of the world make market changing decisions. This level is also where corporate management of existing companies decide to branch off into new uncharted territories and opportunities.

Business Level Marketing

Marketing at the business level asks this question as 'How are we going to compete against the competition?' When Jack Trout says that marketing is 'the war between competitors' and 'the conflict between companies' what he is really doing is defining marketing at the business level. Business level marketing deals with high level strategic marketing concerns. This level deals with long term sustainable advantages and business models.

Functional Level Marketing

Marketing at the functional level (also known as the operating level) ask this question as 'How do we create and keep customers?' This level deals with marketing tactics and the '4ps' of the marketing mix. This level of marketing defines and develops products, prices them, promotes them and then distributes them in a way that helps a company create and sustain demand for their products.

In popular usage, "marketing" is the promotion of products, especially advertising and branding. However, in professional usage the term has a wider meaning which recognizes that marketing is customer centered. Products are often developed to meet the desires of groups of customers or even, in some cases, for specific customers. E. Jerome McCarthy divided marketing into four general sets of activities. His typology has become so universally recognized that his four activity sets, the Four Ps, have passed into the language.

The four Ps are:

- Product: The Product management and Product marketing aspects of marketing deal with the specifications of the actual good or service, and how it relates to the end-user's needs and wants.

- Pricing: This refers to the process of setting a price for a product, including discounts.
- Promotion: This includes advertising, sales promotion, publicity, and personal selling, and refers to the various methods of promoting the product, brand, or company.
- Placement or distribution refers to how the product gets to the customer; for example, point of sale placement or retailing. This fourth P has also sometimes been called Place, referring to the channel by which a product or service is sold (e.g. online vs. retail), which geographic region or industry, to which segment (young adults, families, business people), etc.

These four elements are often referred to as the marketing mix. A marketer can use these variables to craft a marketing plan. The four Ps model is most useful when marketing low value consumer products. Industrial products, services, high value consumer products require adjustments to this model. Services marketing must account for the unique nature of services. Industrial or B2B marketing must account for the long term contractual agreements that are typical in supply chain transactions. Relationship marketing attempts to do this by looking at marketing from a long term relationship perspective rather than individual transactions.

As a counter to this, Morgan, in Riding the Waves of Change (Jossey-Bass, 1988), adds "Perhaps the most significant criticism of the 4 Ps approach, which you should be aware of, is that it unconsciously emphasizes the inside-out view (looking from the company outwards), whereas the essence of marketing should be the outside-in approach". Even so, having made this important caveat, the 4 Ps offer a memorable and quite workable guide to the major categories of marketing activity, as well as a framework within which these can be used.

As well as the standard four Ps (Product, Pricing, Promotion and Place), services marketing calls upon an extra three, totalling seven and known together as the extended marketing mix. These are:

- People: Any person coming into contact with customers can have an impact on overall satisfaction. Whether as part of a supporting service to a product or involved in a total service, people are particularly important because, in the customer's eyes, they are generally inseparable from the total service. As a result of this, they must be appropriately trained, well motivated and the right type of person. Fellow customers are also sometimes referred to under 'people', as they too can affect the customer's service experience, (e.g., at a sporting event).
- Process: This is the process(es) involved in providing a service and the behaviour of people, which can be crucial to customer satisfaction.
- Physical evidence: Unlike a product, a service cannot be experienced before it is delivered, which makes it intangible. This, therefore, means that potential customers could perceive greater risk when deciding whether or not to use a service. To reduce the feeling of risk, thus improving the chance for success, it is often vital to offer potential customers the chance to see what a service would be like. This is done by providing physical evidence, such as case studies, or testimonials.

As well as the other 7 Packaging has been added to this list by some people. The rationale is that it is very important how the product is presented to the customer, and the packaging is often the first contact that a customer has with a product. Although some disagree because packaging is seen as a subfield of promotion.

"Philosophy" is the potential 8th P of marketing. Products (or services) should reflect the underlying philosophy or ethos of the organization. It should also be clear what the philosophy behind the introduction of the particular product is, as well. In his book, "Meeting Need", Ian Bruce explains this concept as it relates to marketing for charities. It also applies to other products and services

Business Models

Marketing in the past focused mainly on basic concepts like the 4 Ps, and primarily on the psychological and sociological aspects of marketing. Competitive advantage was created by directly appealing to the needs, wants and behaviours of customers, better than the competition. Successful marketing was based on who could create the better brand or the lowest price or the most hype. Marketing in the future will be based on a more strategic approach to competitive marketing success. Marketers will consciously build and allocate resources, relationships, offerings and business models that other companies find hard to match.

Companies with a greater amount of resources than their competitors will have an easier time competing in the marketplace. Resources include: financial (cash and cash reserves), physical (plant and equipment), human (knowledge and skill), legal (trademarks and patents), organizational (structure, competencies, policies), and informational (knowledge of consumers and competitors). Small companies usually have a harder time competing with larger corporations because of their disadvantage in resource allocation.

Success in business, as in life, is based on the relationships you have with people. Marketers must aggressively build relationships with consumers, customers, distributors, partners and even competitors if they want to have success in today's competitive marketplace.

Most companies sell a mix of products and/or services. Today's marketplace is often too competitive for "one-trick ponies". Companies that sell the right mix products and services can have a competitive advantage over companies that sell just one product or service.

The concept of product vs. product in competitive marketing is dying. It's slowly becoming business model vs. business model. Business model innovation can make the competition's product superiority irrelevant. Business model innovation allows a marketer to change the game instead of competing on a level playing field.

Customer Focus

Most companies today have a customer orientation (also called customer focus). This implies that the company focuses its activities and products on ever changing consumer demands. Generally there are tthree ways of doing this: the customer-driven approach, the sense of identifying market changes and the product innovation approach.

In the consumer-driven approach, consumer wants are the drivers of all strategic marketing decisions. No strategy is pursued until it passes the test of consumer research. Every aspect of a market offering, including the nature of the product itself, is driven by the needs of potential consumers. The starting point is always the consumer. The rationale for this approach is that there is no point spending R&D funds developing products that people will not buy. History attests to many products that were commercial failures in spite of being technological breakthroughs.

The next big thing is a concept in marketing that refers to a product or idea that will allow for a high amount of sales for that product and related products. Marketers believe that by finding or creating the next big thing they will spark a cultural revolution that results in this sales increase.

Product Focus

In a product innovation approach, the company pursues product innovation, then tries to develop a market for the product. Product innovation drives the process and marketing research is conducted primarily to ensure that a profitable market segment(s) exists for the innovation. The rationale is that customers may not know what options will be available to them in the future so we should not expect them to tell us what they will buy in the future. However, marketers can aggressively over pursue product innovation and try to overcapitalize on a niche. When pursuing a product innovation approach, marketers must ensure that they have a varied and multi-tiered approach to product innovation. It is claimed that if Thomas Edison depended on marketing research he would have produced larger candles rather than inventing light bulbs. Many firms, such as research and development focused companies, successfully focus on product innovation. Many purists doubt whether this is really a form of marketing orientation at all, because of the ex post status of consumer research. Some even question whether it is marketing.

Other Aspects

- An emerging area of study and practice concerns internal marketing, or how employees are trained and managed to deliver the brand in a way that positively impacts the acquisition and retention of customers (employer branding).
- Diffusion of innovations research explores how and why people adopt new products, services and ideas.
- A relatively new form of marketing uses the Internet and is called internet marketing or more generally e-marketing, affiliate marketing or online marketing. It typically tries to perfect the segmentation strategy used in traditional marketing. It targets its audience more precisely, and is sometimes called personalized marketing or one-to-one marketing.
- With consumers' eroding attention span and willingness to give time to advertising messages, marketers are turning to forms of Permission marketing such as Branded content and Reality marketing.
- The use of herd behaviour in marketing.

Some aspects of marketing, especially promotion, are treated as the subject of criticism. It is especially problematic in classical economic theory, which is based on the assumption that supply and demand are independent. However, product promotion is an attempt coming from the supply side to influence demand. In this way producer market power is attained as measured by profits that would not be realized under a free market. Then the argument follows that non-free markets are imperfect and lead to production and consumption of suboptimal amounts of the product.

Critics acknowledge that marketing has legitimate uses in connecting goods and services to the consumers who want them. Critics also point out that marketing techniques have been used to achieve morally dubious ends by businesses, governments and criminals. Critics see a systemic social evil inherent in marketing. Marketing is accused of creating ruthless exploitation of both consumers and workers by treating people as commodities whose purpose is to consume.

Most marketers believe that marketing, like any other technology, is amoral. It can be used for good or evil purposes, but the technique itself is ethically neutral.

The Observer's survey among 1'206 UK adult consumers in 2001 highlighted some of the stark changes our society has gone through in the last two decades. This raises a question on the effectiveness of the CIM's definition of marketing (anticipating, identifying and satisfying customer needs profitably), mainly in consumer marketing. There are similar concerns in industrial markets, also known as business-to-business or B2B.

Core marketing elements such as segmentation, targeting and positioning are still relevant in the modern (or post-modern) world. However, they are complex topics that need a high level of effort, intelligent thinking as well as resources to be implemented successfully. A definitive statement cannot be made whether the conventional marketing concept is applicable in today's environment. Its relevance is very much situational and depends on many factors such as the product, the segment, time, location, political and economic conditions and the inner workings of a company.

However, some scholars such as Stephen Brown challenge the marketing concept in an extreme language. Their statements, though self-contradicting and sometimes unfair, are relevant, which is why Post Modern Marketing 2 was chosen as a key reference point for this chapter.

On the one hand Brown makes positive statements about marketing, e.g. marketing is endowed with considerable personal charm and has enjoyed more than its fair share of conquests; and indeed, the increasing academic attention that is being devoted to marketing and consumption-related phenomena by non-business disciplines such as sociology, anthropology and history; far from being the second-hand rose of the scholarship, marketing is now something of a fashion leader.

On the other hand, he condemns marketing by saying "marketing has to decide whether to expose its intellectual nakedness or press itself against the searing heat of postmodernism"; and using quotes such as "mid-life crisis"; "in decline; failing; anachronistic; being abandoned; no longer appropriate; in an unprecedented state of crisis; delivered nothing of value; failure; confusion; misunderstanding; occasional inexplicable hitting of the jackpot".

This apparent love-hate relationship is proof in itself that even a sceptic Mr. Brown cannot deny the contribution that marketing has made and can make to customer satisfaction and economic value. It has contributed to both customers' and suppliers' quality of life by selecting profitable customer satisfaction as its sole objective. The marketing concept, together with other business disciplines, helped the UK to make the transition from a 19th-century manufacturing economy to a modern model of success in the service industry, creating an economic growth period never seen in UK history before.

It is marketing that has helped create value through customised products, no-questions-asked refund policies, comfortable cars, environmental attention, shopkeepers' smile, and guaranteed delivery dates. Even some government departments address the public not as 'the Queen's subjects' or 'the applicants' any more but as 'customers'. Of course all of the above is done for economic or political gain, for better or worse. Despite all this achievement, to dismiss marketing as a failure is unfair.

Marketing also helps companies avoid unnecessary R&D, operational and sales costs by helping to develop products because customers want them, not for the sake of innovation. Another success is the now commonly implemented value-pricing principle, whereby a product or service is sold for the price the customer is willing to pay, not on a cost-plus basis. This way, both suppliers and customers get a fair deal.

In the context of segmentation, Brown suggests that "the traditional, linear, step-by-step marketing model of analysis, planning, implementation and control no longer seems applicable, appropriate or even pertinent to what is actually happening on the ground". If Mr. Brown had studied "the ground" before making his statement, he would have realised that companies are successful the world over precisely because they implement this model.

They segment their markets, relate their products and services to them, define their value proposition and serve their customers accordingly. Examples are GE, HSBC, PriceWaterhouseCoopers, Smiths Aerospace, BAE Systems, BOC Edwards, Weir Group and BT to name but a few. A brief visit to their websites can make this point clear.

Brown also has a constructive suggestion: "I reckon we need more passion in marketing, not less; it is time we banished banishing passion from works of marketing scholarship" (p. 256). This refers mainly to promotion, which is only one element within the marketing concept. The truth is that marketing today leads the way in segmentation, innovation, pricing, product management, distribution, and last but not least, promotion.

After all the contribution as well as further potential, to deny its successes and try to reduce it to only promotion is a great injustice to the marketing profession as well as to academic insight. Contrary to Brown's suggestion in his final paragraph, we need objectivity, rigour, quantification, models, relationships, paradigm shifts and (some application of) science.

Marketing is not full of holes, but a management process that has helped generate wealth and satisfied millions of customers for the most part of the 20th century. It can do even better in the 21st provided practitioners and scholars do not loose faith and focus. Kotler is not dead, but very much alive, and still kicking.

EXPANDING BUSINESS THROUGH ADVERTISING

The need for advertising of the several prospect of the hotel is utmost important for the development of the business in long term. It will create awareness of the people. Advertising is typically paid communication through a non-personal medium in which the sponsor is identified and the message is controlled. However, it can also include variations, such as publicity, public relations, personal selling, product placement, sponsorship, underwriting, and sales promotion. Major advertisers are typically corporations, but may also include schools, the military, political candidates, advocacy groups, churches, and other organizations that pay to have their message delivered to an audience. The media through which the message is delivered are varied: they include network and cable TV, radio, magazines, newspapers, the internet, billboards, handmade signs, sky writing, and bumper stickers; the list is almost endless.

Strictly speaking, word-of-mouth is not advertising because it is not paid, the message is not controlled, and it is delivered by a personal rather than non-personal medium. Ironically, word-of-mouth communications are often far more effective than advertising campaigns that may have cost many millions of dollars. "Buzz advertising" is a recent term used to describe an attempt by advertisers to simulate word-of-mouth communications.

In ancient times, commercial messages and political campaign displays have been found in the ruins of Pompeii. Egyptians used papyrus to create sales messages and wall posters, while lost-and-found advertising on papyrus was common in Greece and Rome. Wall or rock painting for commercial advertising is another manifestation of an ancient media advertising form, which is present to this day in many parts of Asia, Africa, and South America. For instance, the tradition of wall painting can be traced back to Indian rock-art paintings that goes back to 4000 BC. As printing developed in the 15th and 16th century, advertising expanded to include handbills. In the 17th century advertisements started to appear in weekly newspapers in England.

These early print ads were used mainly to promote books,and newspapers which became increasingly affordable thanks to the printing press, and medicines, which were increasingly sought after as disease ravaged Europe. However, false advertising and so-called "quack" ads became a problem, which ushered in regulation of advertising content.

As the economy was expanding during the 19th century, the need for advertising grew at the same pace. In the United States, classified ads became popular, filling pages of newspapers with small print messages promoting all kinds of goods. The success of this advertising format led to the growth of mail-order advertising such as the Sears Catalog, at one time referred to as the "Farmer's Bible". In 1843 the first advertising agency was established by Volney Palmer in Philadelphia. At first the agencies were just brokers for ad space in newspapers, but it wasn't until N.W. Ayer & Son came along, advertising agencies started to take over responsibility for the content as well. N.W. Ayer and Son was the first full service Ad Agency. They were also the first agency to start to charge commission on ads.

When commercial radio stations began broadcasting in the early 1920's, the programmes were aired without advertising. Many radio stations were established by radio equipment manufacturers and retailers. Programming was provided to sell radio transmitters and receivers. The radio station owners soon realized they could earn more money by selling sponsorship rights to other businesses. In those days, each show was usually sponsored by a single business, in exchange for a brief mention of the sponsor at the beginning and end of the show. This practice was carried over to televsion in the late 1940's and early 1950's.

In the early 1950's, the Dumont television network began the modern trend of selling advertisement time to multiple sponsors. Dumont had trouble finding sponsors for many of their programmes and compensated by selling smaller blocks of advertising time to several businesses. This eventually became the norm for the commercial television industry in the United States. The 1960s saw advertising transform into a modern, more scientific approach in which creativity was allowed to shine, producing unexpected messages that made advertisements more tempting to consumers' eyes. The Volkswagen ad campaign featuring such headlines as "Think Small" and "Lemon" ushered in the era of modern advertising by promoting a "position" or "unique selling proposition" designed to associate each brand with a specific idea in the reader or viewer's mind.

The late 1980s and early 1990s saw the introduction of cable television and particularly MTV. Pioneering the concept of the music video, MTV ushered in a new type of advertising: the consumer tunes in for the advertisement, rather than it being a byproduct or afterthought. As cable (and later satellite) television became increasingly prevalent, "specialty" channels began to emerge, and eventually entire channels, such as QVC and Home Shopping Network and ShopTV, devoted to advertising merchandise, where again the consumer tuned in for the ads.

Marketing through the Internet opened new frontiers for advertisers and led to the "dot-com" boom of the 1990s. Entire corporations operated solely on advertising revenue, offering everything from coupons to free Internet access. At the turn of the 21st century, the search engine Google revolutionized online advertising by emphasizing contextually relevant, unobtrusive ads intended to help, rather than inundate, users. This has led to a plethora of similar efforts and an increasing trend of interactive advertising.

The share of advertising spending relative to total economic output (GDP) has changed little across large changes in media. For example, in the U.S. in 1925, the main advertising media were newspapers, magazines, signs on streetcars, and outdoor posters. Advertising spending as a share of U.S. GDP was about 2.6% in 1925. By 1998, television and radio had become major advertising media. Nonetheless, advertising spending as a share of GDP was slightly lower – about 2.4%.

A recent advertising innovation is "guerrilla promotions", which involve unusual approaches such as staged encounters in public places, giveaways of products such as cars that are covered with brand messages, and interactive advertising where the viewer can respond to become part of the advertising message. This reflects an increasing trend of interactive and "embedded" ads, such as via product placement, having consumers vote through text messages, and various innovations utilizing social networking sites (e.g. Myspace).

Product Advertising

Certain products use a specific form of advertising known as "Custom publishing". This form of advertising is usually targeted at a specific segment of society, but may also "draw" the attention of others.

The same advertising techniques used to promote commercial goods and services can be used to inform, educate and motivate the public about non-commercial issues, such as AIDS, political ideology, energy conservation, religious recruitment, and deforestation.

Advertising, in its non-commercial guise, is a powerful educational tool capable of reaching and motivating large audiences. "Advertising justifies its existence when used in the public interest - it is much too powerful a tool to use solely for commercial purposes." - Attributed to Howard Gossage by David Ogilvy

Public service advertising, non-commercial advertising, public interest advertising, cause marketing, and social marketing are different terms for (or aspects of) the use of sophisticated advertising and marketing communications techniques (generally associated with commercial enterprise) on behalf of non-commercial, public interest issues and initiatives.

In the United States, the granting of television and radio licenses by the FCC is contingent upon the station broadcasting a certain amount of public service advertising. To meet these requirements, many broadcast stations in America air the bulk of their required Public Service Announcements during the late night or early morning when the smallest percentage of viewers are watching, leaving more day and prime time commercial slots available for high-paying advertisers.

Public service advertising reached its height during World Wars I and II under the direction of several governments. Commercial advertising media can include wall paintings, billboards, street furniture components, printed flyers, radio, cinema and television ads, web banners, web popups, skywriting, bus stop benches, magazines, newspapers, town criers, sides of buses, taxicab doors and roof mounts, musical stage shows, subway platforms and trains, elastic bands on disposable diapers, stickers on apples in supermarkets, the opening section of streaming audio and video, posters, chicken niblets, and the backs of event tickets and supermarket receipts. Any place an "identified" sponsor pays to deliver their message through a medium is advertising.

Covert advertising embedded in other entertainment media is known as product placement. A more recent version of this is advertising in film, by having a main character use an item or other of a definite brand - an example is in the movie Minority Report, where Tom Cruise's character Tom Anderton owns a computer with the Nokia logo clearly written in the top corner, or his watch engraved with the Bulgari logo.

Another example of advertising in film is in I, Robot, where main character played by Will Smith mentions his Converse shoes several times, calling them "classics," because the film is set far in the future. Cadillac chose to advertise in the movie The Matrix Reloaded, which as a result contained many scenes in which Cadillac cars were used. Similarly, product placement for Omega Watches, BMW and Aston-Martin cars are featured in recent James Bond films, most notably, Casino Royale.

The TV commercial is generally considered the most effective mass-market advertising format and this is reflected by the high prices TV networks charge for commercial airtime during popular TV events. The annual Super Bowl football game in the United States is known as much for its commercial advertisements as for the game itself, and the average cost of a single thirty-second TV spot during this game has reached $2.5 million (as of 2006).

Virtual advertisements may be inserted into regular television programming through computer graphics. It is typically inserted into otherwise blank backdrops or used to replace local billboards that are not relevant to the remote broadcast audience. More controversially, virtual billboards may be inserted into the background where none existing in real-life. Virtual product placement is also possible. Increasingly, other mediums such as those discussed below are overtaking television due to a shift towards consumer's usage of the Internet as well as devices such as TiVo.

Advertising on the World Wide Web is a recent phenomenon. Prices of Web-based advertising space are dependent on the "relevance" of the surrounding web content and the traffic that the website receives. E-mail advertising is another recent phenomenon. Unsolicited bulk E-mail advertising is known as "spam". Some companies have proposed to place messages or corporate logos on the side of booster rockets and the International Space Station. Controversy exists on the effectiveness of subliminal advertising, and the pervasiveness of mass messages.

Unpaid advertising (also called word of mouth advertising), can provide good exposure at minimal cost. Personal recommendations ("bring a friend", "sell it"), spreading buzz, or achieving the feat of equating a brand with a common noun ("Xerox" = "photocopier", "Kleenex" = tissue, and "Vaseline" = petroleum jelly) – these are the pinnacles of any advertising campaign. However, some companies oppose the use of their brand name to label an object.

The most common method for measuring the impact of mass media advertising is the use of the rating point (rp) or the more accurate target rating point (trp). These two measures refer to the percentage of the universe of the existing base of audience members that can be reached by the use of each media outlet in a particular moment in time. The difference between the two is that the rating point refers to the percentage to the entire universe while the target rating point refers to the percentage to a particular segment or target. This becomes very useful when focusing advertising efforts on a particular group of people.

- For example, think of an advertising campaign targeting a female audience aged 25 to 45. While the overall rating of a TV show might be well over 10 rating points it might very well happen that the same show in the same moment of time is generating only 2.5 trps (being the target: women 25-45). This would mean that while the show has a large universe of viewers it is not necessarily reaching a large universe of women in the ages of 25 to 45 making it a less desirable location to place an ad for an advertiser looking for this particular demographic. Conversely, a TV show with a low overall rating point may be more successful at selling ads when its target rating points are high. In the United States, networks like the WB and FOX have had success with shows based on this premise; the shows had low overall ratings points, but delivered strong target rating points in the desired demographic.

Advertisement Impact

The impact of advertising has been a matter of considerable debate and many different claims have been made in different contexts. During debates about the banning of cigarette advertising, a common claim from cigarette manufacturers was that cigarette advertising does not encourage people to smoke who would not otherwise. The (eventually successful) opponents of advertising, on the other hand, claim that advertising does in fact increase consumption.

According to many media sources, the past experience and state of mind of the person subjected to advertising may determine the impact that advertising has. Children under the age of four may be unable to distinguish advertising from other television programmes, whilst the ability to determine the truthfulness of the message may not be developed until the age of 8.

As advertising and marketing efforts become increasingly ubiquitous in modern Western societies, the industry has come under criticism of groups such as AdBusters via culture jamming which criticizes the media and consumerism using advertising's own techniques. The industry is accused of being one of the engines powering a convoluted economic mass production system which promotes consumption. Recognizing the social impact of advertising, Mediawatch-uk, a British special interest group, works to educate consumers about how they can register their concerns with advertisers and regulators. It has developed educational materials for use in schools. The award-winning book, Made You Look How Advertising Works and Why You Should Know, by former Mediawatch (a feminist organisation founded by Ann Simonton not linked to mediawatch-uk) president Shari Graydon, provides context for these issues for young readers.

Public interest groups are increasingly suggesting that access to the mental space targeted by advertisers should be taxed, in that at the present moment that space is being freely taken advantage of by advertisers with no compensation paid to the members of the public who are thus being intruded upon. This kind of tax would be a Pigovian tax in that it would act to reduce what is now increasingly seen as a public nuisance. Efforts to that end are gathering momentum, with Arkansas and Maine considering bills to implement such taxation. Florida enacted such a tax in 1987 but was forced to repeal it after six months, as a result of a concerted effort by national commercial interests, which withdrew planned conventions, causing major losses to the tourism industry, and cancelled advertising, causing a loss of 12 million dollars to the broadcast industry alone.

An extensively documented effect is the control and vetoing of free information by the advertisers. Any negative information on a company or its products or operations often results in pressures from the company to withdraw such information lines, threatening to cut their ads. This behaviour makes the editors of the media self-censor content that might upset their ad payers. The bigger both companies are, the bigger their relation gets, maximizing control over a single information. Advertisers may try to minimize information about or from consumer groups, or consumer controlled purchasing initiatives (as joint purchase systems), or consumer controlled quality information systems.

Another indirect effect of advertising is to modify the very nature of the communication media where it is shown. Media that get most of their revenues from publicity try to make their medium a good place for communicating ads before anything else. The most clear example is television, where this means trying to make the public stay for a long time and in a mental state that encourages spectators not to switch the channel through the ads. Programmes that are low in mental stimulus and require light concentration and are varied are best for long sitting times. These make for much easier emotional jumps to ads, which can become more entertaining than regular shows. A simple way to understand the objectives in television programming is to compare contents from channels paid and chosen by the viewer with channels that get their income mainly from advertisements.

There have been increasing efforts to protect the public interest by regulating the content and the reach of advertising. Some examples are the ban on television tobacco advertising imposed in many countries, and the total ban on advertising to children under twelve imposed by the Swedish government in 1991. Though that regulation continues in effect for broadcasts originating within the country, it has been weakened by the European Court of Justice, which has found that Sweden was obliged to accept whatever programming was targeted at it from neighbouring countries or via satellite.

In Europe and elsewhere there is a vigorous debate on whether and how much advertising to children should be regulated. This debate was exacerbated by a report released by the Kaiser Family Foundation in February 2004 which suggested that food advertising targeting children was an important factor in the epidemic of childhood obesity in the United States. In many countries - namely New Zealand, South Africa, Canada, and many European countries - the advertising industry operates a system of self-regulation. Advertisers, advertising agencies and the media agree on a code of advertising standards that they attempt to uphold. The general aim of such codes is to ensure that any advertising is 'legal, decent, honest and truthful'. Some self-regulatory organizations are funded by the industry, but remain independent, with the intent of upholding the standards or codes (like the Advertising Standards Authority in the UK).

Naturally, many advertisers view governmental regulation or even self-regulation as intrusion of their freedom of speech or a necessary evil. Therefore, they employ a wide-variety of linguistic devices to bypass regulatory laws (e.g. giving English words in bold and French translations in fine print to deal with the Article 12 of the 1994 Toubon Law limiting the use of English in French advertising); The advertising of controversial products such as cigarettes and condoms is subject to government regulation in many countries. For instance, the tobacco industry is required by law in India and Pakistan to display warnings cautioning consumers about the health hazards of their products.

Linguistic variation is often used by advertising as a creative device to reduce the impact of such requirement.

With the dawn of the Internet have come many new advertising opportunities. Popup, Flash, banner, advergaming, and email advertisements (the last often being a form of spam) abound. Each year, greater sums are paid to obtain a commercial spot during the Super Bowl, which is by most measures considered to be the most important football game of the year. Companies attempt to make these commercials sufficiently entertaining that members of the public will actually want to watch them.

Another problem is people recording shows on DVRs (ex. TiVo). These devices allow users to record the programmes for later viewing enabling them to fast forward through commercials. Additionally, as more seasons or "Boxed Sets" come out of Television shows; fewer people are watching their shows on TV. However, the fact that these sets are sold, means that the company will additionally receive profits from the sales of these sets. To counter this effect, many advertisers have opted for product placement on TV shows like Survivor.

Particularly since the rise of "entertaining" advertising, some people may like an advert enough that they wish to watch it later or show a friend. In general, the advertising community has not yet made this easy, although some have used the Internet to widely distribute their adverts to anyone wishing to see or hear them.

Another significant trend to note for the future of advertising is the growing importance of niche or targeted ads. Also brought about by the Internet and the theory of The Long Tail, advertisers will have an increasing ability to reach narrow audiences. In the past, the most efficient way to deliver a message was to blanket the largest mass market audience possible. However, usage tracking, customer profiles and the growing popularity of niche content brought about by everything from blogs to social networking sites, provides advertisers with audiences that are smaller but much better defined, leading to ads that are more relevant to viewers and more effective for companies marketing products. Among others, Comcast Spotlight is one such advertiser employing this method in their video on demand menus. These advertisements are targeted to a specific group and can be viewed by anyone wishing to find out more about a particular business or practice at any time, right from their home. This causes the viewer to become proactive and actually choose what advertisements they want to view.

Advertising Campaign

An advertising campaign is a series of advertisement messages that share a single idea and theme which make up an integrated marketing communication (IMC). Advertising campaigns appear in different media across a specific time frame.

The critical part of making an advertising campaign is determining a campaign theme, as it sets the tone for the individual advertisements and other forms of marketing communications that will be used. The campaign theme is the central message that will be communicated in the promotional activities. The campaign themes are usually developed with the intention of being used for a substantial period but many of them are short lived due to factors such as being ineffective or market conditions and/or competition in the marketplace.

Communication Design

Communication design is a sub-discipline of design which is concerned with how media intermission such as printed, crafted, electronic media or presentations communicate with people. A communication design approach is more concerned with messages communicated than aesthetics in media. The distinction between communication design and other applied arts is in the motivation: while the communication design process does involve a certain amount of self-expression and creativity, the goals are often those of the commissioning body rather than the artist's, and the parameters set by the commissioning body are often more constraining.

The term communication design is often used interchangeably with visual communication and more specifically graphic design, but has an alternate broader meaning that includes auditory communications as well as visual. Examples of Communication Design include information architecture, editing, typography, illustration and professional writing skills applied to creative industries.

Environmental Scanning

For a company to gain or maintain a sustainable competitive advantage, it must be ever vigilant, watching for changes in the business environment. It must also be agile enough to alter its strategies and plans when the need arises.

There are three ways of scanning the business environment:

- Ad-hoc scanning - Short term, infrequent examinations usually initiated by a crisis
- Regular scanning - Studies done on a regular schedule (say, once a year)
- Continuous scanning - (also called continuous learning) - continuous structured data collection and processing on a broad range of environmental factors

Most commentators feel that in today's turbulent business environment the best scanning method available is continuous scanning. This allows the firm to act quickly, take advantage of opportunities before competitors do, and respond to environmental threats before significant damage is done.

Environmental scanning usually refers just to the macroenvironment, but it can also include industry and competitor analysis, consumer analysis, product innovations, and the company's internal environment. Macroenvironmental scanning involves analysing:

- The Economy
  - GNP or GDP per capital
  - GNP or GDP growth
  - Unemployment rate

  - Inflation rate
  - Consumer and investor confidence
  - Inventory levels
  - Currency exchange rates
  - Merchandise trade balance
  - Financial and political health of trading partners
  - Balance of payments
  - Future trends
- Government
  - Political climate - amount of government activity
  - Political stability and risk
  - Government debt
  - Budget deficit or surplus
  - Corporate and personal tax rates
  - Payroll taxes
  - Import tariffs and quotas
  - Export restrictions
  - Restrictions on international financial flows
- Legal
  - Minimum wage laws
  - Environmental protection laws
  - Worker safety laws
  - Union laws
  - Copyright and patent laws
  - Anti- monopoly laws
  - Sunday closing laws
  - Municipal licences
  - Laws that favour business investment
- Technology
  - Efficiency of infrastructure, including: roads, ports, airports, rolling stock, hospitals, education, healthcare, communication, etc.
  - Industrial productivity
  - New manufacturing processes
  - New products and services of competitors

- New products and services of supply chain partners
- Any new technology that could impact the company
- Cost and accessibility of electrical power

- Ecology
  - Ecological concerns that affect the firms production processes
  - Ecological concerns that affect customers' buying habits
  - Ecological concerns that affect customers' perception of the company or product
- Socio-Cultural
  - Demographic factors such as:
    - Population size and distribution
    - Age distribution
    - Education levels
    - Income levels
    - Ethnic origins
    - Religious affiliations
  - Attitudes towards:
    - Materialism, capitalism, free enterprise
    - Individualism, role of family, role of government, collectivism
    - Role of church and religion
    - Consumerism
    - Environmentalism
    - Importance of work, pride of accomplishment
  - Cultural structures including:
    - Diet and nutrition
    - Housing conditions
- Potential Suppliers
  - Labour supply
    - Quantity of labour available
    - Quality of labour available
    - Stability of labour supply
    - Wage expectations

- Employee turn-over rate
- Strikes and labour relations
- Educational facilities

– Material suppliers

- Quality, quantity, price, and stability of material inputs
- Delivery delays
- Proximity of bulky or heavy material inputs
- Level of competition among suppliers

– Service Providers

- Quantity, quality, price, and stability of service facilitators
- Special requirements

Scanning these macroenvironmental variables for threats and opportunities requires that each issue be rated on two dimensions. It must be rated on its potential impact on the company, and rated on its likeliness of occurrence. Multiplying the potential impact parameter by the likeliness of occurrence parameter gives us a good indication of its importance to the firm.

Sustainable Competitive Advantage

Competitive advantage (CA) is a position that a firm occupies in its competitive landscape. Michael Porter posits that a competitive advantage, sustainable or not, exists when a company makes economic rents, that is, their earnings exceed their costs, especially including cost of capital. That means that normal competitive pressures are not able to drive down the firm's earnings to the point where they cover all costs and just provide minimum sufficient additional return to keep capital invested. Most forms of competitive advantage cannot be sustained for any length of time because the promise of economic rents drives competitiors to duplicate the competitive advantage held by any one firm.

A firm possesses a Sustainable Competitive Advantage when it has value-creating processes and positions that cannot be duplicated or imitated by other firms that lead to the production of above normal rents. An SCA is different from a competitive advantage (CA) in that it provides a long-term advantage that is not easily replicated. But these above-normal rents can attract new entrants who drive down economic rents. A CA is a position a firm attains that lead to above-normal rents or a superior financial performance. The processes and positions that engender such a position is not necessarily non-duplicable or inimitable. It is possible for some companies to make profits for a time above the cost of capital without sustainable competitive advantage.

A key difference between CA and SCA is that the processes and positions a firm may hold are non-duplicable and inimitable when a firm possesses a SCA. Hence a sustainable competitive advantage is one that can be maintained for a significant amount of time even in the presence of competition. This brings us to the question what is a "significant amount of time". A CA becomes SCA when all duplication and imitation efforts have ceased and the rival firms have not been able to create the same value that the said firm is creating.

Analysis of the factors of profitability is the subject of numerous theories of strategy including the five forces model pioneered by Michael Porter of the Harvard Business School.

In marketing and strategic management, sustainable competitive advantage is an advantage that one firm has relative to competing firms. The source of the advantage can be something the company does that is distinctive and difficult to replicate, also known as a core competency – for example Procter & Gamble's ability to derive superior consumer insights and implement them in managing its brand portfolio. It can also be an asset such as a brand (e.g. Coca Cola) or a patent, such as Viagra. It can also simply be a result of the industry's cost structure – for example, the large fixed costs that tend to create natural monopolies in utility industries. To be sustainable, the advantage must be:

1. Distinctive, and
2. Proprietary

Building Sustainable Competitive Advantage

There are basically three types of assets that help build an SCA. These categories are exhaustive and include all of the company's SCAs:

1. Organization and managerial process
   - Coordination and integration: Coordination among teams in organization is key to organizational success. Interdepartmental coordination and resource sharing to reach a common goal is fundamental to creating "value". Integrating resources is key to the success of firms. Firms that are able to integrate resources see synergistic effects of resources coming together.
   - Learning: Organizational learning is key to the success of a firm. It determines how a firm collects, distributes, interprets and responds to market based information collection and changes in the environment. These changes in the environment could be customer based changes, technological developments, legal and government restrictions. Firms have to develop robust market sensing and spanning capabilities to effectively collect information. Once they collect info they have embed this knowledge in the products they produce.
   - Reconfiguring and transformation: The environment for firms is constantly changing and constant reconfiguring and transformation is key to forming SCA. A double loop learning and transformation is key to producing innovative products. Innovative capacity of a firm determines how it reacts and learns from market information.
2. Positions: market positions are the assets of a company. Most of them are self-explanatory:

- Technological assets
- Financial assets
- Reputational assets
- Structural assets: The structure of a company can determine how it performs. The hierarchy of a company can influence its culture, procedure and routines.

3. Paths:
   - Path dependencies: At the birth of a company usually accompanied with certain orientations. The progenitor brings certain orientations and attributes that stay with the company for a long time. The path the company takes then determines the development of its competencies.'
   - Technological opportunities: technology development at a time can determine how a firm can exploit opportunities to form SCA. Very often we see the advent of several technological factors converging into a capability that forms a SCA. An example would be the rise of companies such as Genentech at the turn of the previous century with the advent of gene mapping, significant developments in target selection and databases of previous studies and gene pools.

Strategic Management of hotel

Strategic management is that set of managerial decisions and actions that determines the long-run performance of a corporation. It includes environmental scanning, strategy formulation, strategy implementation and evaluation and control.

An organization's strategy must be appropriate for its resources, environmental circumstances, and core objectives. The process involves matching the company's [internal resources (eg IT) and capabilities (eg quality management)] to the external business environment the organization faces. Strategy formulation involves:

- Doing a situation analysis: both internal and external; both micro-environmental and macro-environmental.
- Concurrent with this assessment, objectives are set. This involves crafting vision statements (long term view of a possible future), mission statements (the role that the organization gives itself in society), overall corporate objectives (both financial and strategic), strategic business unit objectives (both financial and strategic), and tactical objectives.
- These objectives should, in the light of the situation analysis, sugsgest a strategic plan. The plan provides the details of how to achieve these objectives.

This three-step strategy formulation process is sometimes referred to as determining where you are now, determining where you want to go, and then determining how to get there. These three questions are the essence of strategic planning. SWOT Analysis: I/O Economics for the external factors and RBV for the internal factors.

Strategy Implementation involves:

- Allocation of sufficient resources (financial, personnel, time, technology support)
- Establishing a chain of command or some alternative structure (such as cross functional teams)
- Assigning responsibility of specific tasks or processes to specific individuals or groups
- It also involves managing the process. This includes monitoring results, comparing to benchmarks and best practices, evaluating the efficacy and efficiency of the process, controlling for variances, and making adjustments to the process as necessary.
- When implementing specific programmes, this involves acquiring the requisite resources, developing the process, training, process testing, documentation, and integration with (and/or conversion from) legacy processes.

Strategy formulation and implementation is an on-going, never-ending, integrated process requiring continuous reassessment and reformation. Strategic management is dynamic; It involves a complex pattern of actions and reactions. It is partially planned and partially unplanned. Strategy is both planned and emergent, dynamic, and interactive. Some people (such as Andy Grove at Intel) feel that there are critical points at which a strategy must take a new direction in order to be in step with a changing business environment. These critical points of change are called strategic inflection points.

Time Scales

Strategic management operates on several time scales. Short term strategies involve planning and managing for the present. Long term strategies involve preparing for and preempting the future. Marketing strategist Derek Abell (1993), has suggested that understanding this dual nature of strategic management is the least understood part of the process. He claims that balancing the temporal aspects of strategic planning requires the use of dual strategies simultaneously.

Strategic Management is actually a solid foundation or a framework within which all the functionning managerial operations are bundled together. This is the highest level corporate activity that sets the terms and goals for a company that it should follow for prosperity.

In general terms, there are two main approaches to strategic management which are opposite but complement each other in some ways:

- 'The Industrial Organization Approach'
  - Based on economic theory – deals with issues like competitive rivalry, resource allocation, economies of scale
  - Assumptions – rationality, self discipline behaviour, profit maximization
- The Sociological Approach
  - Deals primarily with human interactions

- Assumptions – bounded rationality, satisficing behaviour, profit sub-optimality. An example of a company that currently operates this way is Google

Strategic management techniques can be viewed as bottom-up, top-down, or collaborative processes. In the bottom-up approach, employees submit proposals to their managers who, in turn, funnel the best ideas further up the organization. This is often accomplished by a capital budgeting process. Proposals are assessed using financial criteria such as return on investment or cost-benefit analysis. The proposals that are approved form the substance of a new strategy, all of which is done without a grand strategic design or a strategic architect. The top-down approach is the most common by far. In it, the CEO, possibly with the assistance of a strategic planning team, decides on the overall direction the company should take. Some organizations are starting to experiment with collaborative strategic planning techniques that recognize the emergent nature of strategic decisions.

In most (large) corporations there are several levels of strategy. Strategic management is the highest in the sense that it is the broadest, applying to all parts of the firm. It gives direction to corporate values, corporate culture, corporate goals, and corporate missions. Under this broad corporate strategy there are often functional or business unit strategies.

Functional strategies include marketing strategies, new product development strategies, human resource strategies, financial strategies, legal strategies, and information technology management strategies. The emphasis is on short and medium term plans and is limited to the domain of each department's functional responsibility. Each functional department attempts to do its part in meeting overall corporate objectives, and hence to some extent their strategies are derived from broader corporate strategies.

Many companies feel that a functional organizational structure is not an efficient way to organize activities so they have reengineered according to processes or strategic business units (called SBUs). A strategic business unit is a semi-autonomous unit within an organization. It is usually responsible for its own budgeting, new product decisions, hiring decisions, and price setting. An SBU is treated as an internal profit centre by corporate headquarters. Each SBU is responsible for developing its business strategies, strategies that must be in tune with broader corporate strategies.

The "lowest" level of strategy is operational strategy. It is very narrow in focus and deals with day-to-day operational activities such as scheduling criteria. It must operate within a budget but is not at liberty to adjust or create that budget. Operational level strategy was encouraged by Peter Drucker in his theory of management by objectives (MBO). Operational level strategies are informed by business level strategies which, in turn, are informed by corporate level strategies. Business strategy, which refers to the aggregated operational strategies of single business firm or that of an SBU in a diversified corporation refers to the way in which a firm competes in its chosen arenas.

Corporate strategy, then, refers to the overarching strategy of the diversified firm. Such corporate strategy answers the questions of "in which businesses should we compete?" and "how does being in one business add to the competitive advantage of another portfolio firm, as well as the competitive advantage of the corporation as a whole?"

Since the turn of the millennium, there has been a tendency in some firms to revert to a simpler strategic structure. This is being driven by information technology. It is felt that knowledge management systems should be used to share information and create common goals. Strategic divisions are thought to hamper this process. Most recently, this notion of strategy has been captured under the rubric of dynamic strategy, popularized by the strategic management textbook authored by Carpenter and Sanders. This work builds on that of Brown and Eisenhart as well as Christensen and portrays firm strategy, both business and corporate, as necessarily embracing ongoing strategic change, and the seamless integration of strategy formulation and implementation. Such change and implementation are usually built into the strategy through the staging and pacing facets.

Why Strategic Plans Fails

There are many reasons why strategic plans fail, especially:

- Failure to understand the customer
  - Why do they buy
  - Is there a real need for the product
  - Inadequate or incorrect marketing research
- Inability to predict environmental reaction
  - What will competitors do
    - Fighting brands
    - Price wars
  - Will government intervene
- Over-estimation of resource competence
  - Can the staff, equipment, and processes handle the new strategy
  - Failure to develop new employee and management skills
- Failure to coordinate
  - Reporting and control relationships not adequate
  - Organizational structure not flexible enough
- Failure to obtain senior management commitment
  - Failure to get management involved right from the start
  - Failure to obtain sufficient company resources to accomplish task
- Failure to obtain employee commitment
  - New strategy not well explained to employees
  - No incentives given to workers to embrace the new strategy
- Under-estimation of time requirements
  - No critical path analysis done
- Failure to follow the plan
  - No follow through after initial planning

- No tracking of progress against plan
- No consequences for above

• Failure to manage change
- Inadequate understanding of the internal resistance to change
- Lack of vision on the relationships between processes, technology and organization

• Poor communications
- Insufficient information sharing among stakeholders
- Exclusion of stakeholders and delegates

• Failure to focus
- Inability or unwillingness to make choices which are true to the strategic mission (i.e. to do fewer things, better), leads to mediocrity, inability to compete

Although a sense of direction is important, it can also stifle creativity, especially if it is rigidly enforced. In an uncertain and ambiguous world, fluidity can be more important than a finely tuned strategic compass. When a strategy becomes internalized into a corporate culture, it can lead to group think. It can also cause an organization to define itself too narrowly. An example of this is marketing myopia.

Most theories of strategic management seem to have a lifespan less than that of the popularity of the latest teen music idol. Many critics claim that this is because most of them generally do not work. Keep in mind that this article describes only the 50 or so most successful theories, thus exhibiting survivorship bias (ironically, itself an area of research in strategic management). For every theory that gets incorporated into strategic management textbooks there are many that are quickly forgotten. Many theories tend either to be too narrow in focus to build a complete corporate strategy on, or too general and abstract to be applicable to specific situations. The low success rate is further fueled by the management lecture circuit in which hundreds of self-appointed gurus, many without serious academic credentials or substantial expertise, attempt to sell books and explain their "revolutionary" and "groundbreaking" theories to audiences of business executives for a sizable fee. While there are undoubtedly inspirational ideas contained in these seminars, the theories expounded therein have not, for the most part, been subjected to serious study.

Some critics take the opposite approach claiming effectively that there are not enough theories, and when they arrive they are too late to help managers make any important decisions. These commentators remind us that the basic, everyday purpose of strategic management is to match a company's strategy with the business environment that the organization is in. Because the environment is constantly changing, effective strategic management requires a continuous flow of new theories suitable for the new circumstances. The problem with most theories is that they solve yesterday's problems, similar to a business Maginot Line. Various approaches to solve this problem have emerged, however, including Mintzberg's ideas of 'emergent strategies' and use of ideas from complexity theory in what is often called complexity strategy.

Gary Hamel coined the term strategic convergence to explain the limited scope of the strategies being used by rivals in greatly differing circumstances. He lamented that strategies converge more than they should, because the more successful ones get imitated by firms that do not understand that the strategic process involves designing a custom strategy for the specifics of each situation.

Chapter 5

The Market of Hospitality

A market is a social arrangement that allows buyers and sellers to discover information and carry out a voluntary exchange of goods or services. It is one of the two key institutions that organize trade, along with the right to own property. Allowing markets to arrive at a pareto efficient outcome is one of the key components of capitalism. In everyday usage, the word "market" may refer to the location where goods are traded, sometimes known as a marketplace, or to a street market.

The function of a market requires, at a minimum, that both parties expect to become better off as a result of the transaction. Markets generally rely on price adjustments to provide information to parties engaging in a transaction, so that each may accurately gauge the subsequent change of their welfare. In less sophisticated markets, such as those involving barter, individual buyers and sellers must engage in a more lengthy process of haggling in order to gain the same information. Markets are efficient when the price of a good or service attracts exactly as much demand as the market can currently supply. The chief function of a market, then, is to adjust prices to accommodate fluctuations in supply and demand in order to achieve allocative efficiency. An economic system in which goods and services are exchanged by market functions is called a market economy. An alternative economic system in which non-market forces (often government mandates) determine prices are called planned economies or command economies. The attempt to combine socialist ideals with the incentive system of a market is known as market socialism.

Although many markets exist in the traditional sense—such as a flea market—there are various other types of them and various organizational structures to assist their functions. A market can be organized as an auction, as a shopping center, as a complex institution such as a stock market, and as an informal discussion between two individuals.

In economics, a market that runs under laissez-faire policies is a free market. It is "free" in the sense that the government makes no attempt to intervene through taxes, subsidies, minimum wages, price ceilings, etc. Markets may be distorted by a seller or sellers with monopoly power, or a buyer with monopsony power. Also, the level of organization or negotiation power of buyers, markedly affects the functioning of the market. Markets where price negotiations do not arrive at efficient outcomes for both sides are said to experience market failure.

Most markets are regulated by state wide laws and regulations. While barter markets exist, most markets use currency or some other form of money. Markets of varying types can spontaneously arise whenever a party has interest in a good or service that some other party can provide. Hence there can be a market for cigarettes in correctional facilities, another for chewing gum in a playground, and yet another for contracts for the future delivery of a commodity.

MARKET FAILURE

If advertising is poor, definitely there will be market failure. Market failure is a term used to describe a situation in which markets do not efficiently allocate goods and services. To economists, the term would normally be applied to situations where the inefficiency is particularly dramatic, or when it is suggested that non-market institutions (such as public policing and firefighting) would be more efficient and wealth-producing than their private alternatives.

On the other hand, the term "market failure" is also often used to describe situations where market forces do not serve the perceived public interest. In this article, however, the focus is on market failure as defined by mainstream economics. Economists use model-like theorems to explain or understand such cases. The two main reasons that markets fail are:

- The inadequate expression of costs or benefits in prices and thus into microeconomic decision-making in markets.
- Sub-optimal market structures.

The existence of a market failure in a certain economic activity is often used as an argument that the activity in question should not be directed by market forces. This generally leads to a debate on the question of what - if anything - should be used to replace markets. The most common response to a market failure in the present day is to use the government to produce certain goods and services. However, government intervention may cause nonmarket failure by the intevention itself causing externalitites.

Types of Market Failures

Imperfect Competition

In economic theory, imperfect competition, is the competitive situation in any market where the conditions necessary for perfect competition are not satisfied.

Forms of imperfect competition include:

- Monopoly, in which there is only one seller of a good.
- Oligopoly, in which there is a small number of sellers.
- Monopolistic competition, in which there are many sellers producing highly differentiated goods.
- Monopsony, in which there is only one buyer of a good.
- Oligopsony, in which there is a small number of buyers.

There may also be imperfect competition in markets due to buyers or sellers lacking information about prices and the goods being traded. There may also be imperfect competition due to a time lag in a market. For example, in the 1990s, there was a shortage of computer programmers, but becoming a skilled programmer requires several years of experience. This drove up salaries. Another example is the "jobless recovery". There are many growth opportunities available after a recession, but it takes time for employers to react, leading to high unemployment. High unemployment decreases wages, which makes hiring more attractive, but it takes time for new jobs to be created.

Market Power

In economics, market power is the ability of a firm to alter the market price of a good or service. A firm with market power can raise price without losing all customers to competitors. When a firm has market power it faces a downward-sloping demand curve. In perfectly competitive markets, market participants have no market power. A firm with market power has the ability to individually affect either the total quantity or the prevailing price in the market. If the demand curve is downward sloping (that is, the most common situation where price increases lead to a lower quantity demanded), then the decrease in supply as a result of the exercise of market power creates an economic deadweight loss in comparison with a situation of perfect competition. This is often viewed as socially undesirable, and as a result, many countries have anti-trust or other legislation with the aim of limiting the ability of firms to accrue market power. Such legislation often regulates mergers and sometimes introduces a judicial power to compel divestiture.

A firm usually has market power by virtue of it controlling a large portion of the market. In extreme cases - monopoly and monopsony - the firm controls the entire market. However, market size alone is not a good indicator of market power. Highly concentrated markets may be contestable if there are no barriers to entry or exit, limiting the incumbent firm's ability to raise its price above competitive levels.

Market power gives firms the ability to engage in unilateral anti-competitive behaviour. Some of the behaviours that firms with market power are accused of engaging in include predatory pricing, product tying, and creation of overcapacity or other barriers to entry. If no individual participant in the market has significant market power, then anti-competitive behaviour can take place only through collusion, or the exercise of a group of participants' collective market power.

When several firms control a significant share of market sales, the resulting market structure is called an oligopoly or oligopsony. An oligopoly may engage in collusion, either tacit or overt, and thereby exercize market power. An explicit agreement in an oligopoly to affect market price or output is called a cartel. The behaviour of firms in perfect competition or monopoly can be treated as a simple optimization, but an oligopoly requires game theoretic analysis.

Monopoly power is an example of market failure which occurs when one or more of the participants has the ability to influence the price or other outcomes in some general or specialized market. The most commonly discussed form of market power is that of a monopoly, but other forms such as monopsony, and more moderate versions of these two extremes, exist. Market participants that have market power are sometimes referred to as "price makers", while those without are sometimes called "price takers".

A well known example of monopolistic market power is Microsoft's market share in PC operating systems. The United States v. Microsoft case concerned the allegation that Microsoft illegally exercised its market power by bundling its web browser with its operating system. Some have suggested that Wal Mart exercises monopsonistic market power; its size allows it to extract extremely low prices from its suppliers.

Monopoly

In economics, is defined as a persistent market situation where there is only one provider of a product or service. Monopolies are characterized by a lack of economic competition for the good or service that they provide and a lack of viable substitute goods. Monopoly should be distinguished from monopsony, in which there is only one buyer of the product or service; it should also, strictly, be distinguished from the (similar) phenomenon of a cartel. In a monopoly a single firm is the sole provider of a product or service; in a cartel a centralized institution is set up to partially coordinate the actions of several independent providers.

STRATEGIES IN MARKETING

Marketing strategy is a powerful process that gives an organization a competitive advantage in the marketplace. While just defining a marketing strategy will not automatically create a competitive advantage, it will allow the organization to concentrate its (always limited) resources on the greatest opportunities to increase sales and achieve a sustainable competitive advantage.

The word strategy comes from the Greek word strategos meaning general. Strategy is what generals use to win battles. Thus properly understood, marketing strategy is a high-level exercise involving the "generals" of the organization in determining how to build on the firm's strengths while (ethically) taking advantage of competitors' weaknesses. Marketing strategy is most effective when it is a vital component of corporate strategy, defining how the organization will engage customers, prospects and the competition in the market arena for consistent success.

A marketing strategy also serves as the foundation of a marketing plan. A marketing plan contains a set of specific actions required to successfully implement a specific marketing strategy. For example: "Use a low cost product to attract consumers. Once our organization, via our low cost product, has established a relationship with consumers, our organization will sell additional, higher-margin products and services that enhance the consumer's interaction with the low-cost product or service."

A strategy is different from a tactic. While it is possible to write a tactical marketing plan without a sound, well-considered strategy, it is not recommended. Without a sound marketing strategy, a marketing plan has no foundation. Marketing strategies serve as the fundamental underpinning of marketing plans designed to reach marketing objectives. It is important that these objectives have measurable results. A good marketing strategy should integrate an organization's marketing goals, policies, and action sequences (tactics) into a cohesive whole. The objective of a marketing strategy is to provide a foundation from which a tactical plan is developed. This allows the organization to carry out its mission effectively and efficiently.

Marketing strategies are partially derived from broader corporate strategies, corporate missions, and corporate goals. They should flow from the firm's mission statement. They are also influenced by a range of microenvironmental factors. Marketing strategies are dynamic and interactive. They are partially planned and partially unplanned.

Commercial Planning

In the modern world of business, it is useless to be a creative original thinker unless you can also sell what you create. Management cannot be expected to recognize a good idea unless it is presented to them by a good salesman. The success of a new product depends not only on the idea behind the product, but also on the marketing of the new product before, during and after the product launch. Commercializing a product is commonly known as Commercial Planning. No concrete methods are currently available for New Product Launching (NPL). However, several articles are published about NPL and the essential activities, to launch a new product. This article describes a set of activities and products, that are essential for launching a new product. New Product Launching is part of the New Product Development method.

Strategic Management

An organization's strategy must be appropriate for its resources, environmental circumstances, and core objectives. The process involves matching the company's internal resources (eg IT) and capabilities (eg quality management) to the external business environment the organization faces.

Strategy formulation involves:

- Doing a situation analysis: both internal and external; both micro-environmental and macro-environmental.
- Concurrent with this assessment, objectives are set. This involves crafting vision statements (long term view of a possible future), mission statements (the role that the organization gives itself in society), overall corporate objectives (both financial and strategic), strategic business unit objectives (both financial and strategic), and tactical objectives.
- These objectives should, in the light of the situation analysis, suggest a strategic plan. The plan provides the details of how to achieve these objectives.

This three-step strategy formulation process is sometimes referred to as determining where you are now, determining where you want to go, and then determining how to get there. These three questions are the essence of strategic planning. SWOT Analysis: I/O Economics for the external factors and RBV for the internal factors.

Strategy implementation involves:

- Allocation of sufficient resources (financial, personnel, time, technology support)
- Establishing a chain of command or some alternative structure (such as cross functional teams)
- Assigning responsibility of specific tasks or processes to specific individuals or groups
- It also involves managing the process. This includes monitoring results, comparing to benchmarks and best practices, evaluating the efficacy and efficiency of the process, controlling for variances, and making adjustments to the process as necessary.
- When implementing specific programs, this involves acquiring the requisite resources, developing the process, training, process testing, documentation, and integration with (and/or conversion from) legacy processes.

Strategy formulation and implementation is an on-going, never-ending, integrated process requiring continuous reassessment and reformation. Strategic management is dynamic. It involves a complex pattern of actions and reactions. It is partially planned and partially unplanned. Strategy is both planned and emergent, dynamic, and interactive. Some people (such as Andy Grove at Intel) feel that there are critical points at which a strategy must take a new direction in order to be in step with a changing business environment. These critical points of change are called strategic inflection points.

Strategic management operates on several time scales. Short term strategies involve planning and managing for the present. Long term strategies involve preparing for and preempting the future. Marketing strategist Derek Abell (1993), has suggested that understanding this dual nature of strategic management is the least understood part of the process. He claims that balancing the temporal aspects of strategic planning requires the use of dual strategies simultaneously.

Strategic Management is actually a solid foundation or a framework within which all the functionning managerial operations are bundled together. This is the highest level corporate activity that sets the terms and goals for a company that it should follow for prosperity.

Strategic management techniques can be viewed as bottom-up, top-down, or collaborative processes. In the bottom-up approach, employees submit proposals to their managers who, in turn, funnel the best ideas further up the organization. This is often accomplished by a capital budgeting process. Proposals are assessed using financial criteria such as return on investment or cost-benefit analysis. The proposals that are approved form the substance of a new strategy, all of which is done without a grand strategic design or a strategic architect. The top-down approach is the most common by far. In it, the CEO, possibly with the assistance of a strategic planning team, decides on the overall direction the company should take. Some organizations are starting to experiment with collaborative strategic planning techniques that recognize the emergent nature of strategic decisions.

In most (large) corporations there are several levels of strategy. Strategic management is the highest in the sense that it is the broadest, applying to all parts of the firm. It gives direction to corporate values, corporate culture, corporate goals, and corporate missions. Under this broad corporate strategy there are often functional or business unit strategies.

Functional strategies include marketing strategies, new product development strategies, human resource strategies, financial strategies, legal strategies, and information technology management strategies. The emphasis is on short and medium term plans and is limited to the domain of each department's functional responsibility. Each functional department attempts to do its part in meeting overall corporate objectives, and hence to some extent their strategies are derived from broader corporate strategies.

Many companies feel that a functional organizational structure is not an efficient way to organize activities so they have reengineered according to processes or strategic business units (called SBUs). A strategic business unit is a semi-autonomous unit within an organization. It is usually responsible for its own budgeting, new product decisions, hiring decisions, and price setting. An SBU is treated as an internal profit centre by corporate headquarters. Each SBU is responsible for developing its business strategies, strategies that must be in tune with broader corporate strategies.

The "lowest" level of strategy is operational strategy. It is very narrow in focus and deals with day-to-day operational activities such as scheduling criteria. It must operate within a budget but is not at liberty to adjust or create that budget. Operational level strategy was encouraged by Peter Drucker in his theory of management by objectives (MBO). Operational level strategies are informed by business level strategies which, in turn, are informed by corporate level strategies. Business strategy, which refers to the aggregated operational strategies of single business firm or that of an SBU in a diversified corporation refers to the way in which a firm competes in its chosen arenas.

Corporate strategy, then, refers to the overarching strategy of the diversified firm. Such corporate strategy answers the questions of "in which businesses should we compete?" and "how does being in one business add to the competitive advantage of another portfolio firm, as well as the competitive advantage of the corporation as a whole?"

Since the turn of the millennium, there has been a tendency in some firms to revert to a simpler strategic structure. This is being driven by information technology. It is felt that knowledge management systems should be used to share information and create common goals. Strategic divisions are thought to hamper this process. Most recently, this notion of strategy has been captured under the rubric of dynamic strategy, popularized by the strategic management textbook authored by Carpenter and Sanders. This work builds on that of Brown and Eisenhart as well as Christensen and portrays firm strategy, both business and corporate, as necessarily embracing ongoing strategic change, and the seamless integration of strategy formulation and implementation. Such change and implementation are usually built into the strategy through the staging and pacing facets.

Management by Objectives (MBO) is a process of agreeing upon objectives within an organization so that management and employees buy in to the objectives and understand what they are. Management By Objectives term was first popularized by Peter Drucker in 1954 in his book 'The Practice of Management'.

It is all too easy for managers to fail to outline, and agree with their employees, what it is that everyone is trying to achieve. MBO substitutes for good intentions a process that requires rather precise written description of objectives (for the period ahead) and timelines for their monitoring and achievement. The process requires that the manager and the employee agree to what the employee will attempt to achieve in the period ahead, and (very important) that the employee accept and buy into the objectives (otherwise commitment will be lacking).

For example, whatever else a manager and employee may discuss and agree in their regular discussions, let us suppose that they feel that it will be sensible to introduce a key performance indicator to show the development of sales revenue in a part of the firm. Then the manager and the employee need to discuss what is being planned, what the time-schedule is and what the indicator might or might not be. Thereafter the two of them should liaise to ensure that the objective is being attended to and will be delivered on time.

Organizations have scarce resources and so it is incumbent on the managers to consider the level of resourcing but also to consider whether the objectives that are jointly agreed within the firm are the right ones and represent the best allocation of effort. Also, reliable Management information systems are needed to establish relevant objectives and monitor their "reach ratio" in an objective way.

MBO is often achieved using set targets. MBO introduced the SMART criteria: Objectives for MBO must be SMART (Specific, Measurable, Agreed, Realistic, and Time-Specific). However, it has been reported in recent years that this style of management receives criticism in that it triggers employees' unethical behaviour of distorting the system or financial figures to achieve the targets set by their short-term, narrow bottom-line, and completely self-centered thinking.

Marketing Strategy Tools and Models

Ansoffs Matrix

A common tool used within marketing was developed by Igor Ansoff in 1957. His model gives organisation five strategic business options.

1. Market Penetration: This involves increasing sales of an existing product and penetrating the market

further by either promoting the product heavily or reducing prices to increase sales.

2. Product Development: The organisation develops new products to aim within their existing market, in the hope that they will gain more custom and market share. For Example Sony launching the Playstation 2 to replace their existing model.
3. Market Development: The organisation here adopts a strategy of selling existing products to new markets. This can be done either by a better understanding of segmentation, i.e who else can possibly purchase the product or selling the product to new markets overseas.
4. Diversification: Moving away from what you are selling (your core activities) to providing something new eg Moving over from selling foods to selling cars.
5. Consolidation: Where the organisation adopts a strategy of withdrawing from particular markets, scaling back on operations and concentrating on its existing products in existing markets.

Product Life Cycle

The product life cycle concept suggests that a product passes through four stages of evolution. Introduction, growth, maturity and decline. As a product evolves and passes through theses four stages profit is affected, and different strategies have to be employed to ensure that the product is a success within its market. As a new product much time will be spent by the organisation to create awareness of it presence amongst its target market. Profits are negative or low because of this reason.

Growth: If consumer clearly feels that this product will benefit them in some ways and they accept it, the organisation will see a period of rapid sales growth.

Maturity: Rapid sales growth cannot last forever. Sales slow down as the product sales reach peak as it has been accepted by most buyers.

Decline: Sales and profits start to decline, the organisation may try to change their pricing strategy to stimulate growth, however the product will either have to be re-modified, or replaced within the market.

Value Chain Analysis

Michael Porter in 1985 introduced in his book ' The competitive advantage' the concept of the Value Chain. He suggested that activities within the organisation add value to the service and products that the organisation produces, and all these activities should be run at optimum level if the organisation is to gain any real competitive advantage. If they are run efficiently the value obtained should exceed the costs of running them i.e. customers should return to the organisation and transact freely and willingly. Michael Porter suggested that the organisation is split into 'primary activities' and 'support activities'.

Primary Activities

Inbound logistics : Refers to goods being obtained from the organisations suppliers ready to be used for producing the end product.

Operations : The raw materials and goods obtained are manufactured into the final product. Value is added to the product at this stage as it moves through the production line.

Outbound logistics : Once the products have been manufactured they are ready to be distributed to distribution centres, wholesalers, retailers or customers.

Marketing and Sales: Marketing must make sure that the product is targeted towards the correct customer group. The marketing mix is used to establish an effective strategy, any competitive advantage is clearly communicated to the target group by the use of the promotional mix.

Services: After the product/service has been sold what support services does the organisation have to offer. This may come in the form of after sales training, guarantees and warranties.

With the above activities, any or a combination of them, maybe essential for the firm to develop the competitive advantage which Porter talks about in his book.

Support Activities

The support activities assist the primary activities in helping the organisation achieve its competitive advantage. They include:

Procurement: This department must source raw materials for the organisation and obtain the best price for doing so. For the price they must obtain the best possible quality

Technology development: The use of technology to obtain a competitive advantage within the organisation. This is very important in today's technological driven environment. Technology can be used in production to reduce cost thus add value, or in research and development to develop new products, or via the use of the internet so customers have access to online facilities.

Human resource management: The organisation will have to recruit, train and develop the correct people for the organisation if they are to succeed in their objectives. Staff will have to be motivated and paid the 'market rate' if they are to stay with the organisation and add value to it over their duration of employment. Within the service sector eg airlines it is the 'staff' who may offer the competitive advantage that is needed within the field.

Firm infrastructure: Every organisations needs to ensure that their finances, legal structure and management structure works efficiently and helps drive the organisation forward.

As you can see the value chain encompasses the whole organisation and looks at how primary and support activities can work together effectively and efficiently to help gain the organisation a superior competitive advantage.

SWOT Analysis

A tool used by organisations to help the firm establish its Strengths, Weaknesses, Opportunities and Threats (SWOT). A

SWOT analysis is used as a framework to help the firm develop its overall corporate, marketing, or product strategies. Note:Strengths and Weaknesses are internal factors which are controllable by the organisation. Opportunities & threats are external factors which are uncontrollable by the organisation.

Strength examples could include:

- A strong brand name.
- Market share.
- Good reputation.
- Expertise and skill.
- Weaknesses could include:
- Low or no market share.
- No brand loyalty.
- Lack of experience.
- Opportunities could include:
- A growing market.
- Increased consumer spending.
- Selling internationally.
- Changes in society beneficial to your company.

Threats could include:

- Competitors
- Government policy eg taxation, laws
- Changes in society not beneficial to your company

A SWOT analysis is an excellent tool to use if the organisation wants to take a step back and assess the situation they are in. Issues raised from the analysis are then used to assist the organisation in developing their marketing mix strategy. A SWOT analysis must form the part of any prudent marketing strategy.

Generic Strategies

For an organisation to obtain a sustainable competitive advantage Michael Porter suggested that they should follow either one of three generic strategies.

Strategy one: Cost Leadership

This strategy involves the organisation aiming to be the lowest cost producer within their industry. The orgainisation aims to drive cost down through all the elements of the production of the product from sourcing, to labour costs. The cost leader usually aims at a broad market, so sufficient sales can cover costs. Low cost producers include Easyjet airline, Ryan air, Asda and Walmart. Some organisation may aim to drive costs down but will not pass on these cost savings to their customers aiming for increased profits clearly because their brand can command a premium rate.

Strategy 2: Differentiation

To be different, is what organisations strive for. Having a competitive advantage which allows the company and its products ranges to stand out is crucial for their success. With a differentiation strategy the organisation aims to focus its effort on particular segments and charge for the added differentiated value. If we look at Brompton folding cycles their compact design differentiates them from other folding bike companies. New concepts which allow for differentiation can be patented, however patents have a certain life span and organisation always face the danger that their idea that gives the competitive advantage will be copied in one form or another.

Strategy 3: Niche strategies

Here the organisation focuses its effort on one particular segment and becomes well known for providing products/ services within the segment. They form a competitive advantage for this niche market and either succeed by being a low cost producer or differentiator within that particular segment. Examples include Roll Royce and Bentley.

Are you 'Stuck in the Middle'

The danger some organisation face is that they try to do all three and become what is known as stuck in the middle. The have no clear business strategy, be all to all consumers, which adds to their running costs causing a fall in sales and market share. 'Stuck in the middle' companies are usually subject to a takeover or merger.

Industry Analysis Model

Porters fives forces model is an excellent model to use to analyse a particular environment of an industry. So for example, if we were entering the PC industry, we would use porters model to help us find out about:

1) Competitive Rivalry
2) Power of suppliers
3) Power of buyers
4) Threats of substitutes
5) Threat of new entrants.

The above five main factors are key factors that influence industry performance, hence it is common sense and practical to find out about these factors before you enter the industry.

Competitive Rivalry

A starting point to analysing the industry is to look at competitive rivalry. If entry to an industry is easy then competitive rivalry will likely to be high. If it is easy for customers to move to substitute products for example from coke to water then again rivalry will be high. Generally competitive rivalry will be high if:

- There is little differentiation between the products sold between customers.
- Competitors are approximately the same size of each other.
- If the competitors all have similar strategies.
- It is costly to leave the industry hence they fight to just stay in (exit barriers)

Power of Suppliers

Suppliers are also essential for the success of an organisation. Raw materials are needed to complete the finish product of the organisation. Suppliers do have power. This power comes from:

- If they are the only supplier or one of few suppliers who supply that particular raw material.
- If it costly for the organisation to move from one supplier to another (known also as switching cost)
- If there is no other substitute for their product.

Power of Buyers

Buyers or customers can exert influence and control over an industry in certain circumstances. This happens when:

- There is little differentiation over the product and substitutes can be found easily.
- Customers are sensitive to price.
- Switching to another product is not costly.

Threat of Substitutes

Are there alternative products that customers can purchase over your product that offer the same benefit for the same or less price? The threat of substitute is high when:

- Price of that substitute product falls.
- It is easy for consumers to switch from one substitute product to another.
- Buyers are willing to substitute.

Threat of New Entrant

The threat of a new organisation entering the industry is high when it is easy for an organisation to enter the industry i.e. entry barriers are low.

An organisation will look at how loyal customers are to existing products, how quickly they can achieve economy of scales, would they have access to suppliers, would government legislation prevent them or encourage them to enter the industry.

So to summaries porters five forces model is essential to carry to help you understand your industry in depth before you enter it.

Diffusion of Innovation

This extension of the product life cycle was developed by Everett M. Rogers in 1962 and simply looks who adopts products at the different stages of the life cycle.

Rogers identified five types of purchasers as the product moves through its life cycle stage. He suggested:

1. Innovator who make up 2.5% of all purchases of the product, purchase the product at the beginning of the life cycle. They are not afraid of trying new products that suit their lifestyle and will also pay a premium for that benefit.
2. Early Adopters make up 13.5% of purchases, they are usually opinion leaders and naturally adopt products after the innovators. This group of purchasers are crucial because adoption by them means the product becomes acceptable, spurring on later purchasers.
3. Early Majority make up 34% of purchases and have been spurred on by the early adopters. They wait to see if the product will be adopted by society and will purchase only when this has happened. They early majority usually have some status in society.
4. Late Majority make up another 34% of sales and usually purchase the product at the late stages of majority within the life cycle.
5. Laggards make up 16% of total sales and usually purchase the product near the end of its life. They are the 'wait and see' group. They wait to see if the product will get cheaper. Usually when they purchase the product a new version is already on the market. Some may call Laggards, bargain hunters!

Boston Consultancy Group (BCG Matrix)

This product portfolio matrix classifies product lines into four categories. The BCG models suggests that organisations should have a healthy balance of products within their range. The Boston Consultancy Group classified these products as following:

Question Mark/Problem Child

These are products with low market share but operate in high market growth rates. The company puts a lot of resources in this product in the hope that it will eventually increase market share and generate cash returns in the future.

Star

Stars have high market shares that operate in growing markets. The product at this stage should be generating positive returns for the company.

Cash Cow

Cash Cow are products at the mature stage of the lifecycle, they generate high amounts of cash for the company, but growth rate is slowing. There are chances that the product may slip into decline, appropriate marketing mix strategies should be employed to try to prevent this from happening.

MANAGING INCOME

Accounting (methodology) is the measurement, disclosure or provision of assurance about financial information that helps managers, investors, tax authorities and other decision makers make resource allocation decisions. The names come from the use of financial accounts. Financial accounting is one branch of accounting and historically has involved processes by which financial information about a business is recorded, classified, summarized, interpreted, and communicated. Accounting is also widely referred to as the "language of business".

Auditing, a related but separate discipline, has two sub-disciplines: Internal and External auditing. External auditing is the process whereby an independent auditor examines an organization's financial statements and accounting records in order to express an opinion — that conveys reasonable but not absolute assurance — as to the truth and fairness of the statements and the accountant's adherence to Generally Accepted Accounting Principles (GAAP), in all material respects.

Internal auditing is an examination in which management, and not the external public, is the main beneficiary. It is carried out usually by auditors employed by the company, but sometimes by external service providers. The internal auditor's role is broader, and basically depends on what kind of assurance management wants. It usually certifies the efficiency and effectiveness of processes, departments, projects or internal controls. The Institute of Internal Auditors is generally accepted as the custodian of Internal Auditing best practice.

At the heart of accounting is the measurement of financial transactions which are transfers of legal property rights made under contractual relationships. Non-financial transactions are specifically excluded due to conservatism and materiality principles.

Practitioners of accountancy are known as accountants. There are many professional bodies for accountants throughout the world. Many allow their members to use titles indicating their membership. Examples are Chartered Certified Accountant (ACCA or FCCA), Chartered Accountant (FCA, CA or ACA) and Certified Public Accountant (CPA).

Accountancy attempts to create accurate financial reports that are useful to managers, regulators, and other stakeholders such as shareholders, creditors, or owners. The day-to-day record-keeping involved in this process is known as bookkeeping.

At the heart of modern financial accounting is the double-entry bookkeeping system. This system involves making at least two entries for every transaction: a debit in one account, and a corresponding credit in another account. The sum of all debits should always equal the sum of all credits. This provides an easy way to check for errors. This system was first used in medieval Europe, although claims have been made that the system dates back to Ancient Greece.

According to critics of standard accounting practices, it has changed little since. Accounting reform measures of some kind have been taken in each generation to attempt to keep bookkeeping relevant to capital assets or production capacity. However, these have not changed the basic principles, which are supposed to be independent of economics as such. In recent times, the divergence of accounting from economic principles has resulted in controversial reforms to make financial reports more indicative of economic reality.

Accountancy's infancy dates back to the earliest days of human agriculture and civilization (the Sumerians in Mesopotamia), when the need to maintain accurate records of the quantities and relative values of agricultural products first arose. Simple accounting is mentioned in the Christian Bible in the book of Matthew, in the Parable of the Talents (Matt. 25:19). Twelfth century writer Ibn Taymiyyah mentioned in his book Hisba (verification, calculation), detailed accounting systems used by the Muslims as early as in the mid-seventh century. The accounting practices were influenced by the Roman and the Persian civilizations that Muslims interacted with. The most detailed example of a complex governmental accounting system is the Divan of Umar, the second Caliph of Islam in which all revenues and disbursements were recorded. The Divan of Umar has been described in detail by various Islamic historians and was used by Muslim rulers with mofidications and enhancements until the fall of the Ottoman Empire.

Applied Modern Accountancy in Hotel

The first book on accounting was written by a Croatian merchant Benedetto Cotrugli, who is also known as Benedikt Kotruljeviæ, from the city of Dubrovnik. During his life in Italy he met many merchants and decided to write, Della Mercatvra et del Mercante Perfetto (On Trade and the Perfect Merchant) in which he elaborated on the principles of modern, double-entry book-keeping. He finished his lifework in 1458.

However, his work was not published until 1573, as a result of which his contributions to the field have been overlooked by the general public.

For this reason, Luca Pacioli, also known as Friar Luca dal Borgo, is credited for the "birth" of accounting. His Summa de arithmetica, geometrica, proportioni et proportionalita (Venice 1494), a synthesis of the mathematical knowledge of his time, includes the first published description of the method of keeping accounts that Venetian merchants used at that time, known as the double-entry accounting system. Although Pacioli codified rather than invented this system, he is widely regarded as the "Father of Accounting". The system he published included most of the accounting cycle as we know it today. He described the use of journals and ledgers, and warned that a person should not go to sleep at night until the debits equalled the credits! His ledger had accounts for assets (including receivables and inventories), liabilities, capital, income, and expenses – the account categories that are reported on an organization's balance sheet and income statement, respectively. He demonstrated year-end closing entries and proposed that a trial balance be used to prove a balanced ledger. His treatise also touches on a wide range of related topics from accounting ethics to cost accounting.

The first known book in the English language on accounting was published in London by John Gouge (or Gough) in 1543. It is described as A Profitable Treatyce called the Instrument or Boke to learn to knowe the good order of the kepyng of the famouse reconynge, called in Latin, Dare and Habere, and, in English, Debitor and Creditor.

A short book of instructions was also published in 1588 by John Mellis of Southwark, in which he says, "I am but the renuer and reviver of an ancient old copie printed here in London the 14 of August 1543: collected, published, made, and set forth by one Hugh Oldcastle, Scholemaster, who, as appeareth by his treatise, then taught Arithmetics, and this booke in Saint Ollaves parish in Marko Lane." John Mellis refers to the fact that the principle of accounts he explains (which is a simple system of double entry) is "after the forme of Venice".

A book described as The Merchants Mirrour, or directions for the perfect ordering and keeping of his accounts formed by way of Debitor and Creditor, after the (so termed) Italian manner, by Richard Dafforne, accountant, published in 1635, contains many references to early books on the science of accountancy. In a chapter in this book, headed "Opinion of Book-keeping's Antiquity," the author states, on the authority of another writer, that the form of book-keeping referred to had then been in use in Italy about two hundred years, "but that the same, or one in many parts very like this, was used in the time of Julius Caesar, and in Rome long before."

An early Dutch writer appears to have suggested that double-entry book-keeping was even in existence among the Greeks, pointing to scientific accountancy having been invented in remote times.

There were several editions of Richard Dafforne's book - the second edition in 1636, the third in 1656, and another in 1684. The book is a very complete treatise on scientific accountancy, beautifully prepared and containing elaborate explanations. The numerous editions tend to prove that the science was highly appreciated in the 17th century. From this time on, there has been a continuous supply of literature on the subject, many of the authors styling themselves accountants and teachers of the art, and thus proving that the professional accountant was then known and employed.

The requirements for entry in the profession of accounting vary from country to country. Accountants may be licensed by a variety of organisations, such as the British qualified accountancy bodies including Association of Chartered Certified Accountants (ACCA) and Institute of Chartered Accountants, and are recognized by titles such as Chartered Certified Accountant (ACCA or FCCA) and Chartered Accountant (UK, Australia, New Zealand, Canada, India,

Pakistan, South Africa), Certified Public Accountant (Ireland, Japan, US, Singapore, Hong Kong, the Philippines), Certified Management Accountant (Canada, U.S.), Certified General Accountant (Canada), or Certified Practising Accountant (Australia). Some Commonwealth countries (Australia and Canada) often recognise both the certified and chartered accounting bodies.

The majority of "public" accountants in New Zealand and Canada are Chartered Accountants; however, Certified General Accountants are also authorized by legislation to practise public accounting and auditing in all Canadian provinces, except Ontario and Quebec, as of 2005. There is, however, no legal requirement for an accountant to be a paid-up member of one of the many Institutes and other bodies which are effectively a form of professional trade union. Unlike the Law Society, which can legally stop a solicitor from practising, accountancy institutes do not have such authority. However, auditors are regulated.

Before the Enron and other accounting scandals, there were five large firms and were called the Big Five. Since Arthur Andersen's assurance practice split (after the firm was found guilty in the Enron scandal), with a plurality joining KPMG in the US and Deloitte & Touche outside of the US, Arthur Andersen left from the group. Previous to this there were also groupings referred to as the "Big Six" (Arthur Andersen, plus Coopers & Lybrand before its merger with Price Waterhouse) and the "Big Eight" (Ernst and Young prior to their merger were Ernst & Whinney and Arthur Young and Deloitte & Touche was formed by the merger of Deloitte, Haskins and Sells with the firm Touche Ross).

Enron turned out to be only the first of a series of accounting scandals that enveloped the accounting industry in 2002. This is likely to have far-reaching consequences for the U.S. accounting industry. Application of International Accounting Standards originating in International Accounting Standards Board headquartered in London and bearing more resemblance to UK than current US practices is often advocated by those who note the relative stability of the UK accounting system (which reformed itself after scandals in the late 1980s and early 1990s). Accounting reform of a far more comprehensive sort is advocated by those who see issues with capitalism or economics, and seek ecological or social accountability.

According to Accountancy Age's 2005 league table, fee income amongst the Top 50 accounting firms in the UK rose from £6.3bn to £7.0bn. This followed two successive years in which fee income had declined, largely a result of the sale by some of the larger firms of their consultancy arms. Fee income in most business areas - audit, tax, corporate finance and consultancy - rose in the 2005 survey, with insolvency and wealth management being the only segments where revenue fell.

PricewaterhouseCoopers remains the largest firm with fee income totalling £1,780m followed by Deloitte (£1,350m), KPMG (£1,066m) and Ernst & Young (£945m). The combined revenue of the Big Four accounted for £5.0bn, 72% of the fee income of the Top 50, down from 78-79% in the years up to the 2002 survey and the third year in succession a decline in their share has occurred (Chart 1). Ernst & Young's fee income is the smallest of the largest four firms, but still over three times that of the next largest firm, Grant Thornton. The amount of fee income tapers off amongst the mid-tier firms so that in total there were only 25 firms that each generated more than £15m of revenue in the 2005 survey. For more details regarding British qualified accountancy professionals, please refer to the page of British qualified accountants.

Management Accounting

Management accounting is concerned with the provisions and use of accounting information to managers within organizations, to provide them with the basis in making informed business decisions that would allow them to be better equipped in their management and control functions. Unlike financial accountancy information (which, for the most part, is public information), management accounting information is used within an organization (typically for decision-making) and is usually confidential and access to which is only available to a select few.

According to CIMA, The Chartered Institute of Management Accountants, Management Accounting is "the process of identification, measurement, accumulation, analysis, preparation, interpretation and communication of information used by management to plan, evaluate and control within an entity and to assure appropriate use of and accountability for its resources. Management accounting also comprises the preparation of financial reports for non management groups such as shareholders, creditors, regulatory agencies and tax authorities".

Aims

1. Formulating strategies;
2. Planning and constructing business activities;
3. Making decisions;
4. Well use of resources;
5. Supporting financial reports preparation; and
6. Safeguarding assets.

In the late 1980s, accounting practitioners and educators were heavily criticized on the grounds that management accounting practices (and, even more so, the curriculum taught to accounting students) had changed little over the preceding 60 years, despite radical changes in the business environment. Professional accounting institutes, perhaps fearing that management accountants would increasingly be seen as superfluous in business organizations, subsequently devoted considerable resources to the development of a more innovative skills set for management accountants.

The distinction between 'traditional' and 'innovative' management accounting practices can be illustrated by reference to cost control techniques. Traditionally, management accountants' principal technique was variance analysis, which is a systematic approach to the comparison of the actual and budgeted costs of the raw materials and labour used during a production period.

While some form of variance analysis is still used by most manufacturing firms, it nowadays tends to be used in conjunction with innovative techniques such as life cycle cost analysis and activity-based costing, which are designed with specific aspects of the modern business environment in mind. Lifecycle costing recognizes that managers' ability to influence the cost of manufacturing a product is at its greatest when the product is still at the design stage of its product lifecycle (i.e., before the design has been finalised and production commenced), since small changes to the product design may lead to significant savings in the cost of manufacturing the product. Activity-based costing (ABC) recognizes that, in modern factories, most manufacturing costs are determined by the amount of 'activities' (e.g., the number of production runs per month, and the amount of production equipment idle time) and that the key to effective cost control is therefore optimizing the efficiency of these activities. Activity-based accounting is also known as Cause and Effect accounting.

Both lifecycle costing and activity-based costing recognize that, in the typical modern factory, the avoidance of disruptive events (such as machine breakdowns and quality control failures) is of far greater importance than (for example) reducing the costs of raw materials. Activity-based costing also deemphasizes direct labour as a cost driver and concentrates instead on acitivities that drive costs, such as the provision of a service or the production of a product component.

The most significant recent direction in managerial accounting is throughput accounting, which recognizes the interdependencies of modern production processes and provide managers with a tool that will allow them to measure the contribution per unit of constrained resource for any given product, customer or supplier.

A seldom expressed alternative view of management accounting is that it is neither a neutral or benign influence in organizations, rather a mechanism for management control through surveillance. This view locates management accounting specifically in the context of management control theory.

There are several related professional qualifications in the field of accountancy including:

- Management Accountancy Qualifications
  - CIMA – CMA
  - Institute of Cost and Works Accountants of India
  - AAFM
- Other Professional Accountancy Qualifications
  - Chartered Certified Accountant, (ACCA)
  - Chartered Accountant, (CA)
  - Certified Public Accountant, (CPA)

Accounting Management (Business) is the practical application of management techniques to control and report on the financial health of the organization. This involves the analysis, planning, implementation, and control of programs designed to provide financial data reporting for managerial decision making. This includes the maintenance of bank accounts, developing financial statements, cash flow and financial performance analysis. Accounting management is a mandatory knowledge module of any MBA programme.

Accounting is often referred to as billing management. The goal is to gather usage statistics for users.

Using the statistics the users can be billed and usage quota can be enforced.

Examples:

- Disk usage
- Link utilisation
- CPU time

For non-billed networks, 'Administration' replaces 'Accounting'. The goals of Administration is to administer the set of authorized users, by establishing users, passwords and permissions; and to administer the operations of the equipment such as by performing software backup and synchronization.

Activity-based Costing

Activity-based costing (ABC) is a method of allocating costs to products and services. It is generally used as a tool for planning and control. This is a necessary tool for doing value chain analysis.

The concepts of ABC were developed in the manufacturing sector of the U.S. during the 1970s and 80s. During this time, the Consortium for Advanced Manufacturing-International, now known simply as CAM-I, provided a formative role for studying and formalizing the principles that have become more formally known as Activity-Based Costing. Robin Cooper and Robert Kaplan, proponent of the Balanced Scorecard, brought notice to these concepts in a number of articles published in Harvard Business Review beginning in 1988. Cooper and Kaplan described ABC as an approach to solve the problems of traditional cost management systems. These traditional costing systems are often unable to determine accurately the actual costs of production and of the costs of related services. Consequently managers were making decisions based on inaccurate data especially where there are multiple products.

Instead of using broad arbitrary percentages to allocate costs, ABC seeks to identify cause and effect relationships to objectively assign costs. Once costs of the activities have been identified, the cost of each activity is attributed to each product to the extent that the product uses the activity. In this way ABC often identifies areas of high overhead costs per unit and so directs attention to finding ways to reduce the costs or to charge more for costly products.

Activity-based costing was first clearly defined in 1987 by Robert S. Kaplan and W. Bruns as a chapter in their book Accounting and Management. They initially focused on manufacturing industry where increasing technology and productivity improvements have reduced the relative proportion of the direct costs of labour and materials, but have increased relative proportion of indirect costs. For example increased automation has reduced labour, which is a direct cost, but has increased depreciation, which is an indirect cost.

Traditionally cost accountants had arbitrarily added a broad percentage onto the direct costs to allow for the indirect costs. However as the percentages of overhead costs had risen, this technique became increasingly inaccurate because the indirect costs were not caused equally by all the products. For example one product might take more time in one expensive machine than another product, but since the amount of direct labour and materials might be the same, the additional cost for the use of the machine would not be recognised when the same broad 'on-cost' percentage is added to all products. Consequently, when multiple products share common costs, there is a danger of one product subsidising another.

Like manufacturing industries, financial institutions also have diverse products which can cause cross-product subsidies. Since personnel expenses represent the largest single component of non-interest expense in financial institutions, these costs must also be attributed more accurately to products and customers. Activity based costing, even though developed for manufacturing, can therefore be a useful tool for doing this. This extended use of ABC to financial institutions was presented in 1990 in an article appearing in the Journal of Bank Cost and Management Accounting (Volume 3, Number 2) by Richard Sapp, David Crawford and Steven Rebishcke.

Direct labour and materials are relatively easy to trace directly to products, but it is more difficult to directly allocate indirect costs to products. Where products use common resources differently, some sort of weighting is needed in the cost allocation process. The measure of the use of a shared activity by each of the products is known as the cost driver. For example, the cost of the activity of bank tellers can be ascribed to each product by measuring how long each product's transactions takes at the counter and then by measuring the number of each type of transaction.

Even in activity-based costing, some overhead costs are difficult to assign to products and customers, for example the chief executive's salary. These costs are termed 'business sustaining' and are not assigned to products and customers because there is no meaningful method. This lump of unallocated overhead costs must nevertheless be met by contributions from each of the products, but it is not as large as the overhead costs before ABC is employed.

Although some may argue that costs untraceable to activities should be "arbitrarily allocated" to products, it is important to realize that the only purpose of ABC is to provide information to management. Therefore, there is no reason to assign any cost in an arbitrary manner. Management accountants can be creative in finding other ways to represent these costs on internal reporting statements.

MANAGING BUDGET

Budget generally refers to a list of all planned expenses and revenues. A budget is an important concept in microeconomics, which uses a budget line to illustrate the trade-offs between two or more goods. A personal budget is among the most important concepts of personal finance. In a personal or family budget all sources of income (inflows) are identified and expenses (outflows) are planned with the intent of matching outflows to inflows (Making ends meet). There are a wide variety of personal budgeting methods and tools that can be employed to help individuals and families with the budgeting process. Also the level of planned finance available to a person, corporation or government, as set by a certain person.

The budget of a government is a summary or plan of the intended revenues and expenditures of that government. In the United States, the federal budget is prepared by the Office of Management and Budget, and submitted to Congress for consideration. Invariably, Congress makes many and substantial changes. Nearly all American states are required to have balanced budgets, but the federal government is allowed to run deficits. In the UK the budget is prepared by the Chancellor of the Exchequer, the second most important member of the government, and must be passed by Parliament. The Parliament seldom makes changes to the budget.

The budget of a company is compiled annually. A finished budget usually requires considerable effort and can be seen as a financial plan for the new financial year. While traditionally the Finance department compiles the company's budget, modern software allows hundreds or even thousands of people in the various departments (operations, human resources, IT etc) to contribute their expected revenues and expenses to the final budget.

If the actual numbers delivered through the financial year turn out to be close to the budget, this will demonstrate that the company understands their business and has been successfully driving it in the direction they had planned. On the other hand, if the actuals diverge wildly from the budget, this sends out an 'out of control' signal and the share

Cost-plus pricing is a pricing method commonly used by firms. It is used primarily because it is easy to calculate and requires little information. There are several varieties, but the common thread in all of them is that you first calculate the cost of the product, then include an additional amount to represent profit. Cost-plus pricing is often used on government contracts, and has been criticized as promoting wasteful expenditures.

Calculating Price Using the Cost-plus Method

There are several ways of determining cost, and the profit can be added as either a percentage markup or an absolute amount. One example is:

$$P = (AVC + FC\%) * (1 + MK\%)$$

where:

- P = price
- AVC = average variable cost

- FC% = percentage allocation of fixed costs
- MK% = percentage markup

For example: If variable costs are 30 yen, the allocation to cover fixed costs is 10 yen, and you feel you need a 50% markup then you would charge a price of 60 yen:

P = (30 + 10) • (1 + 0.50)

P = 40 • 1.5

P = 60

An alternative way of doing a similar calculation is:

P = (AVC + FC%) / (1 " MK%)

To make things simpler, some firms, particularly retailers, ignore fixed costs and just use the purchase price paid to their suppliers as the cost term. They indirectly incorporate the fixed cost allocation into the markup percentage. To simplify things even further, sometimes a fixed amount is applied rather than a percentage. This fixed amount is usually determined by head-office to make it easy for franchisees and store managers. This is sometimes referred to as turnkey pricing.

Another variant of cost plus pricing is activity based pricing. This involves being more careful in determining costs. Instead of using arbitrary expense categories when allocating overhead, every activity is linked to the resources it uses.

Cost will need to be recalculated and the percentage markup will likely need to be adjusted as the product goes through its life cycle. This is sometimes referred to as product life cycle pricing, although it is seldom done deliberately or in a planned and organized manner. Price skimming and penetration pricing are also types of product life cycle pricing but they are demand based pricing methods rather cost based.

Advantages of Cost-plus Pricing

1. Easy to calculate
2. Minimal information requirements
3. Easy to administer
4. Tends to stabilize markets - insulated from demand variations and competitive factors

5. Insures seller against unpredictable, or unexpected later costs
6. Ethical advantages

Disadvantages

1. Tends to ignore the role of consumers
2. Tends to ignore the role of competitors
3. Use of historical accounting costs rather than replacement value
4. Use of "normal" or "standard" output level to allocate fixed costs
5. Inclusion of sunk costs rather than just using incremental costs
6. Ignores opportunity costs
7. Contractors may not focus on performance because the cost is always covered by the client

In microeconomics, Production is simply the conversion of inputs into outputs. It is an economic process that uses resources to create a commodity that is suitable for exchange. This can include manufacturing, storing, shipping, and packaging. Some economists define production broadly as all economic activity other than consumption. They see every commercial activity other than the final purchase as some form of production. Production is a process, and as such it occurs through time and space. Because it is a flow concept, production is measured as a "rate of output per period of time". There are three aspects to production processes:

1. The quantity of the commodity produced,
2. The form of the good produced,
3. The temporal and spatial distribution of the commodity produced.

A production process can be defined as any activity that increases the similarity between the pattern of demand for goods, and the quantity, form, and distribution of these goods available to the market place.

A production process is efficient if a given quantity of outputs cannot be produced with any less inputs. It is said to be inefficient when there exists another feasible process that, for any given output, uses less inputs. Some economists (in particular Leibenstein) use the term X-efficiency to indicate that production processes tend to be inherently inefficient due to satisficing behaviour. The "rate of efficiency" is simply the amount of (or value of) outputs divided by the amount of (or value of) inputs. If a production process uses 50 units of input (or $5000 worth of inputs) to produce one unit of output it is more efficient than a process that uses 55 units of input (or $5500 worth of inputs) to produce the same level of output. It is said to be 10% more efficient ({55-50}/50=1/10=10%).

The inputs or resources used in the production process are called factors by economists. The myriad of possible inputs are usually grouped into four or five categories. These factors are:

- Raw materials (natural capital)
- Labour services (human capital)
- Capital goods
- Land

Sometimes a fifth category is added, entrepreneurial and management skills, a subcategory of labour services. Capital goods are those goods that have previously undergone a production process. They are previously produced means of production. Some textbooks use "technology" as a factor of production.

In the "long run" all of these factors of production can be adjusted by management. The "short run" however, is defined as a period in which at least one of the factors of production is fixed. A fixed factor of production is one whose quantity cannot readily be changed. Examples include major pieces of equipment, suitable factory space, and key managerial personnel. A variable factor of production is one whose usage rate can be changed easily. Examples include electrical power consumption, transportation services, and most raw material inputs. In the short run, a firm's "scale of operations" determines the maximum number of outputs that can be produced. In the long run, there are no scale limitations.

The total product (or total physical product) of a variable factor of production identifies what outputs are possible using various levels of the variable input. This can be displayed in either a chart that lists the output level corresponding to various levels of input, or a graph that summarizes the data into a "total product curve". The diagram shows a typical total product curve. In this example, output increases as more inputs are employed up until point A. The maximum output possible with this production process is Qm. If there are other inputs used in the process, they are assumed to be fixed.

The average physical product is the total product divided by the number of units of variable input employed. It is the output of each unit of input. If there are 10 employees working on a production process that manufactures 50 units per day, then the average product of variable labour input is 5 units per day.

The average product typically varies as more of the input is employed, so this relationship can also be expresses as a chart or as a graph. A typical average physical product curve is shown (APP). It can be obtained by drawing a vector from the origin to various points on the total product curve and plotting the slopes of these vectors.

The marginal physical product of a variable input is the change in total output due to a one unit change in the variable input (called the discrete marginal product) or alternatively the rate of change in total output due to an infinitesimally small change in the variable input (called the continuous marginal product). The discrete marginal product of capital is the additional output resulting from the use of an additional unit of capital (assuming all other factors are fixed). The continuous marginal product of a variable input can be calculated as the derivative of quantity produced with respect to variable input employed. The marginal physical product curve is shown

(MPP). It can be obtained from the slope of the total product curve.

Because the marginal product drives changes in the average product, we know that when the average physical product is falling, the marginal physical product must be less than the average. Likewise, when the average physical product is rising, it must be due to a marginal physical product greater than the average. For this reason, the marginal physical product curve must intersect the maximum point on the average physical product curve.

MPP keeps increasing till it reaches its maximum. Up until this point every additional unit has been adding more value to the total product than the previous one. From this point onwards, every additional unit adds less to the total product compared to the previous one. But the average product is still increasing till MPP touches APP. At this point, an additional unit is adding the same value as the average product. From this point onwards, MPP starts to reduce and so does APP because every additional unit is adding less to APP than the average product. But the total product is still increasing because every additional unit is still contributing positively. Therefore, during this period, both, the average as well as marginal products, are decreasing, but the total product is still increasing. Finally we reach a point when MPP crosses the x-axis. At this point every additional unit starts to diminish the product of previous units, possibly by getting into their way. Therefore the total product starts to decrease at this point. This is point A on the total product curve.

Diminishing returns can be divided into three categories:

1. Diminishing Total returns, which implies reduction in total product with every additional unit of input. This occurs after point A in the graph.
2. Diminishing Average returns, which refers to the portion of the APP curve after its intersection with MPP curve.
3. Diminishing Marginal returns, refers to the point where the MPP curve starts to slope down and

travels all the way down to the x-axis and beyond. Putting it in a chronological order, at first the marginal returns start to diminish, then the average returns, followed finally by the total returns.

These curves illustrate the principle of diminishing marginal returns to a variable input (not to be confused with diseconomies of scale which is a long term phenomenon in which all factors are allowed to change). This states that as you add more and more of a variable input, you will reach a point beyond which the resulting increase in output starts to diminish. This point is illustrated as the maximum point on the marginal physical product curve. It assumes that other factor inputs (if they are used in the process) are held constant. An example is the employment of labour in the use of trucks to transport goods. Assuming the number of available trucks (capital) is fixed, then the amount of the variable input labour could be varied and the resultant efficiency determined. At least one labourer (the driver) is necessary. Additional workers per vehicle could be productive in loading, unloading, navigation, or around the clock continuous driving. But at some point the returns to investment in labour will start to diminish and efficiency will decrease. The most efficient distribution of labour per piece of equipment will likely be one driver plus an additional worker for other tasks (2 workers per truck would be more efficient than 5 per truck).

Resource allocations and distributive efficiencies in the mix of capital and labour investment will vary per industry and according to available technology. Trains are able to transport much more in the way of goods with fewer "drivers" but at the cost of greater investment in infrastructure. With the advent of mass production of motorized vehicles, the economic niche occupied by trains (compared with transport trucks) has become more specialized and limited to long haul delivery.

There is an argument that if the theory is holding everything constant, the production method should not be changed, i.e., division of labour should not be practiced.

However, the rise in marginal product means that the workers use other means of production method, such as in loading, unloading, navigation, or around the clock continuous driving. For this reason, some economists think that the "keeping other things constant" should not be used in this theory.

The total, average, and marginal physical product curves mentioned above are just one way of showing production relationships. They express the quantity of output relative to the amount of variable input employed while holding fixed inputs constant. Because they depict a short run relationship, they are sometimes called short run production functions. If all inputs are allowed to be varied, then the diagram would express outputs relative to total inputs, and the function would be a long run production function. If the mix of inputs is held constant, then output would be expressed relative to inputs of a fixed composition, and the function would indicate long run economies of scale.

Rather than comparing inputs to outputs, it is also possible to assess the mix of inputs employed in production. An isoquant relates the quantities of one input to the quantities of another input. It indicates all possible combinations of inputs that are capable of producing a given level of output.

Rather than looking at the inputs used in production, it is possible to look at the mix of outputs that are possible for any given production process. This is done with a production possibilities frontier. It indicates what combinations of outputs are possible given the available factor endowment and the prevailing production technology.

You can use a lot of labour with a minimal amount of capital, or you could invest heavily in capital equipment that requires a minimal amount of labour to operate, or any combination in between. For most goods, there are more than just two inputs. For example in agriculture, the amount of land, water, and fertilizer can all be varied to produce different amounts of a crop. An isoquant, in the two input case, is a curve that shows all the ways of combining two inputs so as to produce a given level of output. In the three input case it will be a surface. Iso is Latin for equal and quant is short for quantity. Movement along an isoquant depicts a constant rate of output, but a changing input ratio. A unique isoquant can be constructed for every level of output, and a family of isoquants can be created to represent various output levels. Isoquants further from the origin represent greater amounts of output. Isoquants are usually considered to be everywhere dense, meaning an infinite number of them could be plotted in any two input space.

A typical isoquant is illustrated in the diagram to the right. At point A in the diagram Ka units of capital are combined with La units of labour to produce 100 units of output. It is downward sloping, convex to the origin, and non-intersecting (additional isoquants, not shown, would be drawn parallel to this one). A complete isoquant is actually a closed curve, but only the "down sloping to the right" portion makes economic sense. The upward sloping parts of isoquants, for example, indicate that that level of output could be produced by less of both inputs so this section is of little interest to decision makers. The economic section of the isoquants is defined by a pair of lines called ridge lines.

The "downward to the right" slope of the economic region of an isoquant is due to the possibility of substituting one input for another in the production process while keeping the level of output constant.

Isoquants are typically convex to the origin reflecting the fact that the two factors are substitutable for each other at varying rates. This rate of substitutability is called the "marginal rate of technical substitution" (MRTS) or occasionally the "marginal rate of substitution in production". It measures the reduction in one input per unit increase in the other input that is just sufficient to maintain a constant level of production. For example, the marginal rate of substitution of labour for capital gives the amount of capital that can be replaced by one unit of labour while keeping output unchanged.

To move from point A to point B in the diagram, the amount of capital is reduced from Ka to Kb while the amount of labour is increased only from La to Lb. To move from point C to point D, the amount of capital is reduced from Kc to Kd while the amount of labour is increased from La to Lb. The marginal rate of technical substitution of labour for capital is equivalent to the absolute slope of the isoquant at that point (change in capital divided by change in labour). It is equal to 0 where the isoquant becomes horizontal, and equal to infinity where it becomes vertical.

The opposite is true when going in the other direction. In this case we are looking at the marginal rate of technical substitution capital for labour (which is the reciprocal of the marginal rate of technical substitution labour for capital). It can also be shown that the marginal rate of substitution labour for capital, is equal to the marginal physical product of labour divided by the marginal physical product of capital. In the unusual case of two inputs that are perfect substitutes for each other in production, the isoquant would be linear (linear, a straight line, with a function y = a - bx). If, on the other hand, there is only one production process available, factor proportions would be fixed, and these zero-substitutability isoquants would be shown as horizontal or vertical lines.

Fixed Assets Management

Fixed assets management is an accounting process that seeks to track fixed assets for the purposes of financial accounting, preventive maintenance, and theft deterrence. Many organizations face a significant challenge to track the location, quantity, condition, maintenance and depreciation status of their fixed assets. A popular approach to tracking fixed assets utilizes serial numbered Asset Tags, often with bar codes for easy and accurate reading. Periodically, the owner of the assets can take inventory with a mobile barcode reader and then produce a report. Off-the-shelf software packages for fixed asset management are marketed to businesses small and large. Some Enterprise Resource Planning systems are available with fixed assets modules.

Free cash Flow

Free cash flow measures a firm's net increase in

- Cash from operations (this includes the reduction for interest),
- Less the dividends paid to preferred shareholders, and
- Less expenditures necessary to maintain assets.

Increases in non-cash current assets may, or may not be deducted, depending on whether they are considered to be maintaining the status quo, or to be investments for growth.

Problems with CapX

1. The expenditures for maintenance of assets is only part of the capx reported on the Statement of Cash Flows. It must be separated from the expenditures for growth purposes. This split is not a requirement under GAAP, and is not audited. Management is free to disclose maintenance capx or not. Therefore this input to the calculation of free cash flow is easy to manipulate. Since it is a very large number, maintenance capx's questionable validity is the basis for some people's dismissal of 'free cash flow'.
2. A second problem with the maintenance capx measurement is its intrinsic 'lumpyness'. By their nature, expenditures for capital assets that will last decades are infrequent, but costly when they occur. 'Free cash flow', in turn, will be very different from year to year. No particular year will be a 'norm' that can be expected to be repeated.

Uses of the Metric

1. Free cash flow measures the ease with which businesses can grow and pay dividends to shareholders. Even profitable businesses may have negative cash flows. Their requirement for increased financing will result in increased financing costs reducing future income. It is easier to grow with organic cash flows than with additional financing.

2. According to the discounted cash flow valuation model, the intrinsic value of a company is the present value of all future free cash flows, plus the cash proceeds from its eventual sale. The presumption is that the cash flows are used to pay dividends to the shareholders. Bear in mind the lumpyness discussed.
3. Some investors prefer using free cash flow instead of net income to measure a company's financial performance, because free cash flow is more difficult to manipulate than net income. The problems with this presumption are itemized at cash flow and return of capital.
4. The payout ratio is a metric used to evaluate the sustainability of distributions from REITs, Oil & Gas Royalty Trusts, and Income Trust. The distributions are divided by the free cash flow. Distributions may include any of income, flowed-through capital gains or return of capital.

This metric is used only by shareholders. Debt holders are not concerned with maintaining the operating capital assets, or with growing the business. Nor are they concerned with taxes paid since their payments come first. The appropriate metric for debt holders is EBITDA.

Change Management

There are several phrases regarding organizational change and development that look and sound a lot alike, but have different meanings. As a result of the prominence of the topic, there seems to be increasingly different interpretations of some of these phrases, while others are used interchangeably. Without at least some sense of the differences between these phrases, communications about organizational change and development can be increasingly vague, confusing and frustrating.

There are different overall types of organizational change, including planned versus unplanned, organization-wide versus change primarily to one part of the organization, incremental (slow, gradual change) versus transformational (radical, fundamental), etc.. Knowing which types of change you are doing helps all participants to retain scope and perspective during the many complexities and frequent frustrations during change.

Successful change efforts often include several key roles, including the initiator, champion, change agent, sponsor and leaders. Organization-wide change in corporations should involve the Board of Directors. Whether their members are closely involved in the change or not, they should at least be aware of the change project and monitor if the results are being achieved or not. As the change agent, you might be performing different roles during the project.

Appreciative Inquiry is a recent and powerful breakthrough in organizational change and development. It's based on the philosophy that "problems" are often caused as much by our perception of them as problems as by other influencing factors. The philosophy has spawned a strong movement that, in turn, has generated an increasing number of models, tools and tips, most of which seem to build from the positive perceptions (visions, fantasies, wishes and stories) of those involved in the change effort.

There are numerous well-organized approaches (or models) from which to manage a change effort. Some of the approaches have been around for many years — we just haven't thought of them as such. For example, many organizations undertake strategic planning. The implementation of strategic planning, when done in a systematic, cyclical and explicit approach, is strategic management. Strategic management is also one model for ensuring the success of a change effort. There are numerous, major methods and movements to regularly increase the performance of organizations. Each includes regular recurring activities to establish organizational goals, monitor progress toward the goals, and make adjustments to achieve those goals more effectively and efficiently.

Any or all of the following approaches will improve organizational performance depending on if they are implemented comprehensively and remain focused on organizational results. Some of the following, e.g., organizational learning and knowledge management, might be interpreted more as movements than organization performance strategies because there are wide interpretations of the concepts, not all of which include focusing on achieving top-level organizational results. However, if these two concepts are instilled across the organization and focus on organizational results, they contribute strongly to organizational performance. On the other hand, the Balanced Scorecard, which is deliberately designed to be comprehensive and focused on organizational results, will not improve performance if not implemented from a strong design.

Index